Gaining Influence in Public Relations

The Role of Resistance in Practice

LEA's Communication Series

Jennings Bryant/Dolf Zillmann, General Editors

For a complete list of titles in LEA's Communication Series, please contact Lawrence Erlbaum Associates, Publishers at www.erlbaum.com

Gaining Influence in Public Relations

The Role of Resistance in Practice

Bruce K. Berger
University of Alabama

Bryan H. Reber
University of Georgia

2006

LAWRENCE ERLBAUM ASSOCIATES, PUBLISHERS
Mahwah, New Jersey   London

Lawrence Erlbaum Associates, Inc., Publishers
10 Industrial Avenue
Mahwah, New Jersey 07430

Cover design by Tomai Maridou

Library of Congress Cataloging-in-Publication Data

Berger, Bruce K.
  Gaining influence in public relations : the role of resistance in practice / Bruce K. Berger and Bryan H. Reber.
       p. cm. — (LEA's communication series)

  Includes bibliographical references and index.
ISBN 0-8058-5292-1 (alk. paper)
ISBN 0-8058-5293-X (pbk. : alk. paper)
1. Public relations. 2. Power (Social sciences).   I. Reber, Bryan H.
   II. Title.   III. Series.
HM1221.B47   2006
659.2—dc22   2005049943
                                                            CIP

Books published by Lawrence Erlbaum Associates are printed on acid-free paper, and their bindings are chosen for strength and durability.

Printed in the United States of America
10   9   8   7   6   5   4   3   2   1

Contents

About the Authors

Bruce K. Berger, PhD, is professor and chairman of the Department of Advertising and Public Relations at the University of Alabama. He received his PhD in Communication at the University of Kentucky. Previously, he was a public relations practitioner and executive for 20 years. At The Upjohn Company he worked on public relations projects in more than 30 countries. At Whirlpool Corporation he was Vice President of Corporate Affairs and was responsible for public relations, government affairs, employee communications, and financial communications in the company's global businesses.

Dr. Berger's research on business and public policy formation, organizational power, and strategic communication practices has appeared in more than 15 scholarly and professional publications, including *Communication Yearbook*, *Journal of Public Relations Research*, *Journal of Asian Pacific Communication*, *Public Relations Review*, *Dartnell's Public Relations Handbook*, *Journal of Employee Communication Management*, and *Business Marketing*.

He is the recipient of a number of awards, including the Robert Heath Top Paper Award in the Public Relations Division of the International Communication Association, a PRSA Silver Anvil Award for a diabetes education program, an *Inside PR All-Star Award* for innovative employee communication leadership at Whirlpool, and the PRSA Big Apple Award for global communication programs.

Bryan H. Reber, PhD, is assistant professor of public relations in the Department of Advertising and Public Relations at the University of Georgia. He earned his PhD in Journalism at the University of Missouri.

His research focuses on public relations theory, organizational roles, factors affecting organizational stance toward stakeholders, and curricular issues.

Dr. Reber has published research articles in *Journalism and Mass Communication Quarterly*, *Journal of Advertising Education*, *Journal of Public Relations Research*, *Public Relations Review*, and *Newspaper Research Journal*, among others.

His professional experience includes more than a dozen years as director of public information at Bethel College in Kansas before embarking on an academic career. He taught journalism at Bethel College, strategic communication management at the University of Missouri, public relations at the University of Alabama, and currently teaches public relations courses at the University of Georgia. He has conducted research through the Institute for Communication Research at the University of Alabama and the Center for Advanced Social Research at the University of Missouri.

Preface

This book examines power and influence in and around the practice of public relations. We explore forces that shape and constrain the practice and argue that professionals must do more to resist these forces and increase their influence inside organizations. The central issue is how to do so, and we enter this ongoing conversation about what public relations is and might be through a power relations perspective.

Understanding operations of power in organizations seems necessary for advancing a profession that advocates for decisions, actions, and communications that fall in the area of doing the right thing. After all, helping organizations do the right things requires a thorough understanding of how things actually get done in those organizations. Michael Foucault (1988) claimed that every relationship is to some extent a power relation, and we are surrounded by ongoing strategic relations. Our own professional experiences suggest we encounter relations of power at our first moments in practice, and such relations attach to us like shadows as we march through assignments and years, whether we so name or engage them.

Our approach is counterintuitive: We argue that public relations professionals can increase their influence and legitimacy with organizational decision makers by engaging in resistance activities against the forces that constrain them. Longtime approaches to legitimate the profession—we call them Alpha approaches—have relied on case studies, accreditation and measurement initiatives, and repeated claims about the value and crucial role of the practice, among others. Despite such efforts to induce support from top decision makers, and there have been some successes, many professionals still do not hold a seat at the table, and the public image of the profession remains tarnished.

We contend that practitioners have many power and influence resources available for use, and they can benefit from developing and mobilizing more of them. They also may gain influence by supplementing traditional Alpha approaches with Omega approaches, which are forms of dissent, professional activism, and more controversial influence tactics that represent potentially rich but largely untapped power sources. Above all, professionals must possess the political will to engage in the often messy and confrontational power relations that occur in organizational decision-making arenas.

Ultimately, our concerns are to first make sense of power relations and then to develop a portfolio of influence resources and tactics that practitioners may call upon when they engage in power relations. To do so, we have grounded the book in the workplace and the routines and structures of practice. Our combined 30 years of professional experience helped us construct our questions about power. For the answers, we turned to those in the practice fields.

Through depth interviews with nearly 200 diverse professionals, and survey responses from more than 1,000 others, we examine perceptions about power, influence, professional roles, constraints on practice, organizational politics, dissent, and activism. We also try to answer a number of related questions along the way. For example, how do PR professionals engage in power relations? What influence resources and tactics do they draw from, which ones are in short supply, and which ones are underdeveloped or underutilized? To what extent, and under what conditions, are practitioners willing to advocate forcefully and use dissent approaches? And what does it mean to "do the right thing" in public relations when organizational leaders make an inappropriate or questionable decision?

The Research Projects

Seven research projects were carried out to provide insights into these little explored topics. Three projects involved in-depth interviews with professionals:

> The *Power Relations Interviews* (Berger, 2005) were conducted with 21 senior public relations executives to learn more about constraints on practice, power relations, and what happens inside dominant coalitions in organizations.

The *Influence Interviews* examined how professionals define influence in practice, the resources and tactics they bring to bear in power relations, their perceptions about Omega approaches, and their ideas for strengthening the power and legitimacy of the profession. Sixty-five professionals from eight countries participated in these interviews in spring 2004.

The *PR Success Interviews* were conducted with 97 high-level public relations executives in spring 2004. These interviews were used primarily to support another research project, which examined success factors in PR leadership positions. However, several questions regarding power sources, influence tactics, and constraints on the profession were the same as those questions raised in the Influence Interviews.

Three survey research projects examined related topics:

The *Most Important Issue in PR Survey* was conducted in spring of 2003 to identify the most pressing issues in the field. More than 200 public relations professionals, teachers, and graduate students participated in the survey.

The *Dissent Survey*, carried out in fall 2004, captured the perceptions of more than 800 diverse professionals regarding dissent practices and tactics, conditions in which practitioners are most likely to dissent, and relationships between PR roles and resistance tactics.

The *Profile Project* was carried out in early 2005 to further assess professionals' views about situational dissent approaches and to construct some preliminary dissent "types" for future research projects. Fifty-one professionals participated in this project.

Finally, a comprehensive case study was prepared to demonstrate how professionals at one large company used a variety of influence strategies and tactics to develop and implement a major employee communication program.

Outline of the Book

Chapter 1 introduces five assumptions on which the book is based, defines power and influence within the practice, and explains how conceptualizing public relations as resistance helps to reflect on the profession. Chapter 2 addresses the longtime issues of public relations roles and service. Data from the Dissent Survey underscore the essential dissonance in the field about these issues and what it means to do the right thing in public relations, our normative framework in the book. Professionals concur that advocacy is the right thing to do, but they disagree about what advocacy approaches are appropriate, for whom they advocate, and the extent to which they should advocate.

In chapter 3, we elaborate a resistance role in public relations and examine organizational politics and three relations of power at work in most decision-making arenas: *power-over, power-with,* and *power-to* relations. The interplay of these relations produces organizational decisions and shapes public relations practices. A conceptual model depicts relationships among the key elements in power relations—social and organizational forces, internal and external influencers, influence resources, political arenas, and political outcomes.

Chapter 4 details five categories of influence resources—personal, relational, structural, informational, and systemic—that professionals may develop, mobilize, and use. Data from the Influence Interviews and PR Success Interviews illustrate the influence resources that professionals use most often, which ones are in short supply, and which ones are underutilized or underdeveloped. We draw from the same data sets in chapter 5 to examine Alpha approaches, or the sanctioned influence tactics that professionals actually use on the job. Practitioners rely most often on rational arguments, coalitions, and pressure in power relations and use consultation, exchange, personal appeals, ingratiation, and legitimation approaches far less often.

Chapter 6 presents a depth case study through the lens of power relations. The case portrays how public relations professionals at Whirlpool Corporation used a range of influence strategies and tactics to develop, sell, and carry out a major internal communication change program during 1992–1995. We assess successes and failures in the change initiative and examine some lessons of power relations in practice.

Chapter 7 explores unsanctioned influence tactics, or Omega approaches, that professionals sometimes use when other tactics don't work. These controversial approaches include planting rumors or information in the grapevine, leaking information outside the company, constructing counternarratives, and whistle-blowing. A small number of professionals reported using such tactics, but a majority said that they were aware of other practitioners who did so.

In chapter 8, we present findings from the Dissent Survey, the first major study to explore organizational dissent in public relations practice. When, how, and to what extent practitioners express dissent in the face of perceived organizational missteps or wrongdoings were found to differ by gender, age, role, type of practice, and professional tenure. Overall, practitioners are more likely to use more extreme tactics to redress illegal, immoral, or unethical decisions or actions. However, about 10% of the 800 participants said they wouldn't express dissent or challenge management decisions in any situation, no matter how egregious.

Chapter 9 explores the issue of political willpower, the resource that may be in shortest supply in the profession. We identify a number of factors that weaken or strengthen the will to engage in power relations and explain why greater willpower is needed at the individual and professional association levels to advance the profession's influence and image.

In chapter 10, we argue that many of the Alpha approaches that professionals have used to try to gain a seat at the table have further rationalized and bureaucratized the practice, but they have not boosted its power or legitimacy. The best opportunities to advance the profession may lie in increased professional activism and accelerated development of systemic influence resources.

Chapter 11 is a brief public relations manifesto, which reflects professional values and beliefs associated with a resistance role in public relations. We call for professionals to push back on the forces that constrain their potential to become more positive and influential change agents in organizations.

Acknowledgments

We want to thank the many individuals who helped us complete this book. The reviewers and editors at Lawrence Erlbaum provided helpful suggestions and excellent support throughout the process. William Blodgett, John Chisholm (The Institute for Communication Research), Chandler Harriss, Stan Kaufman (The Epimetrics Group), Dong-Jin Park, and Jennifer Robinson provided invaluable assistance in carrying out several of the research projects that support claims we make in the book. Many colleagues at the University of Alabama and the University of Georgia provided both technical assistance and intellectual stimulation for our work. Joan and Sharon shared their enthusiasm and unqualified support throughout the project. Finally, we want to thank the hundreds of public relations professionals who generously shared their time and their candid insights and hopes about the practice. Their voices ground and illuminate our work.

—*Bruce K. Berger*
Bryan H. Reber

CHAPTER 1

Influence in Public Relations and Why It's Important

> Public relations has a far greater potential and responsibility in our society than is realized.... I am not upset by its derogation by some elements of the mass media. Of more concern is the prevalent narrow concept of the role of public relations to be found among opinion leaders and public relations practitioners themselves.
>
> —McLaughlin (1972, p. 15)

Concerns about power in public relations may be as old as the practice. Professionals know that power and influence are crucial to getting things done inside organizations. They need a seat at the table, or at least the attention of organizational leaders, when important decisions are being taken or implemented. Many professionals believe they are relatively powerless in these strategic moments, however, and their complaints about the absence of power are often expressed in an all too familiar litany:

"Why don't we report to the CEO?"
"Why do they only listen to us when there's a crisis?"
"Why are we only involved with tactics and execution, never strategy?"
"Why don't *they* understand the real role and value of PR?"

We encountered these and other power concerns frequently in the past 2 years during our discussions and research with hundreds of public relations professionals. Simply put, practitioners told us there are two reasons for a shortage of power and influence in public relations: organizational leaders who just don't get it and professionals who just don't have it. Some said organizational leaders are the problem: They don't understand the role and value of the practice, and they don't view PR practitioners as legitimate members of strategic decision-making circles. Others blamed professionals themselves for being too inexperienced, too passive, or too publicity focused, or for being deficient in leadership and strategic managerial skills.

These are not new findings (L. A. Grunig, J. E. Grunig, & D. M. Dozier, 2002), but they reinforce a widespread belief that the practice is marginalized. As a result, the potential of public relations to help organizations navigate a complex and turbulent world is limited. Moreover, marginalization of the practice makes it difficult to advance the image of professionals beyond widely held perceptions of flacks and publicists. Given this longtime dilemma, what can professionals do about it? How can they increase their influence and acquire legitimacy?

This book attempts to provide some answers. We focus on influence (the use of power) and how professionals can develop, mobilize, and use it to become more active, effective, and ethical agents in organizational decision making. We believe that individual professionals can increase their influence if they become more politically astute, employ more diverse influence resources and tactics, and exert greater political will in organizational arenas where decisions are shaped through power relations. The book provides a descriptive theory of these power relations and then details a lengthy list of influence resources and tactics that professionals may develop, mobilize, and use in such arenas.

But if the profession wants to increase its social legitimacy and influence on a larger scale, we must rethink the practice—what it is and might be, and what it does and might do. If McLaughlin's (1972) assessment in the chapter-opening quotation is right, and many of the professionals we interviewed said it is, the potential of public relations is limited in large measure by how we and others "see" and define the practice. To conceive of public relations as something other than managing communications and making images, we must first extract the practice from some of the myths in which it is embedded, then locate its potential sources of power and examine how public relations power intersects with ongoing relations of power inside organizations.

Rethinking public relations is not a simple matter given its history, prevailing conceptions, and the dominant routines and structures that continue to produce and reproduce professional practice as we know it. To help us reflect on the practice, then, we conceptualize the role of public relations as one of resistance. Though the notion of resistance in practice may seem counterintuitive or even ridiculous, this approach helps because it foregrounds some vital issues and forces in and around the practice that receive limited attention in academic studies and professional forums, for example, power relations, influence strategies and tactics, and dissent and activist approaches.

Our goal in reflecting on public relations in this manner is not to help practitioners become more efficient providers of communication products and services, or to improve relationships with strategic publics, though these outcomes are possible. Nor do we seek to help professionals and their organizations become more controlling in a world that already appears to be dominated by increasingly large global organizations. We also are not interested in just helping the profession "get its way."

Rather, our goal is to help public relations professionals become more influential in ongoing power relations so that they may better help their organizations do the right things. On one level this means making ethical choices and acting and communicating responsibly. On another level it refers to creating an organizational environment conducive to exploring new ideas, raising different views and inviting different voices, and questioning basic assumptions and worldviews. To achieve our goal we develop a descriptive theory of power relations that helps explain why a resistance role is necessary for public relations professionals to increase their influence.

POWER AND INFLUENCE DEFINED

Power and *influence* are closely related terms. Power is often described as a capacity, or something possessed, that allows one to get things done or get others to do what you want them to do (Barbalet, 1985; Cobb, 1984; Greiner & Schein, 1988; L. A. Grunig, 1992b; Hay & Hartel, 2000; Lauzen & Dozier, 1992). In an essay on power and resistance, Barbalet expressed this broad conception of social power: "Ordinarily ... 'power' is understood as the expression of capacity to initiate .... In the broadest terms power has to do with getting things done, or getting others to do them. If it means anything, social power is the generative force through which social relations and institutions are directed" (p. 538).

If power is the capacity or potential to get things done, then *influence* is the use, expression, or realization of power (Hinkin & Schriesheim, 1990; Mintzberg, 1983; Salancik & Pfeffer, 1977). Influence is the process through which power is actually used or realized (Pfeffer, 1992); it is the use of power to get things done, or to accomplish something, for some purpose in organizations (Kanter, 1977; Mintzberg, 1983).

Daudi (1983) reminded us that every individual and group has some power and can exercise it as influence. Every group and individual is also subjected to the power and influence of others, creating complex networks or relations of power in organizations that may be either repressive or productive in nature. The formidable powers and influences of CEOs or other organizational leaders are well documented (Mintzberg, 1983; Pfeffer, 1992), but organizational members at all levels have some power. A receptionist, for example, can influence a visitor's initial perceptions of an organization through his or her conversational tone, responsiveness, and a variety of nonverbal communications. A production worker can influence productivity and product quality through absenteeism, the pace of work, and the extent to which production guidelines are followed.

Power may come from many sources—formal authority, access to decision makers, information, problem-solving expertise, experience, and relationships—and therefore multiple resources exist for those who seek influence (Berger, 2005; A. R. Cohen & Bradford, 1989; French & Raven, 1960; Greiner & Schein, 1988; Kanter, 1977; Kipnis, Schmidt, & Wilkinson, 1980; Mintzberg, 1983; Yukl, Guinan, & Sottolano, 1995). Influence may be directed to achieving self-interests, team or unit goals or interests, organizational objectives, or the interests of others (Hay & Hartel, 2000; Holtzhausen & Voto, 2002; Kipnis et al., 1980; Schriesheim & Hinkin, 1990).

Power is often exercised in organizations to influence actions, agendas, decisions, and resource allocations (Allen, Madison, Porter, Renwick, & Mayes, 1979; L. A. Grunig, 1992b; Mintzberg, 1983; Pfeffer, 1981; Plowman, 1998). Influence also may be used to control access to others or to information (Brass & Burkhardt, 1993; Hardy & Clegg, 1996; Mechanic, 1962); to shape messages, meanings, interpretations, attitudes, and beliefs (M. Edelman, 1964; Ferris, Fedor, Chachere, & Pondy, 1989; Fimbel, 1994; Motion & Leitch, 1996; Tedeschi & Melburg, 1984; Vigoda & A. Cohen, 2002); and to reward, discredit, or punish (French & Raven, 1960; Morrill, 1989; Spicer, 1997).

Though theorists quibble over subtle distinctions between power and influence, most organizational members use the terms interchangeably

(Mintzberg, 1983; Salancik & Pfeffer, 1977). This was the case among the professionals we interviewed, so we use power and influence to mean more or less the same thing, that is: *the ability to get things done by affecting the perceptions, attitudes, beliefs, opinions, decisions, statements, and behaviors of others*. Because we are most interested in the exercise of power through various strategies and tactics, we often use the word *influence*. Public relations professionals have access to a great many influence resources, but they appear to use and rely on relatively few. This is puzzling given the profession's concerns with power.

POWER IS THE NUMBER ONE ISSUE IN PUBLIC RELATIONS

In the spring of 2003, we conducted an online survey of public relations professionals, academics, and graduate students to learn what they considered to be the most important issue in public relations. Drawing from the trade and academic literatures, we constructed a list of 13 professional issues and asked 801 public relations professionals, teachers, and graduate students to select the 2 issues they felt were most important, or to write in others they deemed significant. About 500 professionals were randomly selected from the Public Relations Society of America's (PRSA) membership directory, and 149 educators were randomly selected from membership directories of the International Communication Association (ICA) and the Association for Education in Journalism and Mass Communication (AEJMC). A list of 146 graduate students was developed through contacts with universities offering graduate degrees or advanced courses in public relations. In the end, 219 individuals completed the survey (response rate of 27.3%).

Overall, respondents named 19 important professional issues (Table 1.1), but "gain a seat at the decision-making table" was named the first or second most important issue by 74 respondents (33.8% of total). The number two issue was "measure the value of public relations" (62 respondents, or 28.3% of total). Other issues were named far less frequently, and professional licensing and individual practitioner excellence were identified as significant issues by only a handful of respondents.

Gaining a seat at the decision-making table was the first or second most important issue among most of the demographic "groups" represented in the survey. The issue was the most important and strikingly consistent one for practitioners at agencies (35.7%), nonprofit organizations (39.2%), and corporations (37.0%). It also was the most important issue for public relations graduate students (26.5%), and for women

TABLE 1.1
Most Important Public Relations Issues

Issue	# Responses	% Responses
Gain a seat at the decision-making table	74	33.8
Measure the value of PR	62	28.3
Communicate with diverse publics	37	16.9
Reduce information clutter	32	14.6
Enhance professional image	30	13.7
Strengthen critical-thinking skills in PR	29	13.2
Resolve ethical challenges	25	11.4
Use new technologies appropriately	24	11.0
Reduce "spin" in practice	21	9.6
Increase cross-cultural knowledge	21	9.6
Increase employee trust	18	8.2
Strengthen leadership skills in the profession	15	6.8
Increase individual excellence in practice	7	3.2
License PR professionals	5	2.3
Other issues	15	6.8

(33.3%) and men (35.1%). Among academics, the issue was third (23.3%) behind "measuring the value of public relations" (33.3%) and "enhancing the image of public relations professionals" (26.7%), though a number of academics pointed out the three issues are interrelated.

Through several open-ended questions we encouraged respondents to comment on the issues or explain their selections. The most frequent comments indicated that not having a seat at the decision-making table adversely affected the profession's reputation and its ability to help organizations make important strategic decisions. One agency professional captured this widely expressed belief: "For PR professionals to be taken seriously and seen as a profession, they must have a seat at the head of the table. Only then will the PR field really be able to help organizations make good choices and communicate accurately and receive the respect it deserves."

A corporate PR director was one of a number of respondents who highlighted the important role that public relations might play in ethical decision making if it held a seat at the table: "PR professionals are not considered a part of the decision-making processes in large companies. PR needs to be in on the decision-making process from the start. We represent the ethics of the company but have no voice."

Some respondents blamed professionals themselves for the profession's lack of voice. A corporate media relations director attributed this to professional timidity: "PR practitioners are often just order takers and are too afraid of losing their jobs to strive to be decision makers. We need to take fewer orders and get tougher." Another corporate PR director said, "If we are capable of actual strategic thinking, rather than just being editorialists, we will gain this position naturally. Too many of us are still editorialists."

An agency supervisor indicated the problem had to do with the profession's inability to explain what it actually does: "As professionals, we do a lousy job of explaining to those publics with whom we work what we do .... I think it's our fault, but I don't know what to do about it."

One seasoned professional expressed frustration about the lack of a power seat and wondered when the profession would address it: "We will never be truly part of the management function without a seat at the table. We all know this, PRSA knows this, academics know this. So when are *we* going to do something about it?"

Of course, power relations in organizations are more complex than simply holding a seat at important decision-making tables, and being a member of the dominant coalition or inner circle is no guarantee of influence. Being present and being listened to are not the same thing, and membership in the dominant coalition carries the risk of co-optation of professional voice and values (Holtzhausen, 2000; Holtzhausen & Voto, 2002). At the same time, one does not need to be a member of the inner circle to possess power or exert influence (Mintzberg, 1983; Pfeffer, 1992).

Membership in organizational power circles nevertheless provides some important advantages. It signifies that formal authority has been granted to the public relations professional. This authority embodies two dimensions of power—position power and participation power—that contribute to a third type of power, perceived power (Williams & Wilson, 1997). In addition, membership in the dominant coalition provides regular access to key decision makers and to more strategic information for use (Kanter, 1977). Being present in strategic circles also provides professionals the opportunities to speak, advocate, debate, resist, and participate in decision making, and having "voice" is a critical dimension of influence (Berger, 2005; L. A. Grunig, 1992b).

Though power appears to be a preoccupying concern in the profession, it receives limited attention in public relations research and theorizing. Moreover, public relations power receives almost no attention in trade publications or formal professional association publications, training programs, or professional conferences, as is evident in any review of these publications and conferences over the past 5 years. For example, in the 10th-anniversary issue of *PR Tactics* in July 2004, several dozen public relations executives and leaders were asked to forecast what the profession would be like by 2014 and to express their hopes for it ("PR Blotter," 2004). With few exceptions, these experts said that crucial future issues included professional licensing and accreditation, mastering new technologies, understanding diverse cultures, gaining business knowledge, and improving technical skills.

These are important issues, of course, but the fact that none of these PR leaders mentioned the power issue is striking. Why isn't power a more transparent issue in our academic studies, or in the profession's own public conversations with itself through its journals, conferences, and association forums? Why hasn't the academy and the profession worked harder to understand how power intersects the practice and what public relations professionals might do to become more influential agents in power relations?

Perhaps it's because power has long been a loaded and "dirty" word in organizational studies (Kanter, 1977; Pfeffer, 1992; Porter, Allen, Angle, 1990), or because it might be seen as politically incorrect for public relations professionals, so dedicated to building empowered relationships, to talk about becoming more powerful. Power is often seen in a negative, dominating, and controlling sense, though it may certainly be productive as well as repressive (Daudi, 1983; Holtzhausen, 2000; Holtzhausen & Voto, 2002; Pfeffer, 1992).

Or perhaps power is often absent from professional public relations forums and communications because professionals simply don't want to formally talk about it. They are too busy working to achieve new efficiencies on the job, managing multiple communication projects, and fighting the latest fires. It's difficult enough just keeping up with pressing daily demands, let alone trying to envision and realize a more powerful profession or alternative potentials for the practice. We don't know the answer, but our research suggests that part of the issue is a failure to understand or acknowledge existing power relations and the ways in which they shape organizational decision making and public relations practice.

OUR APPROACH AND ASSUMPTIONS

Management theorists Mintzberg (1983) and Pfeffer (1992) argued that modern organizations will not begin to function better until the power structures and processes in and around them are fully explored and understood. We believe the same argument holds for the public relations profession: Power relations that weave through and around the practice must be examined and understood if the profession is to advance and achieve its greater potential. Before examining public relations power in more depth, however, it's important to outline our approach and disclose some of our assumptions about public relations theory, practice, and the state of the profession.

Our views in the book reflect our scholarly predispositions as well as some biases growing out of more than 30 years of combined public relations professional experiences within corporate and university settings. We cannot fully set aside these professional experiences—nor do we want to—but we do temper them with the views and experiences of others gleaned through the public relations body of knowledge and through empirical evidence obtained in seven research projects carried out for this book. The voices of more than 1,200 public relations professionals whom we interviewed and surveyed, along with those of the theorists and researchers we cite, ground this book both in the workplace and in the academic marketplace of ideas and theories.

Five Assumptions

Our views are further grounded in five assumptions we make about public relations theory and practice, as follows:

1. Public relations theorizing is an ongoing conversation about the nature of the practice. The public relations literature includes a variety of theoretical perspectives that compete to define, explain, and critique the practice. Each perspective is a lens through which public relations may be viewed and interpreted. Each view is accompanied by an ideology or belief system regarding the nature of practice and its roles, purposes, methods, values, and so forth.

These perspectives may be categorized or labeled in various ways. Leichty (2003), for example, used a cultural theory approach to identify five theoretical perspectives, which he referred to as cultural voices or cultural tribes of public relations. In this view, each theoretical perspective is supported by a group of followers or believers who advocate on behalf of the view. Some groups are larger, or noisier, or more visible than others, and sometimes individuals move back and forth from one tribe or group to another because the lines between the groups are blurred to some extent.

Theoretical perspectives also may be grouped around views on a particular issue in practice. If we take the subject of this book, for example, we can locate different perspectives on power in practice. For example, excellence theorists (e.g., L. A. Grunig et al., 2002) see the dominant coalition as the primary power center in organizations and advocate for shared power among members and stakeholders. Rhetorical theorists often focus on how organizations use language to attempt to influence public discourse (Cheney & Vibbert, 1987; Heath, 1993, 1997; Heath & Nelson, 1986) and manage impressions with diverse publics (Cheney, 1991; Cheney & Dionisopoulos, 1989; Toth & Heath, 1992). Critical theorists are directly concerned with power—who has it and who doesn't—and the relations of power in social formations (German, 1995; L. A. Grunig, 1992b; Holtzhausen, 2000; Leitch & Nielson, 1997; Mickey, 1997, 2003).

There are other perspectives and voices, too, including those of chaos theorists, contingency scholars, postmodernists, and occasionally organizational and social theorists. Overall, the voice of each group contributes to an ongoing conversation about public relations; these diverse voices "animate discussions about the nature of public relations" (Leichty, 2003, p. 281). In our view, this ongoing conversation provides richer insights into the practice than any single perspective.

To use an analogy from the online world, each perspective represents a discussion thread in a chat room or on a discussion board. Participants log in and log off and tend to join those discussion threads that are of most interest to them. That is what we do, too. Though we adopt a power relations perspective in this book, we periodically join and draw from a variety of these discussion threads to construct and present our arguments.

2. A practical–critical approach foregrounds power relations and suggests practical actions and consequences. Craig (1989) argued that communication studies and the discipline should be practical; that is, the discipline should "cultivate communicative praxis, or practical art, through critical study" (p. 98). Cheney (1995) made a similar point when he described his essay about workplace democracy as a "theoretical-practical exploration" that was intended to "provoke further thought, discussion, empirical research and social action" (p. 169). More recently, Woodward (2003) suggested that in a practical–critical approach to communication "critical analysis should have practical consequences, specifically to extend participation and to introduce innovative forms of communication" (p. 411).

We follow a practical–critical approach in this book. We examine public relations in a critically reflexive manner and then suggest practical ways in which professionals can become more influential agents in strategic organizational decision making. Our approach draws from a critical theory conversational thread in several senses. First, we examine topics that are most often addressed by public relations critical theorists—power, influence, and forms of professional dissent and resistance (Berger, 2005; German, 1995; O'Connell-Davidson, 1994). We do this to uncover and assess underlying power relations. Second, critical studies can promote self-conscious reflection on the practice and raise alternative views about what it is or might be (Cheney, 1995; Weaver, 2001), and our central intent in this book is to advance a resistance role for public relations.

But we also ground our critical approach in practice, drawing from data systematically collected in the work world. We have conducted more than 180 depth interviews with diverse professionals from nonprofit, agency, corporate, university, religious, and social movement organizations. Through these interviews, and in concurrent surveys involving more than a thousand other professionals, we examine definitions and perceptions of power, preferred influence tactics and strategies, constraints on practice, public relations roles and responsibilities, and forms of professional advocacy, dissent, and activism. In doing so, we hope to provide practitioners with more knowledge about power in practice—how to get it and when and how to skillfully use it—to become more influential agents and help their organizations do the right things.

3. Public relations work is inherently political. Spicer (1997) argued persuasively that a political-system metaphor is the best way to understand relationships between public relations power and organizational power. He contended that power is located in the interactions between people, and "PR positions are political in nature and demand use of influence" (p. 132). To become effective and influential players in the political infrastructure of the organization, practitioners need to become more politically astute.

This view of organizations as political systems is supported by many organizational and management theorists. Organizations are political networks and systems of influences because employees or members have diverse and competing agendas and self-interests (Ferris et al., 1989; Greiner & Schein, 1988); competition exists for scarce resources (Baron & Greenberg, 1990); structural arrangements and hierarchies foster competition (Hay & Hartel, 2000); pressures exist for organizational compliance and survival (Jackall, 1988); and organizational uncertainties and deficiencies produce differing interpretations of, and solutions to, such problems (Mintzberg, 1983, 1985; Salancik & Pfeffer, 1977).

We share the view of these and other theorists that all organizations are political to some extent, falling within a broad range from the nearly apolitical organization (e.g., small start-up companies or community-based service agencies) to organizations so infested with politics and bureaucratic procedures that they are virtually dysfunctional (e.g., U.S. auto manufacturers in the 1980s). In such environments, the practice of public relations is also inherently political, and professionals must therefore possess the political intelligence, skill, and will to effectively use influence resources and compete as agents or players. Otherwise, as professionals told us, they are likely to be order takers who provide and serve a menu of technical support services.

4. Actual public relations practice is governed by how it is defined and by whom. We've all participated in endless discussions about what public relations is, its role, its obligations, and so forth. Though many grow weary of these debates, the discussions underscore the essential dissonance in the field: Who do practitioners serve? Their own career interests? The organization? The profession? Organizational publics or greater society? All of these, somehow? Moreover, who is defining that service (Rakow, 1989)? Practitioners? Theorists? Professional associations? The CEO or top manager? Professions such as advertising, marketing, or human resources? These conflicting interests and perspectives create tension in practitioners and highlight the importance of role definition and the roles actually taken on in practice, which cannot be separated from whom one serves or how one is defined.

Diverse definitions of roles and interests, found even among professionals working in the same public relations team, also make it more difficult to imagine alternative possibilities for the practice. Any future public relations has its roots in public relations of the present and past and is linked to people and events only loosely connected over time. In a sense, our profession is caught up in our current actions and practices as well as those of previous professionals from whom we learned directly or indirectly.

Similarly, perceptions of public relations today are products not only of who we are, what we do, and how we perform, but also of who our predecessors were and what they did and how they performed, and especially how organizational leaders and power holders defined and valued the function. These layers of meanings and definitions, interwoven over time, demarcate what public relations is and isn't.

Two professional roles have grown out of this historical context. Academics call them *technician* and *managerial* roles (Dozier, 1992; Dozier & Broom, 1995), whereas practitioners often refer to them as *order takers* and *strategic advisers* or consultants. Technicians and order takers play important communication production and distribution roles in organizations, whereas managers and strategic advisers are seen to be members of dominant coalitions and to have some role in strategic discussion and decision making. We discuss roles in more detail in the next chapter, but we believe that seeing our practice framed in these two roles limits its potential, and it is time to consider a third role, a *role of resistance* in practice.

For now, we use *resistance* in two senses. It refers to a *process* of mobilizing and using a wide range of advocacy, dissent, and activist strategies and tactics in power relations. The term also is used in the sense of *motivation*, that is, the professional motivation to push back on forces that constrain the profession and to actively engage in power relations in the interests of trying to do the right thing.

We selected the term resistance for two reasons. First, we wanted to encourage professionals to think about the practice in a different way. It seems counterproductive or counterintuitive to define public relations as resistance when the role has been seen for so long as a function for carrying out efficient and effective communication in the service of organizations. We don't mean to imply that public relations shouldn't or doesn't perform such service. Of course it does. But we want to think about the practice in some other ways, too, and a perspective of resistance foregrounds power and influence considerations and forces us to consider their implications in practice.

Second, we think resistance is an appropriate term for this alternative role. To fully understand how public relations can help organizations, it is important to understand both the current role, that is, one often characterized by a strong technical/functional orientation, and the opposite of that role, one wherein public relations is relatively powerful and engaged in strategic organizational decision making.

Several researchers have pursued the notion of resistance in practice. Derina Holtzhausen (2000) focused on resistance in the form of activism at the individual practitioner level. She argued that "public relations is about change or resistance to change" (p. 110), and ethical public relations requires practitioners to become organizational activists who represent the voices of employees and external publics, challenge unjust organizational views and actions, and create opportunities for debate and dissent. Holtzhausen and Voto (2002) later defined an activist role for professionals:

> The practitioner as organizational activist will serve as a conscience in the organization by resisting dominant power structures, particularly when these structures are not inclusive, will preference employees' and external publics' discourse over that of management, will make the most humane decision in a particular situation, and will promote new ways of thinking and problem solving through dissensus and conflict. (p. 64)

According to the researchers, an activist professional becomes influential by building alliances and relationships throughout the organization, creating access to powerful individuals, using professional expertise, and relying on personal characteristics and inner strength or biopower.

Berger (2005) called for resistance activities at the professional association level. Through interviews with 21 senior public relations executives, he examined power relations in corporate inner circles and identified a complex set of constraints that limit public relations, making it difficult for professionals to do the right thing, even if they want to. He suggested that various forms of resistance to a dominance model in corporations could help practitioners become more influential change agents. He urged professional associations to adopt an activist role to help practitioners become more effective participants in power relations and to advance the image of practice.

5. Public relations work is vital, but PR professionals may be expendable. Social theorist James Coleman (1974, 1990) traced out the historical rise and corresponding influences of the modern corporate actor. He argued that these organizations have altered economic, political, social, and communicative arrangements and practices, so that today "power resides in the corporate actor, and the power held by natural persons decreases, while that held by corporate actors increases" (1974, p. 37).

Of primary interest here, Coleman suggested that the rise of the corporation changed personal relations and communications.

Though individuals have always interacted with other individuals, two newer and more formidable types of communication interactions now present themselves to individuals: (a) corporate interactions, or corporate actors communicating with other corporate actors, and (b) corporate actors interacting and communicating with individuals. Because such actors exert control over much of the information about transactions with individuals, issues of information power and information rights become increasingly important and contested (1974, p. 78).

Coleman's insights about communicative practices and the evolution of corporations also apply to some other large organizations, including governments and governmental agencies and departments (e.g., Department of Defense and Environmental Protection Agency), substantive movement or special-interest groups (e.g., Sierra Club or Greenpeace), and some labor unions, among others. In this altered world, then, organizational communication agents, producers, technologists, and decision makers play terribly important roles. Their work may affect not only their own organizations and themselves, but also other individuals, organizations, and the very nature of the communicative arrangements and practices that distribute information power and govern the rights to information. To the extent that practitioners influence communication decisions, as well as what gets communicated and how and when, then the profession has the potential not only to help their organizations survive, compete, and be heard, but also to help organizations do the right things in terms of information power and information rights with stakeholders.

Though we believe that organizations large and small *will* communicate and literally *must* communicate in this social system, we do not take it for granted that public relations professionals per se are required for these communication interactions. Indeed, there are already signs of encroachment in leadership positions in the practice by lawyers, sales and marketing professionals, and specialist business consulting firms (Lauzen & Dozier, 1992; Ruler & Lange, 2003). We see this development as no immediate threat to the 200,000 or so current professionals in the United States, but it does present a challenge to public relations leaders and to the profession. What would be the effects of the wholesale replacement of several thousand public relations leaders by individuals who are not communication specialists, or by individuals with narrower views of the organization, its publics, and its responsibilities? Would it matter?

We think it would, and this possibility underscores the importance of power in public relations, and the need to rethink public relations, for the future of the profession as well as the routines and direction of practice. Though we believe public relations influence is in short supply at all levels, the most critical need is at the leadership level. Powerful PR leaders must overcome a number of constraints on the practice. To do so they draw from power sources, and the literature has highlighted some of them, for example, experience, expertise, enactment of the managerial role, and membership in the dominant coalition (Dozier, 1992; Dozier, L. A. Grunig, & J. E. Grunig, 1995; L. A. Grunig, 1992b; L. A. Grunig et al., 2002; Lauzen & Dozier, 1992).

We describe many more influence resources and tactics that are available for use. Combining these approaches with political intelligence and skill offers opportunities for increased influence, *if* public relations leaders possess the will to engage in power relations. In our view, the issue of political willpower among public relations leaders is an open and crucial question. Before addressing these issues, however, we take a closer look at how professionals see and define public relations influence inside their organizations.

HOW PROFESSIONALS DEFINE INFLUENCE

In the spring of 2004, we conducted interviews with 65 public relations professionals to examine the subject of influence in practice (the Influence Interviews). We asked the professionals how they defined influence, the nature of constraints on their influence, and which influence resources they found to be most valuable on the job and which were in shortest supply. We also asked them about their own dissent activities and unsanctioned forms of resistance. In addition, participants discussed their professional roles and issues of service, and shared their ideas about how the profession might increase its influence and enhance its image. The interviews included semistructured and open-ended questions and averaged about 48 minutes in length. The shortest interview was 24 minutes whereas the longest was 89 minutes.

The sample (Table 1.2) was deliberately constructed to represent diverse professionals and organizations and to create potential for variance in responses and findings. We initially contacted about 30 professionals we knew to solicit their participation. We subsequently asked them and additional interviewees to suggest other candidates who might be interested in the study. In this way, we were able to inter-

TABLE 1.2
Sample for the Influence Interviews

Type of Organization	Female	Male	Total
Corporation	3	20	23
PR agency	7	9	16
Nonprofit	8	1	9
Education	6	2	8
Social movement	2	3	5
Government	2	2	4
Totals	28	37	65

view 65 female and male professionals in diverse companies, agencies, nonprofit organizations, educational institutions, government agencies, and social movement or activist groups.

Thirty-seven (or 56.9%) of the participants were male whereas 28 (43.1%) were female. About one third (23, or 35.4% of total sample) of those we interviewed worked for corporations, whereas 16 (or 24.6%) were employed at public relations agencies. Nonprofit organizations (9), educational institutions (8), social-movement groups (5), and government agencies (4) also were represented in the sample. In addition, 15 of the 65 participants were non-Americans, including professionals in Korea (5), Australia (4), England (2), and 1 each in Canada, China, France, and Sweden. Many of the participants were midlevel public relations managers, though length of professional experience of participants ranged from 2 to 42 years and averaged about 21 years.

We first asked participants to define what public relations influence inside their organizations means to them, and some respondents provided two or three definitions. Overall, we identified two primary definitional themes and four secondary themes in the collective responses that hint at the complexity of perceptions of influence in practice.

Primary Influence Definitions

Public relations influence was defined most often as *holding a seat at the decision-making table.* Somewhat more than half of the participants indicated that being in a position to contribute to and affect strategic discussions, decisions, and actions—participating in the strategic decision-making process—was what public relations influence meant, or should mean. This theme was prominent across genders, organizations, and nationalities; 12 of the 15 non-American professionals defined public relations influence in this way. One longtime corporate practitioner summarized the views of many in this regard: "Influence is one's ability to impact strategic plans of the company—its overall direction, objectives, and so forth. It's also being asked to the table during development of those plans rather than entering the process later to pick up the pieces."

An agency executive noted that a seat at the table was more important than one's rank or reporting relationship, a sentiment shared by others in this group: "I think one of the problems we have in the profession, everyone says they have to report to the CEO to be effective. But that doesn't guarantee you are going to be strategic, or be treated strategically. I think the key point is, are you invited in to help develop strategies and solutions? Do you have a seat at the table?"

About a dozen professionals, however, argued that having a seat at the table was a necessary but not sufficient requirement for influence. They articulated a related subtheme; that is, influence means *having a voice, being listened to, and being heard* when seated at the table. A university information officer expressed this point most directly: "Being influential means that your arguments are listened to, your voice is sought out, and you are paid attention to. In other words, what you say has some weight and counts. You've got a voice they hear."

A public affairs director noted that not all who are seated at the table are recognized or treated equally, so meaningful participation is what counts: "Influence is a little more than just having a seat at the table. A lot of people get a seat at the table as an honorific, but it doesn't mean a hell of a lot because no one listens to them.... So it really amounts to a degree of actual involvement in the decision-making process itself."

A Canadian PR director said the perception by others of one's voice, or political power, also was important: "Are you perceived as a player within the organization? You need to be perceived as someone who has a real voice, someone who's a player, by the CEO or collectively by the decision-making group."

The second most common definition of public relations influence was *having the persuasive power or ability* to convince others of your point of view; to sell your ideas, approaches, and solutions; to get others to do something they don't want to do; and just to "get things done." Having a seat at the table emphasizes the importance of presence in strategic decision-making circles and processes, and having a voice highlights being a player who receives attention and gets listened to. However, having persuasive ability and power refers to "winning out" in addition to participation or voice in strategic discussions. About one quarter of those we interviewed, nearly all whom were corporate and agency professionals, expressed this definition of influence. We should note that the few practitioners who defined public relations influence as the ability to build consensus worked for nonprofit, educational, or activist groups.

From an agency perspective, persuasion is often linked to a client, and one agency executive bluntly articulated what this means: "I'm influential when I convince the client to do something…. Not only do I frame the issues and topics [for clients], but I tell them what to say, what messages to deliver, etc. Left to their own devices, all they would do is come up with sales messages."

A French public affairs director noted a distinction between formal and informal influence and the importance of persuasive ability to the latter:

> Influence in public relations is the power to persuade and convince others to get things done, without necessarily having the authority to do it. In a French company, delegation of authority does not trickle down very far. Many decisions are taken by the most influential persons and rubber-stamped by executive management. Thus, there's formal influence by virtue of one's title, and the more informal influence I'm referring to.

Secondary Influence Definitions

We also identified four secondary definitional themes, each of which was expressed by a handful of respondents. Though these themes collectively represent the views of fewer than one fourth of those we interviewed, they demonstrate some of the diverse ways that professionals see their roles and public relations power. The first theme suggests that influence means *delivering tangible results to support the organization,* that is, favorable publicity, achievement of company or unit goals, and enhanced reputation. In this view, producing results yields influence. As one professional said, "Influence comes from driving an agenda that ultimately influences the internal and external image of the company in a positive way to help the business get results." One's performance record is an important source of influence, and we describe a number of influence resources in chapter 4.

A second minor theme defined influence as *managing the communication production process.* Those who expressed this definition—and they largely represented nonprofits and activist groups—linked public relations influence with control of internal and external communication processes, that is, constructing messages, targeting audiences, selecting channels, producing materials, and so forth. Still others defined influence as effectively advocating for the profession, or *convincing others of the role and value of public relations*. As one director at a large nonprofit organization summarized this view:

> To have influence, people have to understand and value your role. I find that a big part of my job is trying to convince the executives and other key players in the organization of the importance of media relations, marketing, public relations. I don't think many people understand the true benefit.... So we're always trying to convince people that we do a lot more than just handing out press releases.

Finally, a handful of the professionals said that influence means effectively *interpreting the needs and issues of external publics* into responsive and responsible organizational actions. This perspective reflects the boundary-spanning role of public relations and signals the importance of interpreting the external world to those inside organizations, as well as interpreting organizational actions back to external publics. As one corporate VP summarized this view:

> Influence relates to the purpose of PR inside the organization and that is to be a window to the outside world. In terms of your influence on the organization, it has to be in the area of your professional expertise and that consists of the ways you can make the outside world and its issues real to the inside world of the organization.

Proposition Regarding Influence

Findings from the interviews suggest the following proposition regarding the meaning of *influence* in public relations practice:

> **Proposition 1: Public relations professionals define influence in practice in diverse ways, but most practitioners equate influence with having a seat and a voice at the decision-making table.**

Definitions of influence by participants in the Influence Interviews included having a seat at the table, possessing persuasive powers with decision makers, controlling communication production processes, producing results, interpreting the needs of external publics, and advocating for the practice with decision makers. This range of views is valuable in helping us think about an equally diverse set of influence resources that are available for use by professionals. It also helps us begin to see how practitioners' perceptions of power may be closely linked to perceptions of their roles. Professionals who equate influence with control over communication production processes, for example, may see themselves as technicians. Those who define power as a seat at the table possess a more managerial perspective on their role.

This proposition is also supported in findings from the Most Important Public Relations Issue survey, which indicated that gaining a seat at the table was the number one issue for professionals across organizations. At this point, it seems fair to say that many public relations professionals recognize their lack of power and believe they can obtain more by gaining a seat at the table. The most pressing questions then become: What prevents practitioners from gaining a seat at the table, and how can more influence be obtained?

In chapter 2, we examine a number of constraints on practice, including the longtime dissonance among professionals about public relations roles, issues of service, and what it means to do the right thing. Collectively these constraints curb professional power and diminish the profession's image.

Public Relations Roles, Responsibilities, and the "Right Thing"

> *Doing the right thing is basically doing what you are asked to do and doing it well, professionally. PR gets involved in advocating for communication decisions or strategies, but it is not responsible for strategic choices the company executives make.*
>
> *—Corporate practitioner with 7 years of experience*
>
> *As a public relations counselor, I am the keeper of corporate ethics and values.*
>
> *—Agency professional with 30 years of experience*

Public relations struggles with an identity crisis that grows out of long- standing dissensus in the field about what public relations is, who it serves, what its roles and responsibilities are, and what it means to do the right thing in practice. Of course, individual practitioners know what they do and can explain their role on a micro level. However, as evidenced in the chapter-opening quotations, practitioners hold divergent views about their professional responsibilities. To others in their organizations and the public at large, what the profession is and does is even less clear because it has come to mean many things and operate under numerous labels.

Several years ago, for example, a colleague collected more than 150 business cards from professionals who were attending a national conference. He was amazed to discover the diversity of titles and responsibilities on the cards. They included film publicist, speech writer, environmental affairs director, lobbyist, special events coordinator, reputation manager, employee news editor, political affairs analyst, senior counselor, research assistant, thought partner, VNR (video news release) production manager, marketing consultant, social responsibility director, creative services manager, and financial communications leader, among many others. Only a few cards included the words *public relations*, but all of these individuals proclaimed themselves to be public relations professionals.

Agreement on who public relations experts are and what roles they play are essential to understanding their responsibilities to their organizations and society. Yet, public relations is still little understood or misunderstood on a macro level. In this chapter, we explore some of the reasons for this. We examine several divisive issues in the field—public relations definitions, roles, service, and responsibilities—and suggest that these unresolved issues constrain power in practice and diminish professional image. We then review a number of additional constraints on the profession and present some findings from a comprehensive Dissent Survey in which we asked professionals to respond to a hypothetical question about practice: *What does it mean to "do the right thing" in public relations when management makes a poor or inappropriate decision?* The diverse responses to this question provide a window onto a profession today that may be marked more by its differences than its similarities.

DEFINING PUBLIC RELATIONS

The ongoing debate about public relations roles and definitions is a symptom of the profession's struggle with its appropriate use of power and influence. Seitel (2004), in the introduction to his widely used public relations textbook, noted the definitional issue:

> The fact is that there are many different definitions of public relations. American historian Robert Heilbroner once described the field as "a brotherhood of some 100,000, whose common bond is its profession and whose common woe is that no two of them can ever quite agree on what that profession is." (p. 3)

PRSA adopted its broadly accepted definition in 1988: "Public relations helps an organization and its publics adapt mutually to each other." One of the problems with a simple and universal definition like this one is the boundary–spanning nature of public relations practice. As Cropp and Pincus (2001) noted, efforts to define public relations are complicated by segmenting within the discipline. They argued that divisions within public relations included academic versus professional, public relations terminology versus business terminology, and strategic versus tactical (p. 195). These divisions contribute to the bounty of definitions.

Identity and role divisions reach beyond the profession itself. Public relations educators and practitioners have varying views about the skills and knowledge essential to effective practice of public relations. These understandings are logically related to issues of definition of the profession. For example, a definition that emphasizes public relations as a management function would logically be linked to agreement that strategic planning and a place in the organization's dominant coalition would be essential.

Berkowitz and Hristodoulakis (1999) found that although two distinct orientations—management and technician—existed among both public relations students and practitioners, public relations education was associated with the management orientation. But practitioners acknowledge that the majority of the profession is engaged in technician tasks. In addition, Sallot, Cameron and Weaver Lariscy (1998) found that educators and practitioners disagreed on nearly two thirds (62%) of the items on a survey designed to measure opinions about professional standards.

And Who Does Public Relations Serve?

If the practice is difficult for practitioners and educators to define, so are the roles of practitioners. The purview of public relations spans boundaries and contributes to this role confusion. Public relations professionals address the needs of customers, clients, investors, employees, senior management, community members, constituents, volunteers, donors, and on and on. It is understandable, then, why not only what public relations is and what practitioners do, but also who public relations serves is an oft-debated issue. Furthermore, because of the difference in job descriptions, it is understandable that the responses differ so from professional to professional. A professional in a corporate setting may have a rather narrow or focused job description. A practitioner in an agency setting has a job description that varies from client to client and perhaps even from day to day or hour to hour.

Those who practice in a small or nonprofit setting often have an extremely broad job description.

A Servant of Two (or Three or Four) Masters. We explored the issues of roles and service more closely through the PR Success Interviews and the Influence Interviews. The PR Success Interviews were sponsored by Heyman Associates, a public relations executive search firm in New York. Thirty-minute telephone interviews were conducted with 97 senior public relations executives to examine factors contributing to success in the field and to learn more about influence resources and constraints on the job (Heyman, 2004).

CEO and President William Heyman invited 207 of the most senior leaders in the field to participate in the study, and 97 (or 47.5%) of the invited executives subsequently participated in the interviews. The sample was drawn deliberately to ensure that a mix of senior executives from diverse organizations was represented. Those interviewed included 58 male (59.8% of total sample) and 39 female (40.2%) professionals who averaged 23.4 years of experience in the field. Virtually all of the PR executives held the number one or number two communication position in their organizations. The majority of those interviewed were employed by corporations (60 of 97), but public relations agencies (16), nonprofit organizations (9), educational institutions (6), and public service firms (6) also were represented in the sample. Nearly all of the participants were from the United States.

We asked these executives how success is defined and measured in public relations. Their answers provide a window onto how they define themselves and their practice, and ultimately, to whom they feel most responsible. Just under one quarter of respondents (22 of 97) defined success as holding a decision-making position. About one in five (20 of 97) said having a role in helping the business grow was a means of defining success. These were the two top means of defining success, though the executives used more than 90 descriptives in their definitions. Overall, the public relations leaders defined success at three levels—the individual, the organization, and the group or work unit, in that order.

About half of the executives defined success in terms of personal achievements, skills, and character traits that helped them gain respect, influence, and rewards. Fewer executives, about one third of those interviewed, defined success at the organizational level: They view their success largely in terms of organizational achievements. About one in five executives defined their success in terms of those they lead, equating success to effective leadership, talent development, and mentoring. Only a handful of executives defined success in public relations at the societal level or at multiple levels.

How success is measured is another means of determining the primary focus for responsibility by practitioners. The greatest number of the practitioners in the Success Study (39) cited measurement methods such as surveys, feedback from various publics, and other qualitative and quantitative analyzes as how they quantified success. Far fewer (16) said business success was the way public relations measured its own success. A similar number (15) said they believed public relations success was measured based on the media coverage generated. In short, professionals in these interviews held diverse views about what success in practice means and how it should be measured.

Another means of defining the practice of public relations is looking at who practitioners say they serve. We asked the 65 professionals in the Influence Interviews whose interests they served most when trying to influence decisions in their organization (Table 2.1). About two thirds (43 of 65) said they served their organization first. Many of those we talked with rank ordered their devotion, but they were primarily dedicated to their organization.

Seeing oneself as the servant of the organization can be pragmatic. One U.S. corporate practitioner with three decades of experience explained his loyalty to his company in this way: "I mostly serve my company because it's my livelihood; the company pays my bills, not the publics or society at large. That's not to say I don't hear my publics and express their voices in the organization. I do. But in the end, usually, I serve the organization first. I'm just being honest."

Service to the organization was seen by some respondents as the "right" position to take. Another senior corporate practitioner saw or-

TABLE 2.1
Whose Interests Do You Serve First?

Interest Served	Female	Male	Total
My organization	19	24	43
Myself	2	1	3
Organization's publics	0	1	1
Society at large	3	4	7
In combination	3	8	11
Totals	27	38	65

ganizational loyalty as a badge of honor: "There's no better compliment than to say, 'This guy bleeds for his company. It's all about his company, what he does.' And everyone I worked with who had been there long before me; that was their approach towards what they did in PR."

Others believe that the organization demands service and would balk at a practitioner who suggested that service to society was paramount. A U.S. agency practitioner with 35 years experience explained her hierarchy of devotion:

> Society would be pretty much at the bottom of the list, not necessarily through personal choice but through client dictate. They wouldn't want to spend any money on anything that's not directly tied to generating revenue. Sometimes you can combine the [interests of the organization and society]. For example, ... we promoted the concept of alarms to protect the elderly and disabled. And since the client was the market leader, they would benefit more than anybody else. So, you might say it was a self-serving responsible attitude.

The rationale for devotion to the organization was put succinctly by one practitioner: "There are times you can advocate a position that's primarily in the interest of the general public, but you'd better get the boss's agreement."

However, others believed that it was the role of the public relations practitioner to expand the vision of the organization and its leadership. One corporate practitioner saw his role as helping the organization see opportunities to address the needs of society:

> That's one of the influencer's tricks, I think: to get management to understand that line of sight ... to see that the altruistic thing might be in the best interests of the business as well, that it might be a long-term decision, but at the very least the decision ought to be made that will maintain public approval, sanction your right to exist and operate. And that, by definition, will be aligned with the interests of society at large.

Some practitioners see their role as a calling to help the organization be ethical and altruistic. Many practitioners, when prodded, will share stories about how their organization was going to make one decision, but they suggested a different route that addressed the interests of the organization as well as those of a public or publics.

Public relations scholars often propose a role for the public relations practitioner in which he or she advocates for both the organization and its publics. The goal of this model of practice is for all parties in a situation to "win." This model suggests that the most effective way to practice public relations is to focus on ethics and the needs of society, publics, and the organization in tandem. Some in the Influence Study agreed. One leader in the field said public relations should help the organization see beyond itself:

> I see PR positioned as a very effective check and balance on activities by financialists, by corporate counsel, by CEOs. So that fulfilling a role that ensures that the organization is, for example, financially and legally compliant with federal regulations, which has a positive affect on society at large.... You need a voice of reason. You need credible, honest public relations that focus on truth and honesty rather than the value of the stock price or the valuation of the company.

Another agency practitioner with 30 years of experience lamented the dearth of ethics in companies and provided a vivid example of his own complicity in one such situation:

> As I get older, I worry more about the ethics of the company and the real value it brings to the marketplace. Company X is a good example. I did some work for them preparing comments for the chairman and president for an employee-wide meeting. They presented an image of their company as launching hundreds of new stores around the country ... moving away from an old product line, bring back some things, and so forth. The employee meetings were spectacle. The management came out in T-shirts pumping their fists to rock-and-roll music. Six months later they filed for bankruptcy. It was completely dishonest, and on the way out the door, management loaned themselves millions, which didn't have to be repaid. I almost become physically ill thinking about it, and the fact that I had worked on the messages for that program.

Some respondents strongly disagreed with the idea of the public relations practitioner advocating for society versus their organization. One corporate practitioner with two decades of experience said:

> I've heard more than one PR person over the years try to refer to themselves as the conscience of the corporation. That just goes right through me. That's the most presumptuous statement a person could make regardless of their function. It implies you are leading your company to the betterment of society at large. I'm altogether confident in the good consciences of the people who lead this organization, and they don't need me to tell them what the right thing to do is.

The findings from the Influence Interviews suggest a general change in attitude compared to findings in a survey 15 years earlier by Judd (1989). He surveyed 100 practitioners and found that 65% said they serve society first; 35% said their first responsibility was to their organization or client. This seems to endorse the corporate-conscience role that was so chafed at by the practitioner quoted earlier. It also suggests a change in professional attitudes when two thirds of our respondents pledged primary service to their organization or client, and only about 1 in 10 said they served society first.

Though allegiance to one's employer is important, there should be ways to serve multiple publics. Public relations' role *is* to be the servant of multiple masters. Public relations' role is to help organizations succeed while contributing to society in a positive way. Blind allegiance to an organization, its leadership circle, or chief executive might, in fact, be detrimental to the organization, its publics, and society at large. The examples of such a high price to loyalty are legion and have expanded exponentially in recent years.

Technicians, Strategists, or Both? The role of public relations has been studied for decades. Pasadeos, Renfro and Hanily (1999) found in a bibliometric study of public relations scholarship that public relations roles research was the "largest category of most cited works" (p. 39). Glen Broom and colleagues began a stream of roles research, developing metrics to measure those roles in the 1970s. More recently, Larissa Grunig et al. (2002) provided an extensive review of roles research literature and described metrics used in the Excellence Study.

In 1979, Broom and G. D. Smith defined and tested five practitioner role models. The five models were: the expert prescriber, technical services provider, communication process facilitator, problem-solving process facilitator, and acceptant legitimizer. Broom and Dozier (1986) conducted a panel survey, comparing findings from Broom's work in 1979 to data gathered in 1985. They suggested that, because three of the four roles were not empirically distinct, the best role generalizations would be manager, which included expert prescriber, communication facilitator, and problem-solving process facilitator, and technician. This study (Broom & Dozier, 1986) was found by Pasadeos et al. (1999) to be the most cited article on roles research in the public relations literature.

Roles in public relations are important because they are linked to professional behaviors and to perceptions of others about the practice (Mechanic, 1962). Dozier (1992) noted findings that "practitioners playing the manager role are more likely to be strongly committed to their organization and highly ethical in their view of public relations practices. They see public relations evolving into a management function and they like that trend" (pp. 350–351).

Of course, influence within the organization is generally stronger for a public relations practitioner whose role is more strategic—that of a manager—than production oriented—that of a technician. Though most practitioners play both roles within the workplace, experience suggests that one role is usually dominant over the other. We explore these roles, as well as a resistance role, in chapter 3.

What Constitutes "Doing the Right Thing" in Public Relations?

Ethical Frameworks. Bring up the words *ethics* and *public relations* at any dinner party and you're likely to hear sneers, guffaws, or both. Society, it seems, views the phrase "public relations ethics" as an oxymoron. Even many public relations professionals and educators have been known to quietly chortle at the suggestion that public relations practice should have an ethical focus. Usually the "ethics chapter" falls at the end of textbooks and trade tomes. Unfortunately, news reports all too frequently tell stories of unholy alliances, front groups, and video news releases without journalistic merit, which feed this disreputation. We suggest that public relations practitioners *should* consider their own and society's ethical frameworks. And we believe they should be central to practices rather than a footnote.

Ethicists have identified several ethical frameworks. A teleological framework "emphasizes outcomes; simply put, the ends justify the means. Ethical actions are those that result in the greatest good" (Curtin & Boynton, 2001, p. 411). Utilitarianism is a common form of teleology. Utilitarianism takes a societal view, suggesting that ethical decisions are those that have the greatest impact on society at large. Utilitarianism has been discussed and conceptualized by philosophers such as John Stuart Mill. Philosophy and ethics scholar Sissela Bok (1989) wrote, "For utilitarians, an act is more or less justifiable according to the goodness or badness of its consequences" (p. 48).

Deontological frameworks can be compared to rules. "Deontologists believe that good consequences are not in and of themselves sufficient to guarantee good actions; some acts must be done regardless of their consequences" (Curtin & Boynton, 2001, p. 412). Professional codes of ethics such as those by PRSA or the International Association of Business Communicators (IABC) would be an example of deontological frameworks.

Philosopher John Rawls epitomizes a third common ethical framework based on justice. Rawls introduced a concept he termed the "veil of ignorance" (1971). Rawls suggested that individuals should make ethical decisions based on imagined ignorance of their place in the situation. In short, we make decisions behind a veil based on the understanding that, when stepping out from behind the veil, we might find ourselves on the giving or receiving end of the decision.

In summary, these three common ethical frameworks focus on greatest good (teleology/utilitarianism), agreed–upon rules (deontology), or justice and fairness. From a public relations perspective, teleology might come into play when considering decisions that will affect society as a whole. Deontology, as previously mentioned, is comparable in public relations practice to professional and organizational codes of ethics. Justice ethics might come into play when considering the good of a particular public compared to the good of the organization.

Organizational Ethics. Organizational ethics can be viewed through the frameworks outlined previously, but there are additional corporate-specific ideals at play. To illustrate these frameworks, we provide examples from three points on the spectrum.

Economist Milton Friedman argued that organizations are morally obligated to their stockholders and are thereby required only to make money and obey the law. Friedman's ideas about organizational ethics imply that unethical organizations will not survive because they will not be profitable (M. Friedman, 1970).

Clifford Christians, John Ferre, and Mark Fackler (1993) applied organizational ethics models to media organizations. They argued for a communitarian ethic in which the organization considers not only what is good for itself, but for the community or communities it serves.

Social responsibility as an ethical model for organizations arose as a response to demands for corporations to be involved in more than profit making (Daugherty, 2001, p. 392). This model argues that an ethic of returning to society is essential. Social responsibility may come in the form of charitable giving or community enrichment programs.

Professional Ethics. As noted previously, professional organizations such as PRSA and IABC follow a deontological framework as they outline codes of ethics. PRSA introduces its member code of ethics by stating "Ethical practice is the most important obligation of a PRSA member" (Public Relations Society of America, 2000, p. 5). The association suggests that a professional code of ethics is set on a foundation of professional values that include: advocacy, honesty, expertise, independence, loyalty, and fairness (pp. 6–7).

The 2000 code also contains six provisions. The first code provision requires "protecting and advancing the free flow of accurate and truthful information" (p. 8). Among the goals of this code is to contribute to informed decision making. The second code provision endorses "healthy and fair competition" (p. 9). The third code requires the disclosure of information, stating an intent of building "trust with the public by revealing all information needed for responsible decision making" (p. 10). The fourth code requires practitioners to protect confidentiality (p. 11). The fifth code demands that practitioners avoid "real, potential, or perceived conflicts of interest" (p. 12). The final code asks that professionals "work constantly to strengthen the public's trust in the profession" (p. 13).

IABC's code of ethics for professional communicators includes 12 articles with themes that are similar to the PRSA code. The IABC code embraces free speech, free flow of "essential" information, dissemination of accurate information, abiding by the laws and regulations, protection of confidentiality, and dedication to client or employer. The final IABC code states: "Professional communicators are honest not only with others but also, and most importantly, with themselves as individuals; for a professional communicator seeks the truth and speaks that truth first to the self" (IABC Code, 2005, p. 12).

Enforcing codes of ethics is problematic, and one might ask whether ethics can really be "enforced" at all. PRSA notes that enforcement of its membership codes may result in revocation of membership, though this rarely if ever happens. Central to our thesis is that ethical behavior requires serving as counsel to management and sometimes dissenting with management. This approach is supported by PRSA's code that requires professional members to inform decision making and build trust with publics.

Laws and Regulations.   Nearly all codes of ethics cite duty to societal laws and regulations. Indeed, much of what professional communicators do is either regulated or protected—regulated by governmental organizations such as the Securities and Exchange Commission (SEC) or the Federal Trade Commission (FTC), protected by the First Amendment to the U.S. Constitution or copyright laws. Our purpose here is not a thorough review of communication law, but to acknowledge that following legal and regulatory rules is essential to an ethical practice of public relations.

Briefly stated, in the United States the primary legal protection for speech arises out of constitutional law in the form of the First Amendment. Freedom of speech applies not only to individuals but also to institutions. And those institutions may be the press or corporations. Freedom of speech affects corporate speech, which is not sales-oriented advertising or marketing, but rather a corporation's stance on an issue of public or social interest (Gower, 2003, p. 25). Commercial speech is distinct from corporate speech and is not afforded the same protections. Whereas corporate speech addresses an organization's perspective on a matter of public importance, commercial speech is aimed at promoting a product or service (Gower, 2003, pp. 28–29).

Beyond concerns related to First Amendment issues, the popular and trade media are full of examples of ethical and legal issues that have an impact on the practice of public relations and organizational viability. Some of these newsmakers' names have become nearly synonymous with corporate malfeasance.

Ethical Dilemmas. What is the role of the public relations practitioner when laws or regulations may be or have been broken by their organization or client? Does the public relations counselor simply step aside and defer to the legal counselor? Does the public relations counselor vocalize opposition or work to sidestep potentially damaging organizational behavior? What does ethical practice demand? Clearly, professional codes of ethics require adhering to legal and regulatory constraints. But how can an individual or department help steer an organization away from the rocks and into safe water?

Doing the right thing from an ethical perspective is more difficult than from a legal perspective. Oftentimes, even recognizing the right choice is difficult. Pfeffer (1992) suggested that it is virtually impossible to know what is the right or best decision in some instances. He noted that even the right decision is meaningless without appropriate implementation. Therefore, without a plan of implementation and organizational support for such a plan, a "right" decision is only conjecture. Even knowing the appropriate plan may only be possible as consequences unfold, according to Pfeffer. Finally, he observed that knowing the correct route is complicated by the fact that we spend far more time living with consequences than we do making the decision.

Public relations practitioners have a variety of ways to deal with this uncertainty. One senior public relations counselor we interviewed suggested adopting a best-practices model as a means to inform decision making. He said: "If I don't happen to have experience on my own, I will usually find another organization or another person that can point me to the best practices that have been effective in solving a particular dilemma. I find executives who are involved in such solutions in the past and ask them their experiences."

Although the right answers are sometimes tough to identify, practitioners at a variety of levels can help answer these questions and others. The insight of these practitioners, together with a review of scholarly and trade literature, provide some useful guides for such ethical and legal practice.

What Are Constraints to "Doing the Right Thing" in Public Relations?

Support From the Executive Suite. Though many factors constrain the practice, there is near universal agreement among public relations academics and professionals that for practitioners to be effective they must have support from the executives within their organization and be members of the decision-making structure (Dozier, 1992; Dozier & Broom, 1995; L. A. Grunig, 1992b; L. A. Grunig et al., 2002).

When asked about influence in public relations practice, the highest percentage of practitioners in the PR Success Study said the factor that most impeded public relations practice and influence is the view of public relations among organizational executives. Nearly half (45 of 97) of the executives said that misunderstanding the role of public relations, or the perceptions or view of public relations, by other organizational executives was a substantial hurdle in their influence on decision making.

Results in the Influence Interviews were very similar: 29 of the 65 practitioners said the leading constraints on public relations practice were executive perceptions of the role and the often low position of public relations in the organization's hierarchy. Additionally, about 10% of professionals in each study indicated that lack of access to decision makers adversely affected the practice.

One practitioner summarized this widely held view: "Too often there is an ignorance among leadership about the impact certain decisions can make on public relations. Executives don't have a good understanding of what PR can do. We are always an afterthought." Another linked effectiveness in practice to the degree of executive support: "We succeed as communicators by having the support of senior-most management."

In the Right Place at the Right Time. Not only must public relations professionals have the ear of senior management, they need to be present when organizational strategy is formed in order to convey the interests of various publics. Professionals often complain that they are called upon to put out fires once they erupt, but they are not present in strategic planning sessions to suggest tactics that might keep the fire from occurring in the first place. One public relations executive said, "People do not devote the time and energy to include PR until something has gone wrong. Then they invite them in for 'clean-up.'"

As noted in chapter 1, practitioners most frequently defined their influence as the ability to be heard, or to have input into institutional decisions. But their answers to other questions suggested they are often not in the right place at the right time. Out of 65 respondents in the Influence Interviews, for example, 18 said that public relations' influence is limited by organizational structural or reporting issues (12) or public relations not being in the dominant coalition (6). Of equal importance, 17 said that influence is reduced by a lack of understanding or respect among organizational leadership for the contribution of public relations (see Table 2.2).

One senior practitioner noted the importance of organizational structure: "If you're not at the top in terms of reporting relationships, you may not get heard. Your ideas and recommendations may get filtered along the way, or never even reach decision makers." Berger (2005) found that decision-making structures can be affected in a variety of ways. He noted that the idea that there is a single dominant coalition in large organizations is a myth. Although there are formal decision-making structures such as boards of directors, decision making happens in a variety of structured and unstructured coalitions. Because decision making is diffused, political astuteness is required to understand where the power lies. Therefore, Berger noted, "Many of the

TABLE 2.2
What Limits Your Influence?

Source	Female	Male	Total
Organizational/reporting structure	2	10	12
Lack of resources	7	6	13
Weak PR team	1	5	6
Not in dominant coalition	4	2	6
Lack of understanding/respect for PR	7	10	17
Organizational culture/politics	3	3	6
Other	3	2	5
Totals	27	38	65

Note. $N = 65$.

public relations executives indicated that venues for dominant coalitions often shift from formal to informal settings, effectively closing out or reducing the participation of public relations or other functions in the coalitions" (p. 11).

The fluid nature of decision-making coalitions affects the influence of public relations professionals, even when they have input into those decisions. According to Berger (2005), multiple dominant coalitions contribute to a "porous" structure in large organizations. This can benefit public relations because it provides many points of entry into the process. On the other hand, this porous structure also allows others to have an impact on public relations strategy even after a course has been set, as well as on the content of communication materials as they undergo reviews (p. 12).

When the Public Relations Function Is Directed by Others. In many organizations, the public relations function reports to a manager in some other field of expertise, such as a general legal counsel, a senior vice president of marketing, or a human resources executive. Lauzen (1992) conducted some of the early research on encroachment on the public relations function. She defined encroachment as when professionals from other disciplines are assigned management of the public relations function (p. 61). Of course, such lack of autonomy contributes to a diluting of influence at executive levels. Lauzen argued that establishing centrality of the public relations function is essential in securing influence and staving off encroachment. She found that as public relations professionals demonstrated and believed in the value of the function, encroachment decreased.

More recently, Ruler and Lange (2003) surveyed Dutch organizations and found that more than 60% had one department that coordinated communication activities, but only 42% of those in charge of communication management had job titles that related in any way to communication. Ruler and Lange noted that communication is not an "emancipated specialty" (p. 150) but is frequently encroached on by other professions.

Controllable Constraints. Some of the aforementioned constraints are more easily controlled or changed than are others. It takes cultivating political savvy to increase influence among executives or to ensure that public relations concerns are heard when PR has a place in the dominant coalition. Several professionals said that influence came from political intelligence; however, these PR pros were in the minority (only 6 of 65).

One practitioner said, "You have to have a deep understanding of how a decision is made in your organization because that controls all the ways you use your expertise." Another told us, "The ability to have your views heard and acted on requires being properly wired into the organization, that is, knowing who are the decision makers."

Too often, however, this political intelligence is lacking. As Lauzen (1992) noted regarding encroachment, the best way to hold authority is to identify unique contributions that public relations can make and subsequently make them known. Without the will or skill to identify power brokers in the organization and persuade them of the contributions of public relations, encroachment on the function is more likely.

Practitioners often complain of their influence being eroded by a lack of skill or will within the profession. Sallot et al. (1998) found that public relations practitioners hold "their peers in comparatively low esteem, viewing others collectively as somewhat naive, unprofessional and unenlightened" in comparison to themselves (p. 1). This opinion of the profession was affirmed in our interviews. "I don't think there are all that many great people in the overall profession today," one said.

As noted earlier in the chapter, the highest number of professionals we talked with said that their influence was eroded by the view of public relations or a lack of understanding of the function. Such a lack of respect or understanding might be attributed to public relations selling itself. One senior practitioner was frustrated that the profession "still undersells what we do" and said "we are our own worst enemy."

Removing constraints on public relations practice and influence begins with increasing political intelligence, identifying influence resources, building or selling skills, and showing the will to "do the right thing." What does this mean in practice, especially when professionals find themselves between a rock (the right thing) and a hard place (constraints to influence)? We explore the answer to this question in depth in the remainder of this chapter.

DOING THE "RIGHT THING" IN PUBLIC RELATIONS

In the Dissent Survey (see chap. 8 for more details on the study), we asked respondents to answer this question: *What do you think it means to "do the right thing" in public relations when management is making decisions that you believe are inappropriate?* We purposefully left open the issue of what "inappropriate" might mean so that respondents would provide their own interpretations of the term. We hoped this would increase potential variance among responses. Of the 808 survey participants, 707 (87.41%) answered the question. The number of responses by gender (255 men, or 36.07%, and 452 women, or 63.93%) closely paralleled those in the overall survey. The collective responses yielded 56 pages of single-spaced text that were subjected to qualitative analysis and data reduction following Lindlof (1995). Responses were read and subsequently sorted, categorized, and interrelated according to the emerging patterns and schemes of interpretation.

Some of the responses were brief, for example, "follow the PRSA code," whereas others were mini essays that ran more than 300 words in length. Nearly all of the participants said that doing the right thing meant using professional advocacy to attempt to correct or mitigate an inappropriate decision. Many noted that doing the right thing was contingent on the type or degree of inappropriateness; that is, ineffective or annoying decisions should be treated differently than unethical or illegal decisions. Some also noted the complexity of doing the right thing in situations where there was not always a clear choice between right and wrong. One PR executive captured this view in the following statement:

> Sometimes you are in a difficult situation where there are losers on both sides of a cause. Product liability, moral dilemmas in international labor issues, etc., complex subjects that have negative consequences regardless of the decision. I think communications professionals must be able to look at situations objectively, but each person must decide what they can and will do in terms of ethics, morals, and doing the right thing. There is no clear cut definition for what exactly that means.

Eight respondents said that "pre-emptive advocacy" was the right thing to do; that is, PR professionals should do their jobs so well that inappropriate decisions aren't ever made by organizational executives. They argued that when PR practitioners are members of the dominant coalitions in their organizations, they can help head off poor decision making. A half dozen participants indicated that they were too new to the profession, or had never experienced a situation like the one in question, to be able to know what doing the right thing meant.

A handful also indicated that they couldn't answer the question because it was "too subjective" or "too far beyond the reality of ethical or legal issues which actually occur in organizational environments." On the other hand, 12 of the participants reported that they had been fired from their jobs, or resigned their positions or client accounts, when they refused to carry out management decisions that they believed were unethical, illegal, or immoral.

Seven Categories of Advocacy

The responses of most participants, however, were reflected in seven categories of advocacy in which doing the right thing varied by (a) the extent to which PR professionals would advocate, (b) the types of advocacy approaches they would use, and (c) the framework or perspective from within which they would advocate. The frequencies of responses for each of the seven categories are presented in Table 2.3, and each category is subsequently defined and analyzed.

Loyal Advocates.   Loyalty advocacy (53 professionals) refers to first expressing concerns about an inappropriate decision and attempting to change it. But once you've made the case as a professional, "you've done all you can do." At this point, doing the right thing means supporting the decision and executing professionally. Respondents in this category argued that professionals need to stand by the company and its decision and do what they are asked to do because executives are ultimately responsible for making strategic organizational decisions, not PR professionals. This perspective is represented in the following types of responses to the open-ended question:

- As a public relations professional, it's your job to advise management and stand by management. Doing your job is the right thing.

TABLE 2.3
Seven Categories of Advocacy

Category	F	M	Total	% Sample
Loyalty advocacy	35	18	53	7.50
Self-protective advocacy	29	11	40	5.66
Rational advocacy	113	61	174	24.61
Stakeholder advocacy	23	11	34	4.81
Ethical advocacy	113	55	168	23.76
Activist advocacy	37	22	59	8.35
Exit advocacy	78	63	141	19.94
Other	24	14	38	5.37
Totals	452	255	707	100.00

Note. N = 707.

- I believe that if I express myself clearly on a given topic and a decision is made to the contrary of my opinion, I have done all that I can do.
- In this position, you are always expected to give your opinions, possible media spins, and other useful tips, but in the end, once the decision is made, you must support it, even if you disagree with it.
- Once a decision has been questioned and stands, the role of the PR person is to support that decision.
- Doing the right thing is standing by your company—no matter what .... There are many times when management may have information that you don't have and therefore makes a decision that you may not think is a good decision, but in reality it is—you just don't know it because you don't have all the information.

Eight professionals in this category added that doing the right thing meant "spinning" the decision in the best possible way, as reflected in these statements:

- We as PR professionals must examine the decision and find the positive attributes and create the spin.
- I would try to find the positives in the news and gloss over the negatives.
- Your job as their subordinate is to make the boss (and their decisions) look good.
- It is my responsibility to tell management why I think the decision is inappropriate and what the potential ramifications are. It is then my job to stand by their decision and prepare a plan and materials to help put it in the best light—and be prepared for the worst.

Self-Protective Advocates.   Self-protective advocacy (40 professionals) means discussing an inappropriate decision with management, pressing for change, and documenting and recording your advocacy and actions. Once the decision is final, public relations professionals should then "get as far away from it as possible," or perhaps even refuse to carry out communications in support of the decision. The most important thing from this perspective is to protect yourself so that you don't lose your job or damage your career. This approach to doing the right thing is captured in the following examples of responses:

- Doing the right thing means trying to influence appropriate decision making but I stop short of pushing so hard that my job is jeopardized.... If someone wants to pay me to be their PR person and then ignore my advice and do something stupid, I'm not going to lose my job over it.

- Voice concerns to your superior; document your actions. If severe situation such as legal, get as far away from it as possible.
- Give advice and make the case and if the decision is made that goes against doing the right thing, then you know you did everything in your power to change their minds. Document to CYA.
- I think it depends on the situation. In this day and age, job security is important, so I would carefully evaluate the situation before deciding on what the right thing is.
- I feel that confronting management about policies and issues that are clearly unfair would be career suicide and negatively impact my job in this organization.

Rational Advocates.   Rational advocacy (174 professionals), the largest category, focuses on professional counseling approaches and "good reasons" that practitioners use to attempt to change inappropriate decisions. Rational advocates follow the chain of command and marshal and use data, cases, laws, rational arguments, and their professional experience and expertise to attempt to persuade decision makers and negotiate better solutions. Responses in this category were typically somewhat neutral in that they did not indicate what the rational advocate would do if these approaches failed to overturn an inappropriate decision. The following responses are representative of this perspective:

- Gather evidence to support my point of view and engage the management team in a discussion of the issue. If their decision is truly inappropriate, then presenting a well-thought-out rationale and proposing an alternative solution to their decision should be sufficient to change their minds.
- It is always important to respect the chain of command .... Doing the right thing would involve compiling factual evidence ... and letting that evidence tell its own story.
- Provide professional PR consultation by bringing to the attention of management facts, pros and cons of situation, examples from other organizations, provide alternative options or solutions, provide feedback (research) regarding what key stakeholders have to say. In short, providing accurate information on which to base decisions and the possible outcomes of each decision.

- Get your facts together and make a persuasive argument for your case to management. You can't attack or be defensive—you have to try to get them to see another point of view. I feel one of the responsibilities of a PR person is to present different points of view to decision makers.
- Provide well-reasoned input, making a persuasive argument against the decision, outlining the potential consequences and outcomes. If the argument can be made passionately without being overly emotional, and without letting emotions control the debate, then I think that's appropriate in certain circumstances.
- Think the situation through, from as many angles as possible; formulate as much credible thought as possible to bulwark my opinions; prepare a cogent memo to the highest ranking supervisor in my chain of command.

Stakeholder Advocates.   Stakeholder advocacy (34 professionals) refers to doing the right thing in the interests of an organization's stakeholders, for example, employees, customers, contributors, shareholders, the general public, and so forth. PR professionals who use this approach speak on behalf of such stakeholders, and they believe they are doing the right thing when they demonstrate how inappropriate decisions are likely to adversely impact stakeholders, pose risks to them, or damage relationships with them. The following participant comments reflect this perspective:

- You have a responsibility to represent the rights of your company's stakeholders—shareholders, customers, employees, the community—in guiding senior management.
- It means doing what is necessary to protect the integrity of the organization and the safety of its publics.
- Make sure the decision is fair to all publics.
- Ask is it right for the constituents, right for the mission, should we be doing this?
- The number one trait a PR practitioner needs is courage. Courage to challenge management in an appropriate venue. Courage to stand up in a meeting to represent those who aren't there but will be affected.... PR people are there for the company and its employees and customers. Keeping them in the forefront is our role, and we must have the courage to challenge questionable decisions.

Ethical Advocates.   Ethical advocacy (168 professionals) refers to advocating for decisions that are based on human values and codes of ethics that apply at the personal, organizational, professional, and societal levels. In this perspective, doing the right thing means acting and communicating honestly, with integrity, and according to established laws and regulations. Many of the professionals who described doing the right thing in this way mentioned strong personal values, the PRSA and IABC Codes of Ethics, and organizational codes of conduct as important decision-making frameworks. The following participant responses to the question capture this perspective:

- It means to tell the truth.
- I ask, if it were my family, what would I do? Or I ask, what would Jesus do?
- I follow three codes of ethics: IABC, PRSA, and my own, using the most stringent of the three as it applies to the situation in question.
- Doing the right thing means to strictly adhere to the ethics, morals, and values that I believe in and those set forth in the mission and vision of the company. Doing the right thing also means to adhere to the corporate responsibility we have to our customers, shareholders, and analysts.
- The role of the PR practitioner is to point out how the decisions being made are inconsistent with the organization's, culture's, or society's code of ethics.
- To always act with integrity in the practice of public relations, even when others may not; to do what's right, because it's right, always.
- Are we doing the right thing should be the key question that any organization should ask of management and PR counsel. A company's reputation, financial standing, and ultimately its future, rely on an unwavering commitment to safety, honesty, integrity, accountability, caring and respect.

Twenty-one of the professionals in this category also mentioned that they viewed their role as one of "organizational conscience." They labeled this role variously as: moral compass, social conscience, guardian of corporate values, ethical gatekeeper, soul of the organization, voice of public responsibility, and so forth. This role is perhaps most explicitly stated in this participant comment: "To do the right thing to me means to be the conscience of the organization and to make sure that the law is being followed and that information is timely, honest, and accurate, and that the respect and dignity of employees and stakeholders are being considered."

Activist Advocates.   Activist advocacy (59 professionals) refers to making persuasive arguments with decision makers and, if those are unsuccessful, to using a variety of established internal approaches and more extreme outside approaches to attempt to change inappropriate decisions. Inside approaches include compliance hot lines, employee coalitions, audit boards, and governance committees. Outside approaches include leaking information to the press, mobilizing external stakeholders, and whistle-blowing to authorities. Ethical advocates in the survey often said that outside approaches are unprofessional and unethical, but activist advocates feel that under certain conditions such tactics are both justified and necessary to pressure decision makers and expose inappropriate actions. The following participant responses characterize an activist perspective:

- If the decision is just irritating or stupid, the best thing is to try to change it from the inside but not to advertise it outside. If the decision is illegal or immoral, the best thing is to try to change it from the inside…. If that doesn't work, then tell other employees and shareholders about the decision so they can exert pressure to change it, too. Only if that doesn't work do you go to the press.
- If, despite my counsel, management was intent on making an inappropriate decision, I would use our appropriate methods of recourse, including using our compliance hot line, contacting the appropriate ethics/corporate governance/compliance officers, and even the chairman of the audit committee of the board of directors.
- Doing the right thing means voicing your concerns to the top members of management. If your concerns are ignored, then doing the right thing extends to making decisions based upon your moral and ethical standards—that may include leaving the position, leaking information to stakeholders, or rallying others to help change the position.
- I speak from some experience as, after [a number] of years at [organization], I was laid off on a pretext following my complaint about illegal campaign contributions made by [organizational executives].
- If there were something completely egregious going on, I would make my strongest case, and, if management disregarded, would

work my way up the chain. If still no results, blow the whistle by leaking or reporting to a regulatory agency.

- Advocating as forcefully as possible to try to convince management to change an inappropriate decision. On rare occasions, doing the right thing may mean leaking information outside the organization, or using the grapevine. I think most people and PR professionals know what the right thing is in their hearts. The issue usually is are you prepared to take some risks, maybe significant risks, to do something about it, to take some action that is risky. Knowing and acting may be light years apart. I don't consider a lot of PR professionals to be courageous in this regard.

Exit Advocates.   Exit advocacy (141 professionals) refers to using professional experience and persuasive arguments to attempt to overturn inappropriate decisions. In this regard, it is similar to rational advocacy. However, if advocacy efforts fail, professionals in this category indicated that they would leave the organization if the issue were a legal or ethical one. The following responses to the question capture this perspective:

- If I disagree strongly with the policies of my company, it is my responsibility to change them or remove myself from such a company.
- I believe that doing the right thing means to do everything possible to persuade management to make a more appropriate decision and consider the consequences of their decision. If this does not produce results, I believe that the PR practitioner should leave the organization.
- There were times when a client wanted me to lie—not a white lie—and I said no. I've refused to misrepresent who I am when a client requested it. It would have been mostly harmless but I still thought it was crossing a line that I didn't want to cross.... I have fought to get rid of clients that I thought were unethical or engaged in unethical practices. I wasn't always successful which is one of the reasons I left my last position, even though it was a key career position.... As I interviewed this past year, I came across an agency engaged in some seriously unethical practices and I was torn about how to respond. In the end, I attempted to notify the PRSA, which was non-responsive simply because of poor organization.
- First, take steps to inform immediate supervisors of the concern and offer suggestions on how to rectify the situation. If no action is

taken, or if the action that is taken is unsatisfactory, make attempts to discuss with upper management, again, offering suggestions and solutions. If these options fail, leave the organization rather than leak information or report to external publics.

- It is the responsibility of the public relations officer to confront management, point out the consequences of the decision, and strongly urge a change in the company's position. If management refuses the counsel and continues down an illegal or unethical path, the public relations officer should resign his position so as not to support the decision but without undermining management through unethical acts of his/her own, such as leaking information or sabotaging the decision.

- It means effectively confronting management, advising and counseling them with a clear case against their position. If their decision stands, depending on the implication (against the law, etc.), I would likely resign or recuse myself. I have done it once in my career.

Advocacy is the "Right Thing"

Participants in the Dissent Survey provided diverse responses to the hypothetical question of "doing the right thing" when confronted with an inappropriate management decision. However, one common thread ran throughout virtually all of the answers: advocacy. PR professionals said that they have a responsibility—it is part of their role—to advocate with decision makers to try to change or modify an inappropriate decision. Beyond that fundamental professional responsibility, respondent answers varied according to the extent of their advocacy, the type of advocacy approaches they used, and the framework from within which they made decisions about advocacy.

Some professionals said advocacy was important up to the point of a final decision, at which time their loyalty to the organization took over and they carried out the decision as effectively as they could. Other professionals said that job concerns and future career opportunities curbed the extent of their advocacy. On the other hand, a much larger number of professionals indicated they would exit, or had exited, companies where illegal, unethical, and immoral ends were being pursued.

Nearly one quarter of the respondents indicated that their advocacy was governed by personal, organizational, and professional codes of ethics. We had imagined that an even larger number of respondents might answer in this manner, given promotion of such codes in recent years and pervasive publicity about accounting scandals and corresponding SEC requirements for ethical guidelines and practices.

A small number of professionals said they would advocate based on stakeholder interests, whereas the largest group said they would use rational arguments and data to counsel management and negotiate better solutions. These rational advocates did not attempt to explain what they might do if advocacy failed, perhaps implying that such persuasive approaches were or could be sufficient to change decisions. Finally, another large group of professionals said they would use both established internal channels to change decisions, as well as more controversial external approaches to pressure or expose inappropriate decisions.

Hirschman's (1970) exit-voice-loyalty (EVL) model of employee dissatisfaction provides one way of delineating such differences among these seven groups of responses. The EVL model describes several ways in which employees may react to dissatisfaction in organizations (in this case, dissatisfaction with an inappropriate decision). According to Hirschman, employees can choose to exit the organization when they are dissatisfied, or they can try to change the dissatisfactory condition by voicing their concerns. Loyalty to the organization is seen as a moderating variable that affects decisions to exit or voice.

Nearly all of the respondents said they would voice concerns about an inappropriate decision because advocacy is part of the professional role. Given that they all voice, the issues then become how do they voice and how long do they voice. It appears that five of the groups—loyalty, self-protective, rational, stakeholder, and ethical advocates—voice in a constructive manner; that is, they use dialogue and persuasive arguments in appropriate forums inside the organization to try to change inappropriate decisions. Factors that influence how and how long they voice include loyalty, job security concerns, and particular decision-making frameworks (rationality, stakeholder interests, and ethical guidelines).

Activist advocates and possibly exit advocates, however, voice in a constructive manner up to the point of a final decision. At that time, if the decision is still deemed inappropriate, exit advocates are likely to leave the organization. Activist advocates are prepared to continue to voice concerns, but in a more adversarial and retaliatory manner—using other internal and external approaches—to increase pressures on decision makers and to make the decision visible to other audiences. They may subsequently exit the organization, too.

Five Propositions About the "Right Thing" in Public Relations

Clearly, there is dissensus in the field about a number of aspects of practice, including the question of doing the right thing. Understanding how the profession is defined by practitioners and others, the various roles public relations professionals are expected to play, the legal and ethical limits to practice, and personal differences all help in wrestling with what doing the right thing means in public relations practice. Though no pat answers exist, it is useful to analyze the question of what is "the right thing." Practitioners' responses to depth interviews and surveys help bring this issue into focus. We close this chapter by briefly discussing five propositions about this issue.

> **Proposition 2: Practitioners define public relations practice as a strategic management function that can help organizations solve problems and achieve success.**

As noted previously, public relations scholars have increasingly defined effective public relations as a management or strategic function within an organization. Public relations practitioners in our studies agreed. The largest percentage of respondents to the PR Success Interviews defined success in public relations as holding a decision-making post (22.7%) or helping business grow (20.6%). These responses affirm public relations as a managerial and strategic function more than a tactical function.

Practitioners further defined public relations as a results- and bottom-line-oriented profession. The highest percentage of practitioners defined public relations success as quantifiable. They do not accept any arguments about public relations results being impossible to measure.

Scholars have noted that managers wield more power and influence than do technicians. Practitioners in the Influence Study identified managerial issues as their definition of influence. The largest number of respondents (24/65 or 36.9%) said that having a voice in organizational issues is how they defined influence; the second-highest number (18/65 or 27.6%) said they defined influence as having direct input into a decision.

Public relations practitioners increasingly define the profession as a management or strategic function within organizations in which public relations practitioners who are successful or influential have input into important decisions.

Proposition 3: The allegiance that public relations professionals feel to their organizations trumps devotion to stakeholders or society.

The Influence Interviews suggest that practitioners further define the profession as asymmetrical in terms of its advocacy. It is clear that public relations practitioners serve multiple interests or "masters." But, it is equally clear that they cede their primary devotion to their organization. Though such allegiance is logical, it runs somewhat counter to the notion that many practitioners have about serving as an organizational conscience and as an internal voice for external and unempowered internal stakeholders. Two thirds of practitioners in the Influence Study said their primary allegiance was to their organization. Only 1 in 10 said their primary devotion was to society. Therefore, public relations practitioners in this study, and we suspect generally, define themselves, their interests, and their focus largely by the organization for which they work.

Proposition 4: Practitioners draw the devotion line to their organizations at legal or moral wrongdoing.

Even though practitioners give their utmost dedication to their organizations rather than society-at-large, they also pledge allegiance to deontological and teleological ethics. They value organizational codes of conduct and societal laws and norms. This value of ethical conduct is succinctly stated by the aforementioned quote of one of the Dissent Survey respondents: "Follow the ethics of PRSA, the ethics of your company, and all the laws of the land."

Among participants in the Influence Interviews, 73.8% (48/65) said they would never employ activist tactics such as whistle-blowing. But they find other ways to resist unethical or illegal behavior. In the Dissent Survey, 23.76% of respondents were classified as ethical advocates. This was the second-largest group among respondents to the question of "What is doing the right thing in public relations" (rational advocates accounted for 24.61% of responses).

This suggests that most public relations practitioners embrace traditional ethical models, especially when faced with legal or moral wrongdoing by an organization. This is addressed in more detail in chapter 8.

Proposition 5: Doing the right thing in practice is still limited by others' perceptions about public relations and by organizational and professional constraints.

Public relations practitioners said their influence was impeded by how others perceive or interact with PR. Literature has focused on the need to be in the dominant coalition, although Berger (2005) pointed out that traditional views of the dominant coalition may be oversimplified. Public relations literature has also expressed concerns about encroachment on the public relations function by other professions, such as marketing, law, or human resources.

The 65 practitioners in the Influence Interviews affirmed these views. When asked what limits their influence, the highest percentage 26.2% (17/65) said a lack of understanding of the role of public relations by others was a limiting factor. If a public relations practitioner does not control resources, then their influence is affected. The second-highest number of responses to the question of limits to influence was a lack of resources 20.0% (13/65). The third-highest category of influence impediments was organizational structure or reporting position 18.5% (12/65). Each of these suggests that others—in their lack of understanding or their control of resources—limit public relations' ability to wield influence. The problem of organizational structure or reporting position also suggests that public relations is not being given access to decision makers and, therefore, likely not contributing to organizational strategy.

Some practitioners argued that public relations' greatest limitation is placed on it by other practitioners. These respondents argued that public relations as a profession is not stepping up to the plate to advocate for itself and its causes effectively. Therefore, in addition to the organizational others who impede influence, there are others within the profession who serve to limit public relations effectiveness.

> **Proposition 6: Public relations advocacy strategies focus on reasoning, reporting, or relinquishing when practitioners pursue "doing the right thing."**

Three dominant advocacy strategies emerged among the 700+ respondents who answered the survey question about "doing the right thing." They are rational advocacy, ethical advocacy, or exit advocacy.

Rational and ethical advocacy were within a percentage-point difference. Rational advocacy, which is advocacy that is based on logical appeals and arguments, was the advocacy practiced by the highest percentage of respondents (24.61%). This affirms the ideas that being a decision maker or, at least, having the ear of a decision maker is a defining factor of success or influence. Ethical advocacy involves using professional, organizational, or cultural standards as a measure of appropriate behavior and decisions. Many ethical advocates subscribe to deontological standards put forth by PRSA, IABC, or similar professional organizations. Ethical advocates make up the second-largest category at 23.76%.

Exit advocacy is practiced by those professionals who say they offer their superiors the best ethical advice they can, and if wrong decisions or wrongdoing persists, then this professional chooses to leave their organization. Exit advocates accounted for 19.94% of respondents.

These three categories of advocates make up about 68% of responses to this survey item. Therefore, we conclude that "doing the right thing" from an advocacy point of view is to reason, report, or relinquish. That is, most practitioners use reason and logic, report ethical standards, or relinquish their position in an organization.

Scratching Beneath the Surface

In this chapter, we explored a number of issues that divide public relations professionals and discussed some of the constraints on practice. The data presented from the two sets of interviews largely confirm previous findings and reinforce what many in the field suspect or experience in practice. In our view, the combination of divisive issues and constraints limit the influence of professionals inside their organizations. They also serve to diminish or at the very least muddy the public's image of the profession.

Understanding how power relations shape decision making in organizations is a first step toward resolving or mitigating these two professional problems. In the next chapter, we develop a theory of power relations that describes this process. We then elaborate a resistance role and explore how this role may help public relations professionals increase their influence and professional stature.

CHAPTER 3

Resistance, Politics, and Power Relations

> I find that unconventional tactics are often times the only way you can succeed. The reason is because … public affairs officers aren't given a formal inclusion or respect in top levels of organizations, so you sometimes have to resort to unconventional means to get the influence you require to make a difference.
>
> —Australian Public Affairs Consultant

The public relations profession has tried many approaches over the years to increase its influence with organizational decision makers and acquire social legitimacy, but these approaches haven't worked to the extent desired. Many professionals still don't hold a seat at the table, and public perceptions of practitioners as flacks and publicists remain pervasive. To better understand this dilemma, we must take a more realistic view of the extent of power in and around the practice.

In this chapter, we explore the practice through a power relations lens that magnifies the ways in which power shapes strategic decisions and the practice itself inside organizations. Focusing on power relations illuminates a wide range of influence resources and tactics that may be mobilized and used in decision-making arenas. It also helps us begin to understand how resistance may strengthen influence and legitimacy of the practice. We first describe what a resistance role means in public relations and examine three broad forms of resistance—advocacy, dissent, and activism. We then explore organizational political systems and arenas where relations of power come into play. The chapter concludes with a presentation and discussion of a conceptual model of power relations.

A RESISTANCE PERSPECTIVE

Many persuasion studies and persuasive influence attempts themselves have focused on what Knowles and Linn (2004) called the "approach forces" in communication that "increase the motivation to move toward the goal" desired by the persuader (p. 119). These approaches, which they labeled "Alpha strategies," include crafting more compelling messages, constructing more convincing arguments, offering more attractive incentives, and including more credible sources to motivate or induce individuals toward a desired goal.

To a large extent the public relations profession has employed Alpha strategies over the years to try to legitimate itself with organizational decision makers and the general public. The profession has marshaled more arguments to support the value of practice, assembled a burgeoning collection of successful case studies, and crafted more compelling messages about the need for PR in today's wired 24/7 world. It also has established professional accreditation programs and codes of ethics, built a body of knowledge about the practice, and incorporated business and political leaders in its conference programs to endorse the practice. Though these efforts have produced some successes in some organizations, we nevertheless seem to have arrived at a destination Lesly (1991) predicted more than a decade ago when he said: "PR will probably go on growing in numbers and in universality of its use—while slipping in stature and influence. There will be more people doing more things—except having a role in the top levels of our institutions" (p. 6).

One way out of this continuing dilemma may begin with conceptualizing and practicing the role differently. Recent research in persuasion, for example, has begun to examine its opposite—resistance—to gain new insights into the dynamics of resistance and how it can be used to reduce, overcome, or even promote persuasion. Knowles and Linn (2004) contended that looking at resistance in this way foregrounds a second set of persuasive approaches—Omega strategies—that may stimulate change and persuasion by reducing the resistance to change or minimizing avoidance forces. They cited such strategies as seeking incremental gains rather than large changes, directly confronting resistance to try to defuse its power, making repeated requests, and reframing messages so that resistance to them actually promotes change.

Applying a similar resistance perspective to public relations provides a way to "see" the practice in a different light and to illuminate a diverse repertoire of Alpha and Omega approaches that professionals can develop and use to increase their influence. As we saw in chapter 2, dissensus among professionals about roles and service, along with a variety of structural, relational, and procedural forces, constrain the influence of public relations. These constraints are manifested in low-level reporting positions, limited resources, extensive editorial and process controls, executive perceptions of the role, and restricted access to strategic decision makers. Though Alpha strategies have mitigated some of these constraints, coupling these approaches with Omega strategies may accelerate changes in the profession.

A Resistance Role

According to Webster's, resistance is "the act of resisting, opposing, withstanding." In the persuasion literature the "clear core of the definition of resistance is that it is a reaction against change," a behavioral outcome (Knowles & Linn, 2004, p. 4). When we talk about a resistance role for public relations, then, we use resistance in two senses. First, we refer to a resistance *process* in which public relations practitioners deliberately select and use influence strategies and tactics to engage and oppose others in power relations. Second, we refer to resistance as a *motivation*; that is, practitioners are motivated or driven to actively push back on the forces and structural arrangements that constrain the practice and curb its potential to help organizations do the right thing. They see it as an essential part of the job.

Public relations executive Katherine Delahaye Paine (2001) didn't use the term *resistance* in her pointed description of what she sees as a new role for professionals, but she called for increased influence in the practice to help organizations not just say but also do the right things:

> The role of the PR person as we've defined it in the last half century is over. We will no longer be the ones guiding "spokespeople" into communicating key messages.... The role of the PR person in the 21st century should not be one of managing "reality." We should be shaping the actions and deeds of our companies, not just words ... helping guide our organizations to new heights of social responsibility and institutional respect, not just crafting messages. (p. 47)

Paine didn't explain how this new role might be achieved, but we believe it requires some alternative approaches to supplement traditional advocacy efforts. Seen as part of a resistance process, such approaches include developing and mobilizing a number of underutilized influence resources and engaging in forms of dissent and activism. These alternative approaches have been little explored in the public relations literature, but collectively they represent a significant repertoire of resistance strategies and tactics. Each approach is described in more detail in the following sections.

Advocacy—Resistance. *Advocacy* is often defined in an extraorganizational sense as "the act of publicly representing an individual, organization, or idea with the object of persuading targeted audiences to look favorably on—or accept the point of view of—the individual, organization, or idea" (Edgett, 2002, p. 1). Though public relations scholars are divided on whether advocacy is a legitimate function of practice today, most practitioners consider advocacy—speaking in favor of, promoting, advancing, or supporting—to be a central function of public relations.

Professionals regularly advocate for their organizations, products, services, issues, positions, strategic developments, results, and accomplishments with a variety of publics. Carried out through many print, electronic, and interpersonal channels, these advocacy efforts represent an increasingly voluminous set of organizational discourses through which organizations compete with each other for attention; "talk" to other organizations, publics, and individuals; and attempt to influence individuals and groups (Coleman, 1974, 1990).

Our primary interest is with advocacy that occurs inside organizations. Whenever a public relations professional (or other organizational member) expresses his or her point of view or puts forth arguments against those of others, that professional is counterarguing or resisting the other's point of view or influence attempts. Advocacy in this sense represents a relatively common form of resistance in organizational settings to others and to proposed policies or plans, issue definitions, established practices or procedures, dominant or controlling perspectives, particular ideologies, and so forth. In fact, organizational members advocate points of view and beliefs in a variety of internal settings virtually all of the time, for example, performance reviews, team or staff meetings, committees, employee forums, teleconferences, training sessions, and dominant coalitions.

Advocacy, and especially rational advocacy, is widespread inside organizations because it is an acceptable form of voice or resistance, up to a point. Advocacy is accepted or sanctioned as a form of influence so long as it is seen to be in the interests of the organization and its objectives and is institutionalized within the office or position of the advocate (Mayes & Allen, 1977; Porter et al., 1990; Vigoda & A. Cohen, 2002). Hay and Hartel (2000) referred to this type of influence as *formal influence*, which refers to the "institutionalized right to use power vested in an office or position ... in ways that have been sanctioned by the organization to achieve ends that also have been sanctioned by the organization" (p. 136). On the other hand, *informal influence* is "unauthorized, illegitimate, and unsanctioned" because it represents individual or group interests over those of the organization (p. 136). We address informal influence shortly.

Public relations professionals who enact a managerial role are viewed as primary communications advocates who attempt to influence organizational decisions, actions, and ideologies (Dozier, 1992; Dozier & Broom, 1995; Dozier et al., 1995; L. A. Grunig et al., 2002). Advocacy in this sense relates to formal or acceptable influence attempts: Experienced public relations managers use their expertise, experience, knowledge of the environment, and research and problem-solving skills to advocate "excellent" public relations practices. In this way, they help organizations resolve conflicts, deal with uncertainties, and balance self-interests with the interests of others (Dozier et al., 1995; L. A. Grunig et al., 2002).

To do so, however, PR managers require a seat at decision-making tables (L. A. Grunig, 1992b): "Only as part of the dominant coalition could public relations professionals be influential enough to shape the organization's ideology. Presumably, these boundary spanners would appreciate the point of view both of their employers and their relevant external publics" (p. 491). L. A. Grunig et al. (2002) later modified this perspective, equating power in public relations to empowerment of everyone in the organization. According to excellence theory, empowered public relations professionals need to be present in the dominant coalition not to shape or influence organizational decisions, but rather to "allow the organization to benefit from the expertise of the public relations profession" (p. 142).

But how practitioners become empowered, and what they need to do to advance excellent communications, is less clear. In addition, little direction is provided for dealing with problematic ethical, legal, and moral situations where formal influence or advocacy efforts just aren't enough—they just don't get the job done despite best efforts—and an organization makes a poor decision or decides to communicate poorly. Should practitioners accept such decisions and carry them out in these situations? Should they advocate more passionately to continuing deaf ears? Do they simply look away, or walk away to work elsewhere? Or do they decide to resist or to attempt influence through other forms of dissent and activism?

Forms of Dissent. Kassing's research in organizational communication studies has advanced our understanding of employee dissent and dissent practices (Kassing, 1997, 1998; Kassing & Avtgis, 1999). He described dissent as feeling apart from one's organization and expressing disagreement or contradictory opinions about the organization in the workplace. Employee dissent may occur for many reasons, for example, safety issues, impractical or inefficient organizational decisions, moral or ethical concerns, political constraints, exercise of free speech, or simply as a means of participating in organizational discussions (Kassing, 1998). Dissenting may be seen as a political right, a moral obligation, an enlightened management practice, or a punishable violation (Sprague & Ruud, 1988).

The typical dissent process includes a triggering event, selection of a dissent strategy, and the actual expression of dissent (Kassing, 1997). Employees may express themselves directly, passively, or aggressively. *Direct* or *articulated dissent* refers to upward communication and attempts to change things by working within the system. Articulated dissent "occurs when employees express their dissent within organizations to audiences that can effectively influence organizational adjustment" (Kassing, 1997, p. 326). This type of dissent expression may be likened to forceful or persistent advocacy.

Antagonistic or *latent dissent* "occurs when employees believe they will be perceived as adversarial, but also feel they have some safeguard against retaliation," for example, seniority, vital expertise, family ties, minority status, and so forth (Kassing, 1997, p. 326). This type of dissent is often concerned with personal advantages, or threats to them. It challenges the organization directly but does so largely to ineffectual audiences, for example, subordinates or other employees in work or social units or groups.

Displaced dissent "occurs when employees believe their dissent will be perceived as adversarial and lead to retaliation" (Kassing, 1997, p. 327). Such dissent is typically shared outside the workplace with nonwork audiences like family members, members of professional associations, community clubs or groups, media personnel, or even public officials. This is a form of disagreeing without directly challenging or confronting the organization (Kassing, 1997).

Dissent episodes also influence sensemaking. By discussing their own expressions of dissent, or those of others in the organization, members may "make sense of such experiences, refine their sense of organizational tolerance for dissent, determine what issues merit dissent, and reform their future dissent strategy choices" (Kassing, 2001, p. 459). Kassing also found that employees express dissent about significant issues of ethics and harm more often outside rather than inside the organization (Kassing & Armstrong, 2002). He found no significant differences for dissent type and gender of the dissenter in his various studies. However, articulated and antagonistic dissenters were perceived quite differently in the organization. Articulated dissenters were seen to be less argumentative and to have more influence in their organizations than antagonistic dissenters (Kassing, 2001).

Dissent activities can range from grumbling with others about organizational matters to whistle-blowing, one of the most extreme forms of dissent. Apart from whistle-blowing, other types of dissent approaches have been little explored, though they have been characterized by some critical theorists. O'Connell-Davidson (1994), for example, noted that dissent and resistance activities can range from outright sabotage to withholding information to creating counternarratives for organization realities:

> Resistance can encompass anything and everything that workers do which managers do not want them to do, and that workers do not do that managers wish them to do. It can take in both the collective and the individual: it can embrace actions that are specifically designed to thwart management (such as strikes and work-to-roles), and those which may not be (such as alcoholism). (p. 94)

Deetz (1992) described employee resistance in a metaphorical sense when he suggested that resistance could mean selecting the game itself rather than choosing a move or an action from a set of moves or actions in a game prescribed by someone else. Such forms of resistance might include using contract-free forms of working relationships or agreements, for example, or voting through stock ownership to change governing structures in organizations. Mumby (1997) described how workers used low-profile dissent practices to construct interpretations and shared meanings that run counter to the dominant and hegemonic discourse in organizations. Through these counternarrative approaches, "subordinate groups can outwardly or denotatively express acquiescence to the prevailing order, while simultaneously and connotatively denying it" (p. 363).

Studies of dissent activities by public relations professionals are rare. Through depth interviews with 21 corporate public relations executives, Berger (2005) identified a handful of dissent activities that some of the executives indicated they had carried out. These included leaking information to the press, using the grapevine to plant rumors, and constructing their own interpretations of formal corporate decisions and official communications. They subsequently shared these counternarratives with other members of the PR unit. One VP, for example, described a situation in which his company decided to "officially" explain the loss of a major business contract as a product quality problem attributable to poor production performance. He used the grapevine to express his dissent with this decision:

> The reality was, we lost the business because we took too long to respond to a customer bid. It wasn't a product quality issue at all—it was a decision-making problem. But my protests were overruled and I was given my directives, which I carried out. But I also shared the story with a friend in production, who spread the rumor on the grapevine, and someone, maybe him, posted anonymous memos with the story on bulletin boards. Within 24 hours management was retreating, and the incident became an important marker in future communication decisions. (Berger, 2005, p. 20)

About one quarter of the 65 diverse professionals who participated in the Influence Interviews shared examples of similar dissent activities, and many of those we interviewed said they knew other public relations professionals who had dissented in these or other ways. These dissent approaches are explored more fully in chapter 7. Many forms of dissent, and especially those that Kassing defined as nondirect or nonarticulated dissent expressions, are unacceptable or unsanctioned by the organization because they represent informal influence and are seen to privilege individual or group interests over those of the organization (Hay & Hartel, 2000). In this sense, dissent approaches are similar to activist approaches.

Activism and Activist Approaches.   *Activism* refers to the efforts of groups that organize to influence public policy, organizational practices and policies, and social values and norms through action (L. A. Grunig, 1992b; M. F. Smith, 1997). Activist concerns may be political, social, or economic in nature, but typically they seek to rectify or change specific practices, customs, policies, or regulations that are in place (M. F. Smith & Ferguson, 2001). To do so, they use a variety of informational, symbolic, legalistic, organizing, and civil-disobedience tactics (Jackson, 1982).

The public relations literature regarding activism often focuses on activist groups as external threats to organizations and is primarily concerned with how professionals and their organizations respond to these pressures (L. A. Grunig, 1992a; M. F. Smith, 1997; M. F. Smith & Ferguson, 2001; Werder, 2003). Some scholars, however, look at activism from the point of view of public relations professionals themselves, calling for professionals or professional associations to become more activist-like in their work (Berger, 2005; Holtzhausen, 2000; Holtzhausen & Voto, 2002; Mickey, 2003). One approach (J. E. Grunig, 1989) calls for professionals to become organizational activists in the academic world to help increase resources for public relations education programs and to develop autonomy in academia for such programs: "Political change occurs most often when individuals develop activist groups to pressure for change ... public relations practitioners should use their financial and political clout to pressure for resources in public relations and to support the universities that support public relations education" (p. 21).

Another approach (Holtzhausen, 2000; Holtzhausen & Voto, 2002) urges practitioners to become activists in their own organizations and to work within those organizations to make the practice more ethical and representative of others:

> The practitioner as organizational activist will serve as a conscience in the organization by resisting dominant power structures, particularly when these structures are not inclusive, will preference employees' and external publics' discourse over that of management, will make the most humane decision in a particular situation, and will promote new ways of thinking and problem solving through dissensus and conflict. These actions will contribute to a culture of emancipation and liberation in the organization. (Holtzhausen & Voto, 2002, p. 64)

In this view, practitioners who lack authoritative or structural power can become influential activists by relying on strong personal characteristics, building relationships and alliances in the organization, creating access to powerful individuals, and using personal inner power (self-knowledge and moral consciousness). To practice ethical public relations and institutionalize such practices, professionals-as-activists must challenge unjust views or actions in their organizations, help create opportunities and forums for members to dissent and debate, and work to make organizations more transparent in their communications and interactions with publics (Holtzhausen, 2000).

A third perspective (Berger, 2005) focuses on activism at the professional-association level. It highlights the potential contributions these associations might make through activist approaches to increasing public relations power and legitimizing the profession. Berger suggested associations can play a valuable activist role by preparing case studies of power issues inside organizations, establishing working groups to address issues of resistance and influence, and issuing statements or staging demonstrations to protest deplorable organizational or public relations practices. He contended that association activism can help legitimate the profession and provide mechanisms for organizational learning and professional self-reflection on the practice.

Advocacy, dissent, and activist approaches provide public relations professionals with a potentially powerful repertoire of resistance strategies and tactics that may be used in organizations to gain influence. Consideration of all approaches seems warranted given the political nature of most organizations and the complex set of power relations that come into play in organizational decision-making arenas.

ORGANIZATIONAL POLITICS AND POLITICAL SYSTEMS

Practitioners are quick to acknowledge that "politics" play a central role in getting things done inside organizations. Organizational politics refers to those activities undertaken "to acquire, develop, and use power and other resources to obtain one's preferred outcomes in a situation in which there is uncertainty or dissensus about choices" (Pfeffer, 1981, p. 7). Politics are pervasive in many organizations due to competition among members for scarce resources, differing unit or individual agendas, environmental uncertainties that produce conflicting interpretations and solutions, and hierarchies and inequalities in the workplace (Baron & Greenberg, 1990; Ferris et al., 1989; Fimbel, 1994; Hay & Hartel, 2000). The role that politics plays in organizational life ranges from a nearly invisible background game to a dominant system of influence that can sap vital resources and render an organization virtually dysfunctional (Mintzberg, 1985).

In contrast to formal power or authority vested in an office and prescribed in policies and procedures, organizational politics are usually seen to represent illegitimate authority that operates outside of established policies and structural authority. Hay and Hartel (2000), for example, defined organizational politics as "the use of power, in a way that is not formally sanctioned by an organization, to have an effect on the making of decisions or their implementation in the workplace" (p.

146). Similarly, Porter et al. (1990) defined organizational politics as "social influence attempts that are discretionary (outside behavioral zones prescribed or prohibited by the formal organization) that are intended ... to promote the self-interests of others" (pp. 111–112). More explicitly, Mintzberg (1983) described politics as "individual or group behavior that is informal, ostensibly parochial, typically divisive, and above all, in the technical sense, illegitimate—sanctioned neither by formal authority, accepted ideology, nor certified expertise" (p. 172).

Four comprehensive treatments of organizational politics and power help depict the complex and dynamic environment of shifting forces and influences in which PR managers and other organizational members attempt to shape decisions, actions, ideologies, and communications. Management theorist Henry Mintzberg (1983) described organizations as political arenas where organizational politics unfold in a "power game in which various players, called *influencers*, seek to control the organization's decisions and actions" (p. 22). These influencers draw from power sources, expend energy (will), and use skillful political approaches to affect outcomes and distribute benefits and organizational power. Mintzberg's diverse cast of political players includes external influencer groups—owners, associate suppliers and customers, employee associations, and various traditional publics—and internal influencer groups—the CEO, line managers, operators, analysts, and support staff.

Each group possesses some form(s) of power and therefore potential influence, Mintzberg (1983) argued, and each group and individual also may draw from four broader systems of influence that operate within the organization: systems of formal authority, organizational ideology, professional expertise, and politics. These systems may be integrated reasonably well, or, at any given time, one or two of the systems may come to dominate the others, thereby creating imbalances or dysfunctions and shifting coalitions. In this view, organizational power is not fixed and stable but rather ebbs and flows from the center to the peripheries and back again, depending on the relative strengths of internal and external influencers.

Mintzberg (1983) assigned public relations to a support staff position in this model and suggested that the profession's greatest power lies in the system of expertise. Support staff members also draw from the system of politics, however, and politics occur more often among staff personnel than among line managers or operators (Madison, Allen, Porter, Renwick, & Mayes, 1980; Morrill, 1989). Applying Mintzberg's comprehensive political systems view to public relations, then, suggests that the most effective and influential public relations professionals are likely those with (a) a high level of formal authority and (b) high levels of vital expertise, who (c) understand the system of ideology and (d) are active and savvy participants in the system of politics.

Pfeffer (1981, 1992) focused on conditions that produce organizational politics and the use of power. In this power-control perspective, organizational governance and decision making grow out of conflict and struggle among competing interests and actors. Much of the political struggle in organizations is therefore aimed at gaining membership in, or influencing those members in, the organization's dominant coalition. This group(s)—usually senior or high-level executives—makes strategic decisions, allocates resources, dictates policies, and shapes the organization's ideology, sometimes to advance and benefit the organization and sometimes to benefit self-interests and maintain existing power relationships. Pfeffer argued that the point is to get things done in organizations, and power—neither good nor bad in itself—is what gets things done, whereas "politics and influence are the processes, the actions, the behaviors through which ... potential power is utilized and realized" (Pfeffer, 1992, p. 30). Success in organizations therefore requires knowing how to get things done and actually being willing to try to do them.

Pfeffer provided a number of insights into how organizational members may identify, gain, and use power and influence resources, as well as particular types of influence tactics and strategies. His comprehensive tour of power resources calls attention to individual attributes of power, structural or formal sources of power, the crucial role of political knowledge in organizational politics, and the need to match influence resources and tactics with specific issue contexts. In this view, any individual in the organization who wants to "manage with power" must know where power resides, know how and when to use various types of influence, and possess the willpower to engage in conflict.

Jackall (1988) provided a fascinating if discouraging look at how organizational managers attempt to balance self-interests with those of their bosses and organizations. Based on extensive interviews with managers in several organizations, Jackall portrayed modern corporations as so fraught with politics that individual success and survival are more important than meeting organizational goals. In this world, individuals compete for favors, promotions, and other benefits from those in the inner circle. Hard work may lead to rewards, but so too can self-promotion, cloaked intentions, powerful patrons, glib responses, and simply outrunning one's mistakes. The pressures for compliance in this work world are unrelenting.

Jackall (1988) suggested that public relations practitioners hold particularly difficult positions because they must be especially attentive to the demands and whims of senior executives, and they must manipulate meanings to serve the interests of their bosses, their organizations, and themselves. In addition, they must "above all satisfy [the] clients' desires to construct the world in certain ways" (p. 170). In this view, the influences and interests of PR professionals are closely tied to those in power, and the way to gain power therefore is to anticipate and effectively satisfy the needs and desires of those in power. There appears to be little room for resistance in this organizational world unless such resistance is covert, subtle, calculating, and perhaps carefully coordinated with others in coalitions or alliances.

Spicer (1997) took a distinctly political perspective on practice, arguing that a political system metaphor is the best way to understand the relationships between PR power and organizational power. He contended that "public relations positions are political in nature and demand use of influence" (p. 132). In this view, power is located in the interactions between people, and the decisions and actions flowing out of these interactions are grounded in the organization's political infrastructure:

> It is in this nether world of organizational life—the intersection of good intentions, selfishness, power, concern for others, survival, retreat, advocacy, and collaboration—that decisions about public relations are born. Understanding how to better negotiate the political system of the organization will help PR practitioners better achieve their dual interests of serving both the organization and the public good. (p. xiii)

To successfully negotiate this infrastructure, practitioners must become politically astute. This means gaining knowledge of formal and informal decision-making processes in the organization and knowing other key players and their "strengths, weaknesses, penchants, hidden agendas, personal likes and dislikes" (Spicer, 1997, p. 145), as well as their own levels of political intelligence and knowledge. According to Spicer, political astuteness helps practitioners become more effective advocates, a sanctioned form of resistance described earlier that relies on rational arguments, the use of data and measures, the power of performance, and the art of persuasion.

Collectively, these four works portray a politicized organizational world of competing and colliding forces and influences that render public relations practice difficult. The theorists highlight the interplay of competing influencers in the organization; the power resources, tactics, and strategies they use; and the requirements for individual political astuteness, skill, and willpower to engage in conflict and confrontation. Though these researchers tend to focus on corporations, our own research has identified similar forces and influences in varying degrees in nonprofits, academic institutions, and social-movement or special-interest groups.

For example, about one third of the 65 professionals who participated in the Influence Interviews underscored the value of political knowledge and knowing how to get things done inside their organizations. Political knowledge was seen as a valuable influence resource by professional women and men alike in corporations, agencies, nonprofits, and educational institutions *because their organizations are political arenas*. One corporate VP compared politics in his company to federal politics:

> My company is a lot like Washington. Inside the Beltway, you have to know the players, who's heading up a committee, what their agenda is, what the timetable is, who's coming to hearings, and so forth. Same in my company: who's involved, what the agendas are, how they operate, how they can be approached and convinced, etc. Big companies are probably as political as Washington, so you absolutely have to understand the politics and get good at playing them to be effective and get things done.

Another company public relations director highlighted the importance of organizational knowledge in knowing how to get things done:

> You have to have a deep understanding of how a decision is made in your organization because that controls all the ways you use your expertise.... I call this the "internal reality" of the company. Next is understanding the people that play the key roles in making decisions. So what you are continually doing is trying to inject what you know and believe and propose through the various openings that exist in the organization that allow them to be heard.

A female PR director at a university described the cumulative powers of political knowledge this way: "Organizational politics plays a crucial role. The more you understand the politics [of decision making], the more key decision makers will take your counsel. The more you're in a position to be on these key committees and share in the decisions ... then the more you're empowered to communicate about them."

The communications director of an Australian nonprofit called attention to the relationships between political knowledge and political skill in his organization:

> I know how to push and how to defer, and when to be aggressive and when
> to be patient. I know intimately how the organization works.... There are in-
> ternal politics. There are ways of doing things, and you have to understand
> those ways if you're going to get the organization to accept the viewpoint
> you're putting across.

These and other comments about organizational politics, cultural influences, and constraints on practice resonate with the organizational
worlds portrayed in the four books briefly reviewed in this section. We
now take a closer look at the nature of power relations that occur within
organizations and shape both strategic decisions and the practice of
public relations.

POWER RELATIONS IN ORGANIZATIONS

Foucault (1988) contended that power is so thoroughly embedded in the
fabric of our social lives that "every human relationship is to some degree a power relation. We move in a world of perpetual strategic relations" (p. 168). Daudi (1983) likened the social world to an "infinitely
complex network of micro-powers, of power relations, that permeates
every aspect of social life" (p. 320). Power-control theorists believe that
power is also woven deeply into the fabric of organizational lives and is
located in the interactions, or relations of power, between people (L. A.
Grunig, 1992b; Pfeffer, 1981, 1992; Spicer, 1997).

Many aspects of organizational life exemplify relations of power in
practice. These include job performance reviews, the distribution of project assignments, the implementation and enforcement of policies and
procedures, the assignment of titles and designation of awards and recognition, the selection of committee members, the construction of meeting agendas, and especially the pervasive decision-making processes
that govern matters large and small in organizations. To the extent that
the internal business of any organization is concerned with these interactions and with selecting, implementing, and communicating choices
and decisions, then ongoing power relations constitute an important
dimension and dynamic of organizational life.

Power relations help define not only who participates, who gets
what, and what gets done, but also what the organization means to its
members, how it acts and speaks publicly, how it is seen and perceived
by its publics, what it might become, and so forth. The study of power
relations, therefore, seems vital to public relations professionals because those relations profoundly structure the practice (Berger, 2005;
L. A. Grunig, 1992b; Holtzhausen, 2000). In short, public relations are

practiced the way they are by organizations "because the people who have power in an organization choose that behavior" (J. E. Grunig, 1992, p. 23).

Power may be the most valuable and important resource in organizations (Bolman & Deal, 1991), and every organizational member possesses and may exercise some power and is at the same time subjected to the power of others. Power comes from many sources, including individual characteristics, formal authority or reporting position, professional expertise, experience, relationships, access to decision makers, information, and political intelligence. The influence growing out of these potential power sources comes into play when organizational members meet in formal or informal political arenas to interact, discuss, advocate, and make choices and decisions.

At the same time that members attempt influence in these interactions, they are aware of and subjected to the many kinds of power that others in the arena possess, and they must make choices about what influence tactics or approaches will best serve them. These choices are based on the perceived powers of others, the type or nature of particular issues under discussion, the relative importance attached to an issue by the organization, and the quality of relationships with others in the arena.

Three Systems of Power Relations

Actual public relations practices grow out of three systems of power relations that may come into play in the dominant coalition—the most powerful arena—or other political arenas. One set of power relations—*power-over* relations—refers to a dominance model, that is, an instrumental or controlling orientation in discourse and decision making. This top-down managerial model is reflected in Marxist and Weberian theoretical traditions wherein power is equated with structures that dominate particular interests (Hardy & Clegg, 1996). It also may be equated with an asymmetrical worldview in the public relations literature (J. E. Grunig, 2001) and, as some theorists have suggested, with actual capitalist management structures and discourse practices (Deetz, 1992; Weaver, 2001).

Today, power-over relations are often linked with "hegemony," a noncoercive form of domination through which "subordinated groups actively consent to and support belief systems and structures of power relations that do not necessarily serve ... those groups' interests" (Mumby, 1997, p. 344). Prevailing organizational discourses and practices, along with existing dominance structures, manufacture a world-view that is "acceptable" to both the powerful and those who are relatively powerless (Deetz & Mumby, 1990). Public relations critical theorists contend that practitioners knowingly or unknowingly support such relations of power through the production of persuasive texts and strategic attempts to shape internal and external discourse (Gandy, 1992; Leitch & Neilson, 1997; Weaver, 2001), or to "manage reality" (Paine, 2001).

The existence of power-over relations, however, creates the conditions and environment for resistance (Barbalet, 1985; Hardy & Clegg, 1996; Wrong, 1979). There can be "no adequate understanding of power and power relations without the concept of resistance" (Barbalet, 1985, p. 532), and the power to resist can only be enacted when power-over relations exist (Wrong, 1979). Such resistance comes through two other systems: *power-to* relations and *power-with* relations. Power-to relations refer to approaches, processes, and actions that public relations professionals and others may use to try to counter or push back on a dominance or instrumental model and its corresponding power-over system of relations. As noted earlier, such approaches include a variety of Alpha and Omega strategies that are detailed in subsequent chapters.

Power-with relations refer to shared power and collaborative decision making (Kanter, 1977; Rakow, 1989), and the advocacy of power-with relations constitutes another form of resistance to an instrumental model. The ideology of shared power underscores the values of interaction, dialogue, cooperation, and relationships rather than dominating power conceptions (Bologh, 1990; Hartsock, 1981; Rakow, 1989; Shepherd, 1992). The two-way symmetrical model of excellent public relations emphasizes shared power with stakeholders that may be achieved through dialogue, negotiation, collaboration, and substantive relationship building (J. E. Grunig, 2001; L. A. Grunig, Toth, & Hon, 2001). Some researchers have suggested that two-way symmetrical public relations approaches may be gender loaded; that is, they are associated with a feminine worldview, whereas instrumental orientations in practice may be rooted in male values (L. A. Grunig, Toth, & Hon, 1999; Kanter, 1977; Rakow, 1989).

Relations of Power and PR Roles

Ongoing interactions among these three systems of power relations occur to some extent in many political areas. Power-over relations are manifest when organizational members in such arenas advocate or support decisions and actions that are self-interested, nondialogic, and restrict other points of view. Power-with relations are in play when members advocate or support decisions or decision-making processes that are more self-reflective, noncoercive, and inclusive of other points of view. Power-to relations are evident whenever members overtly or covertly resist a prevailing system of power-over relations. Though both power-with relations and power-to relations represent forms of resistance to an instrumental model, they differ in approaches and strategies. Power-with relations appear to rely primarily on sanctioned persuasive advocacy and relationship-building approaches. Power-to relations may combine these approaches with unsanctioned dissent and activist approaches.

Each system of power relations suggests a somewhat different role for public relations in the organization:

- In the power-over system, public relations is seen as an influence variable, one used instrumentally on behalf of the organization to accomplish its goals, or on behalf of those in power to advance self-interests. The job of public relations professionals is to efficiently and effectively do whatever those in charge direct them to do.
- In the power-with system, public relations is considered to be a relationship variable that is essential to gaining an interactive, relational perspective with others. The job of public relations is to advocate the primacy of relationships and to help the organization gain respect for, respond to, and construct mutually beneficial relationships with its many diverse publics.
- In the power-to system, public relations is viewed primarily as a political variable, a political actor that competes with others to influence organizational decisions, actions, and communications. The job of public relations professionals is to engage in power relations; they must use political intelligence, resources, and willpower to push back on the forces, processes, practices, and structural arrangements that otherwise constrain their abilities to help organizations do the right thing in a complex world.

Public relations professionals confront power relations at virtually every turn in the organization. They come into play in the dominant coalition and in major strategic decisions, of course, but they also touch such routine practices as the preparation and production of news releases. Power relations may determine whether a news release is selected as an appropriate communication channel, who writes the release, how the contents of the release are framed and structured, what sources are cited, who reviews and approves the release, when the release is distributed and to whom, whether subsequent interviews will be allowed and with whom, and so forth. Choices of one kind or another are made at virtually every step. Though practitioners are likely to be involved in such decisions, their recommendations do not always prevail. They then must decide whether to carry out the decisions and directives of others, to resist them, and if so, to what extent and using which approaches and tactics.

There are many reasons why professionals may choose to go along and execute, rather than resist the directives of others regarding the production of news releases or other weightier matters. Some of the professionals we interviewed, for example, said they needed to carefully select battles and battlefields so they wouldn't "burn up their influence." Others indicated that some processes and practices are so thoroughly established in organizations that one simply follows them without considering whether they are appropriate practices and procedures. As one PR director in the technology industry said, "Should the HR VP always review and edit our news releases? Well, probably not. But he's always done it so far as I know, so we don't really even think about that."

Hardy and Clegg (1996) provided two answers to their own question about why there is so little resistance in most organizations: The powerless remain relatively powerless because (a) they are ignorant about power and don't know how, or don't have the skills, to effectively resist, or (b) they understand power and how to resist, but they believe the costs of resistance outweigh their chances for, or the benefits of, success: they can't win or can't win enough (p. 628). Others may lack the self-confidence or willpower to engage in resistance activities, or seek to avoid the conflict and confrontation that are likely to accompany them (Pfeffer, 1992). In addition, resistance of any sort to a prevailing set of power relations is always risky but perhaps especially so in the current economic climate where downsizing has become a naturalized practice and employees and members are easily displaced or replaced.

A MODEL OF POWER RELATIONS

In this chapter, we have defined resistance in practice and described three broad types of resistance approaches: advocacy, dissent, and activism. We also sketched out the political nature of organizational life and decision making and examined the systems of power-over, power-with, and power-to relations in organizational politics. In our view organizational decisions and actual public relations practices are defined and structured through these systems of power relations and the political outcomes emerging from them. Organizational politics and power relations are produced by pressures from social and organizational forces and driven by various internal and external political influencers (L. A. Grunig, 1992b; Holtzhausen, 2000; Mintzberg, 1983; Pfeffer, 1992; Spicer, 1997). Drawing from these theorists, then, we depict the relationships among these forces, political influencers, political arenas, power sources, and power relations in Fig. 3.1.

Social-system forces include cultural values and practices, political events, economic developments, laws and regulations, public opinion, changes in technologies, and the rise and fall of advocacy and social-movement groups, among others.

Social-system forces exert varying pressures on the *organizational system*, which includes its own set of forces, that is, the organization's culture, history, structure, hierarchy, policies, practices and procedures, distribution of resources, and prevailing ideology. To some extent organizational system forces also may push back on the larger social system through public affairs programs and political activities, economic performance, strategic initiatives, social actions, and policies and practices.

Both social-system and organizational-system forces act on external and internal influencers, who to some degree also may push back on these systems. *External political influencers* include various publics or groups who have interests in and potential influences on the organization's economic and social performance, decisions, actions, communications, and so forth. They represent the more traditional "publics" in public relations, for example, customers, suppliers, unions, activist groups, professional associations, competitors, media organizations, governmental units, and financial institutions.

Internal political influencers include individual organizational members; formal groups of members who constitute specialized functions or units, work or project teams, and committees; and informal networks and coalitions of members who share common interests or seek to achieve common goals.

Internal and external influencers may compete with and pressure each other, or they may form coalitions or activist groups to pursue shared interests. Public relations practitioners, for example, may draw upon resources in professional associations, or they may join with professional associations or community groups to exert greater influence in

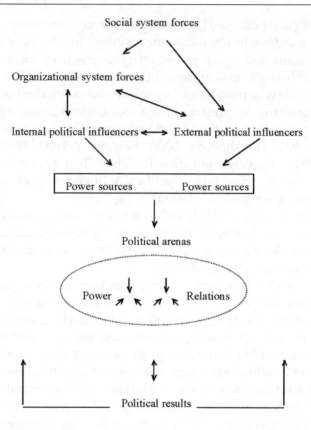

FIG. 3.1. This model depicts key elements and relationships among them in power relations in organizations.

power relations. They also may form coalitions with individuals or groups inside or outside the organization to increase political intelligence, resources, and influence. Much of the political conflict in organizations, however, occurs among competing internal influencers who engage in power relations in diverse organizational political arenas.

A *political arena* is a site of conflict, a space wherein political influencers interact to raise and define issues, discuss and debate solutions, negotiate, compromise, pose and posture, play power games, and use a variety of influence resources in order to take decisions and set courses of action. Political arenas are somewhat porous, and influencers may gain access to arenas through a variety of approaches. Common political arenas include offices, boardrooms, and traditional meeting rooms, but they also may include hallways, cafeterias, parking lots, company limousines and aircraft, as well as shared spaces created through tele-conferences, video conferences, chat rooms, discussion boards, videos, and so forth.

Political arenas are not the only place, of course, where power is evident. It is also present in organizational culture, structural arrangements, architecture, protocols and procedures, and so forth. Nevertheless, power relations frequently occur among individuals in decision-making moments within group venues of one form or another.

In his study of dominant coalitions, Berger (2005) found that in large corporations power groups or coalitions of influencers often intersect each other and may be loosely or tightly coupled in myriad political arenas in organizations. Some power groups are relatively fixed (e.g., strategic planning or budget review committees), whereas others are ad hoc and contingency based. According to public relations executives participating in the study, the existence of multiple political arenas means that any active political issue may move across multiple sites, making it difficult for public relations professionals to remain engaged with the issue.

Deliberately shifting issues from one arena to another is a common political tactic, according to the executives. The idea is to locate the most favorable venue for decision making for particular issues, or to exclude the participation of other political influencers from the decision-making process. To counter this approach, practitioners must anticipate arena shifts and insert themselves into the process, or try to create informal briefing sessions with key decision makers to stay in the process (Berger, 2005).

Influencers operate in political arenas by drawing from various *power sources* to capture the attention of decision makers and attempt to influence political results or outcomes. Power sources include personal characteristics, experience, expertise, structural authority, relationships, access to decision makers, political skill and will, professional associations, and a variety of influence strategies and tactics, among others.

Political results refer to the outcomes of power relations, that is, the organization's decisions, goals, resource allocations, actions, policies, implementation plans, and ideologies. Because political results are power based and reflect who gets what and what gets done, they exert pressures back onto internal and external political influencers, as well as the systems of power relations themselves.

Having briefly described the elements in our power relations model (Fig. 3.1), we note that all models are simplified representations of some reality. They focus on certain "key elements or parts of the object or process and the connections among them" (Shoemaker, Tankard, & Lasorsa,

2004, p. 110). Our model helps us "see" and think about power relations and relationships among elements or variables in this system. In this way, models can assist theory development.

At the same time, models are always partial and incomplete representations that conceal other variables or researcher assumptions (Shoemaker et al., 2004). The power relations model, for example, tells us nothing about individual influencer skills, the types of issues being contested, or the relative weight of diverse power sources. Yet, each of these and other variables factor into power relations.

The Importance of Resistance in Public Relations Thinking and Practice

Some may be uncomfortable with our use of "resistance" as a label for a public relations role. However, seeing and practicing public relations as forms of resistance in politically charged organizational environments helps crystallize the political nature of several key constraints on the profession, that is, lower-level reporting positions, comparatively limited program and staffing budgets, and limited participation in strategic decision making. Defining these constraints as political problems may direct our thinking away from doing more of the same to solve them to employing dissent, activist, and other alternative approaches that address their political nature.

This resistance perspective underscores two additional propositions:

> **Proposition 7: Because relations of power shape public relations practices as well as organizational decisions and actions, practitioners must better understand and engage in power relations.**

If organizations are political arenas where power relations are in play, and if public relations practices are shaped and defined by power relations in these arenas, then public relations professionals must become more adept at power relations, which includes forms of resistance. We can no longer professionally or theoretically ignore the pervasiveness and complexity of power relations in organizations. If the interviews told us anything, it is that power relations touch and shape professional practice at virtually every turn in every kind of organization.

This is not to suggest that the profession is nothing but organizational politics, but rather that practitioners must better understand power relations and more effectively use power sources to gain legitimacy and influence. At a minimum this requires public relations professionals to:

1. Understand the political infrastructure of the organization, the key political players, and how to get things done.
2. Recognize, marshal, develop, and use a variety of influence resources.
3. Select appropriate political strategies and tactics for influence attempts.
4. Employ influence strategies and tactics skillfully.
5. Possess the political will to engage in what are often confrontational power relations.

Proposition 8: Public relations professionals can increase their power by developing, mobilizing, and wisely employing a greater number and more diverse range of Alpha and Omega influence resources.

Practicing public relations as resistance increases the number of influence tactics and approaches available for use. Recognizing and using more influence resources wisely has the effect of increasing the potential power of the profession. However, simply recognizing the potential power sources that are available in practice may be an issue. When we asked practitioners to identify the influence resources they used most effectively on the job, nearly half of them found it difficult without prompting to name such resources, or to name resources beyond the proverbial time, money, and experience. This may have been due to the way the question was worded, or it may be that some professionals simply don't think of such resources in terms of their potential power.

We believe that practitioners have many influence resources available for use, but too often they may go unrecognized or underutilized. In the next chapter, we examine five types of influence resources and the extent to which practitioners actually use them.

CHAPTER 4

Identifying and Using Influence Resources in Public Relations

> *Most problems are framed, alternatives specified, and proposals pushed ... by Indians. Indians fight with Indians of other departments.... But the Indians' major problem is how to get the attention of Chiefs, how to get an issue on an action-channel, how to get the [organization] to do what is right.*
>
> *—Allison (1971, p. 177)*

Political influencers mobilize and use a variety of influence resources in political arenas to attempt to shape organizational decisions, actions, and communications. In this chapter, we identify and explore five types of influence resources that are available for use in power relations. We then draw from interviews with 162 public relations professionals to examine the influence resources they consider most valuable, which ones are in short supply, and what situations or circumstances provide greatest opportunities for public relations influence.

TYPES OF INFLUENCE RESOURCES

Influence resources are virtually anything perceived as valuable in getting things done in organizations (Pfeffer, 1992). In a classical treatment of power in organizations, French and Raven (1960) described five types of power sources or bases. *Authoritative* or *legitimate power* is based on reporting position or hierarchy in the organization. *Coercive power* is based on control over punishments or reprimands, whereas *reward power* comes from control over the distribution of organizational rewards and resources. These three types of power are structurally based, growing out of the position one holds in an organization. Two other forms of power have their bases in individual or personal attributes or characteristics. *Expert power* grows out of specialized knowledge or expertise, whereas *referent power* is similar to charisma. Bachrach and Lawler (1980) later added a sixth base of power to this typology, *information power*, which refers to power based on access to important information, or controls over such information.

Kanter (1977) identified other individual sources of power, including being visible and taking risks. She also called attention to a third category of power—relational influence resources—which includes mentors, sponsors, networks of contacts, coalitions, and access to those in power. In a comprehensive review of communication influence tactics, Waldron (1999) argued that relationships with mentors, peers, and other organizational members can facilitate or impede upward influence attempts and affect influence tactics. He suggested conceptualizing the influence process horizontally, as a "web of relationships" that might be activated, as opposed to a dyad relationship.

A. R. Cohen and Bradford (1989) noted that relationships are especially valuable when an individual's formal or structural authority is limited. They found that organizational members often "fail to recognize just how much ability they have to influence others … through mutually beneficial exchanges" (p. 5). By exchanging information, inspiration, support, and favors, organizational members can accomplish tasks and achieve their own influence goals even as they help others meet their needs. Public relations researchers also have underscored the importance of relational resources to practitioners when they possess limited formal power (L. A. Grunig, 1992a; Hatch, 1997; Holtzhausen & Voto, 2002).

In a survey of 309 corporate public relations practitioners, O'Neil (2003) found that the use of internal coalitions contributed positively to the practitioner's influence. She also found that both relational power and structural power exerted moderate and positive effects on perceived organizational influence. In the PR Success Interviews, nearly half of the 97 executives said that relationships with others in their organizations provided as much or more influence than their structural power (Heyman, 2004).

Individual Influence Resources

These three categories of influence resources—individual, structural, and relational—capture many of the types of power that are available for use. Individual or personal influence resources include professional experience and expertise; accomplishments and performance record; organizational knowledge; and a number of skill sets, for example, problem solving, environmental scanning, conflict resolution, interpersonal communication, and impression management. They also include personal attributes like intelligence, creativity, integrity, charisma, character, vision, and risk taking. However, Pfeffer (1992) argued that these conventional attributes were less important in power relations than were high energy, endurance, flexibility, the ability to "read" and be sensitive to others, and the willingness to engage in conflict in political arenas.

Other researchers have highlighted the importance of willpower in gaining influence. Mintzberg (1983) contended that "political power inevitably requires political will" (p. 187). Lauzen (1992) argued that the PR function can be powerful only if the top public relations leader believes that PR *is* a powerful organizational function. Holtzhausen and Voto (2002) emphasized the importance of *biopower*, or personal inner power, in gaining influence in public relations. In our view, resistance in practice requires the use of political will and a commitment to engaging and confronting others in political arenas.

Structural Influence Resources

Structural or formal influence resources include hierarchical position in the organization; membership and location in committees and other decision-making groups; formal authority provided in job descriptions, policies, role tasks, and project assignments; the structure and size of the unit or department; and controllable resources (money, people, technologies, etc.). Structural power tends to become institutionalized over time into established and taken-for-granted practices, policies, protocols, committees, rules, and distribution schemes (Pfeffer, 1992; Salancik & Pfeffer, 1977). In an example cited earlier, the human resources VP retained review and editorial power over news releases because that's the way it has been done for so long that no one could remember when the practice started: It had become an institutionalized practice.

Pfeffer (1992) argued that other structural influence resources also have value. These include the use of time (especially the timing and application of tactics), unit strength and the power of a unified unit voice, and the control of physical space. Several of the professionals we interviewed described how they used space to enhance their visibility and influence in employee communication programs.

Following a series of demoralizing employee opinion surveys that were sharply critical of internal communications efforts, practitioners in one unionized manufacturing plant decided to relocate their offices out of the administrative center and into the heart of production activities. They established a small communication center on one of the most heavily trafficked aisles on the plant floor. This dramatically increased the unit's visibility with its primary audience and allowed the practitioners to interact regularly with production employees. More importantly, the move provided them with immediate intelligence about employee issues and hot buttons, which they were quickly able to address. Over time, the unit gained the employees' confidence and became a more powerful voice for timely and substantive two-way communication between production employees and plant management.

Another professional in a large midwestern corporation described how his unit used office space no one else wanted to strengthen employee communications. The office was located just inside a rear entrance door to the administrative office building, an entrance used largely by mid- and upper-level executives. Because the office was small and situated where there was a lot of foot traffic, the space wasn't highly valued by others in the large facility.

The employee communications professionals reasoned, however, that the space provided an opportunity to make their products and programs more visible to the very people who made decisions about the unit's work. They set about removing a wall and "opening" the office to all who passed by. Then they professionally displayed their communication products, greeted executives each day, and put a face on their work.

The unit also began to conduct monthly telephone surveys of randomly selected employees to identify issues of greatest concern. They began posting a list of "Top 5 Employee Issues" on a bulletin board just inside the entrance door. The executives took notice of the issues and would stop to discuss them briefly with the public relations professionals. In this way, the unit was able to draw the attention of decision makers to key issues that otherwise might have remained below the surface.

Relational Influence Resources

These refer to relationships with others inside and outside of organizations, especially those in positions of power and authority. Relationships inside organizations grow out of interactions with mentors and sponsors; organizational and social networks; coalitions and alliances with other members; shared identity groups (gender, ethnicity, profession, etc.); and teams, committees, and routine working interactions. Relationships also may be located and developed with others in community, professional, and social networks outside of the organization.

About half of the professional men and women we interviewed said that internal relationships were one of their most valuable influence resources. As one professional put it, "Influence is all about relationships—in the beginning, the middle, and the end." Relationships can create access to powerful individuals or influential groups and lead to challenging and career-enhancing assignments. They can provide crucial information, organizational knowledge, and political intelligence for use. Relationships can multiply the number of other influence resources available for use, and strengthen and amplify voices in political decision-making arenas. Relationships represent a powerful multidimensional influence resource, a web of connections that can be cultivated and activated (Waldron, 1999) in public relations practice.

Informational and Systemic Influence Resources

Individual, structural, and relational influence resource categories are cited most often in the literature, but other resources also are available for use. Some researchers have argued that political influence may be gained though the communicative processes of framing and defining terms, issues, goals, and roles (M. Edelman, 1964; Ferris et al., 1989; German, 1995; Spicer, 1997). Brass and Burkhardt (1993) suggested that political activity itself is a form of power: "Strategic action can be used to compensate for relatively weak resources. Skillful political activity is one tool for overcoming a lack of resources or making less visible resources more potent" (p. 406). Similarly, Allison (1971) described influence as "an elusive blend of ... bargaining advantages and skill and will in using bargaining advantages" (p. 168).

Information is another form of power, and controlling access to vital information or its use, content, and distribution represents influence resources in political arenas (Bachrach & Lawler, 1980; Berger, 2005). Vital information includes material information about an organization's performance, strategies, and decisions; political information concerning other political players, agendas, and processes inside the organization; and empirical data gathered through research projects, case study analyses, and benchmarking activities, among others. Informational resources cross individual and relational categories, but we treat them as a separate category of influence in this research.

Systemic power sources represent an important fifth category. Systemic resources refer to professional organizations and associated codes, standards, established measures of professional value, and reputation. Systemic resources also include social, economic, and political developments and institutions in the larger social system that surround and intersect the organization (Barbalet, 1985). New communication and information technologies, for example, provide practitioners (and others) with potentially significant influence resources in the forms of greater access to information from publics and increased opportunities for dialogue with organizational members and external publics (Johnson, 1997).

Established measures of professional value or worth can help legitimate a profession and enhance its reputation and power. Professional associations and occupational communities also provide potential power through collective member knowledge, pooled experiences, and shared advocacy and activist initiatives (Waldron, 1999). Power in the systemic context has many points of contact or bases, and individuals or groups excluded from one power source or base may find access at another.

Overall, then, political influencers may draw from at least five interrelated categories of influence resources—individual, structural, relational, informational, and systemic—when they compete in political arenas in organizations. Examples of resources in each category are summarized in Table 4.1. In the next section, we discuss the influence resources that public relations professionals consider most valuable, as well as those that are in short supply.

THE USE OF INFLUENCE RESOURCES IN PUBLIC RELATIONS

We discussed influence resources and tactics with public relations professionals in two research projects carried out in the spring of 2004—the Influence Interviews and the PR Success Interviews. The Influence Interviews included 65 generally midlevel managers who represented diverse organizations, nationalities, and years of experience. The 97 partici-

TABLE 4.1
Categories of Influence Resources

Category	Examples of Resources
Individual	*Professional:* expertise, education, years and types of experience, performance record, organizational knowledge.
	Skills: interpersonal, technical, leadership, managerial, problem solving, political, and conflict resolution.
	Personal characteristics: intelligence, charisma, integrity, energy, willpower, character, risk taking, endurance, flexibility, focus, and vision.
Structural	*Authority:* reporting position, memberships in decision-making groups, job description, project responsibilities, policies, and practices.
	Controllable resources: budgets, personnel, technologies, physical space, equipment, and time/timing.
	Communication team: size and capabilities of work unit, collective voice, training, and development programs.
Relational	*Internal:* mentors, sponsors, access to decision makers, teams, coalitions, alliances, shared identity groups, and social networks.
	External: other professionals, associations, coalitions, clubs, community organizations, and social networks.
Informational	*Access to information:* research data, case studies, benchmarking results, organizational memory, material information, and political intelligence.
	Control over information: control the access to, collection of, or timing and distribution of information; editorial control over content.
Systemic	Professional associations; professional codes and standards; image or reputation of profession; measures of professional value; alliances and activist groups; and developments in political, social, and economic systems and institutions.

pants in the PR Success Study were almost exclusively high-level American executives.

We asked participants in both research projects to name two or three influence resources they valued the most (used most often on the job). Because a large number of professionals were interviewed in each project, frequency tables are used to present their responses before the results are assessed qualitatively. The influence resources named most often by participants in the PR Success Interviews are presented in Table 4.2.

TABLE 4.2

Most Valuable Influence Resources—PR Success Interviews

Influence Resource	Females	Males	Total
Relationships with others	18	21	39
Professional experience	15	21	36
Performance record	9	17	26
Persuasive skills with top executives	10	14	24
Professional expertise	7	14	21
Reporting (hierarchical) position	12	8	20
Data and research results	4	15	19
Political knowledge	6	12	18
Access to decision makers	12	5	17
Interpersonal skills	3	9	12
Information	6	6	12
Integrity, personal credibility	2	9	11
Knowledge of organization	2	6	8
Business knowledge	2	6	8
Education	4	1	5
Capabilities of PR team	2	2	4
Risk taking, political will	2	2	4
Others	4	6	10
Totals	120	174	294

Note. N = 97.

Clearly, public relations professionals consider many influence resources to be valuable. However, more than one third of the executives said that relationships with others (39, or 40.2% of total) and professional experiences (36, or 37.1%) were their most valuable influence resources. Many types of internal relationships were identified, but 15 of the 39 respondents specifically noted that relationships with decision makers and top executives were most valuable.

About one quarter of the participants said their performance records and accomplishments on the job (26), and their persuasive communication skills with top executives (24), were among their most valuable influence resources. Five other influence resources were mentioned by about one fifth of participants: professional expertise (21), reporting position (20), data and research results (19), level of political knowledge (18), and access to decision makers on the job (17).

Other influence resources that were mentioned only once by interview participants included financial resources and a handful of personal skills or characteristics, for example, critical-thinking skills, self-confidence, intelligence, analytical skills, and good judgment.

Some modest gender differences are evident when the results are assessed proportionally; that is, two female respondents are proportionally about the same as three male respondents in the sample. The top two influence resources on the list—relationships and experience—were seen by both female and male professionals to be among their most valuable influence resources. However, female professionals somewhat more often than male professionals highlighted the value of reporting position, access to decision makers, and education in gaining influence. On the other hand, male practitioners somewhat more often than female practitioners underscored the importance of data and research results, interpersonal skills, and integrity and credibility.

When examined in terms of categories of influence, there is a pronounced emphasis on individual influence resources. More than half of the resource mentions (155 of 294, or 52.7%) fall into the personal or individual category. These include professional experience, performance record, persuasive skills, expertise, interpersonal skills, integrity and credibility, knowledge of the organization and business, education, and political risk taking and willpower. Relational influence resources, that is, relationships with others and access to decision makers, were mentioned 56 times (19% of all mentions), whereas informational resources (data and research results, political information, and information generally) were mentioned 49 times (16.7%). Structural influence resources, that is, reporting position and PR team capabilities, were mentioned infrequently (24 times, or 8.2%), and systemic resources were not mentioned by any of the executives.

Responses by the 65 participants in the Influence Interviews to the same question about their two or three most valuable influence resources are presented in Table 4.3.

Professionals in this study also reported a wide range of influence resources on the job, mentioning more than two dozen. However, more than half of those interviewed indicated that professional experience (39, or 60.0% of participants) and relationships with others (36, or 55.3%) were among their most valuable influence resources. More than one third of participants said their performance record (27, or 41.5%) and professional expertise (25, or 38.5%) also were valuable resources.

TABLE 4.3

Most Valuable Influence Resources—Influence Interviews

Influence Resource	Females	Males	Total
Professional experience	16	23	39
Relationships with others	17	19	36
Performance record	13	14	27
Professional expertise	8	17	25
Reporting (hierarchical) position	14	5	19
Political knowledge	10	6	16
Data and research results	2	13	15
Knowledge of organization	6	9	15
Interpersonal skills	5	7	12
Access to decision makers	6	4	10
Integrity, personal credibility	4	5	9
Risk taking, political will	4	3	7
Capabilities of PR team	2	4	6
Information	2	3	5
Business knowledge	0	5	5
Education	3	1	4
Financial resources	1	3	4
Others	6	10	16
Totals	119	153	272

Note. N = 65.

These top four influence resources were followed by four others that were closely grouped: reporting or hierarchical position (19), political knowledge (16), data and research results (15), and organizational knowledge (15).

Both male and female practitioners rated most highly the value of professional experience and relationships with others. However, female professionals somewhat more often than male professionals emphasized the importance of reporting position, political knowledge, access to decision makers, and education. Male professionals highlighted somewhat more often than female professionals the influence value of professional expertise, data and research results, and business knowledge.

Other influence resources that were mentioned only once or twice by interview participants included high energy, intelligence, charisma, humor, personality, ambition, analytical skills, good judgment, and language skills.

Given the diversity of nationalities and types of organizations in this study, some other modest differences also were noted. For example, female practitioners who emphasized the importance of reporting position, political knowledge, and access to decision makers largely represented noncorporate organizations. Also, male practitioners who underscored the importance of data and research results worked almost exclusively in corporations and public relations agencies. Finally, the non-American professionals mentioned somewhat more often (proportionally) than American participants the influence value of their interpersonal skills and personal integrity.

When examined in terms of categories of influence, there is again a pronounced emphasis on personal or individual influence resources. More than half of the influence resources mentioned (147 of 272, or 54% of all mentions) qualify as personal or individual resources. Relational influence resources (relationships with others and access to decision makers) were mentioned 46 times (16.9%), whereas informational resources were mentioned 36 times (13.2%). Structural influence resources (reporting position and PR team capabilities) were mentioned even less frequently (29 times, or 10.7%), and systemic resources were not mentioned by any of the practitioners.

Though the samples in the two research projects were different, the similarities in responses among public relations professionals in the two groups are striking, with one notable exception. Comparisons of the top 10 influence resources for the two research studies are depicted in Table 4.4.

Public relations professionals in both studies assign more or less similar values to these 10 influence resources and believe their greatest sources of power reside in professional experiences and relationships with others. Nearly half (75, or 46.3%) of those in the two research projects ($N = 162$) said that relationships and professional experience were among their most valuable influence resources.

The only notable exception to these comparisons is #4 in the PR Success Interviews—persuasive skills with top executives—which was not mentioned by any of the participants in the Influence Study. This may be due to the fact that most of the professionals in the PR Success Interviews reported directly to the CEO or president of the organization, and they indicated they often engaged in discussion and debate with top ex-

TABLE 4.4
Comparisons of Top 10 Influence Resources in the Two Studies

Influence Resource	Success Study Rank (Number)	Influence Study Rank (Number)	Total Mentions
Relationships with others	#1 (39)	#2 (36)	75
Professional experience	#2 (36)	#1 (39)	75
Performance record	#3 (26)	#3 (27)	53
Persuasive skills with top execs	#4 (24)	——	24
Professional expertise	#5 (21)	#4 (25)	46
Reporting position	#6 (20)	#5 (19)	39
Data and research results	#7 (19)	#7 (15)	34
Political knowledge	#8 (18)	#6 (16)	34
Access to decision makers	#9 (17)	#10 (10)	27
Interpersonal skills	#10 (12)	#9 (12)	24

ecutives. In these political arenas, professional advocacy and persuasive skills come directly into play. It's also possible that some participants equated persuasive skills with interpersonal skills and reported them that way.

Professional Experience and Performance Record

Many of the professionals said that experience is a valuable influence resource because it provides knowledge in use and practical lessons that can inform and shape decision making. One corporate PR director in the Influence Interviews summarized this view: "Experience is a great teacher that shows the way and guides us. Experience gives us examples, cases, practical knowledge we can use to try to persuade or convince others in the company when a decision is needed."

Others emphasized the value of lessons learned over time and the kind of storehouse of professional solutions that grow out of repeat experiences, as indicated in these comments by an agency executive:

> I've been in a hundred situations in the past 30 years, each with a lesson or several lessons learned.... I find that experience gained with a wide range of organizations in a wide range of industries is a key resource. I'll go to a client and he'll say, "We have this situation." Immediately, I'll think of six re-

lated situations that I've been in with other clients, and I can tap into those and say, "In my experience, this is typically what happens, or this is typically the best approach to take." Your ability to influence is shaped by experience and the ability to say, "I've seen this situation before," or "I have a store of analogs in my head, and I can share with you what other organizations I've worked for have done in past when faced with similar circumstances, and here were the outcomes."

Of course, experience is a resource for most influencers in organizations, and sometimes one's experience doesn't outweigh that of others, or the formal authority of others, as one PR director at a nonprofit noted: "It doesn't seem that our experience makes a difference often enough. People get it in their minds that this is the way we're going to do it, or this is the way we've always done it, right or wrong, especially if we're trying to plan certain events or programs."

The PR Success Interviews added another dimension to considerations of professional experience. The researchers identified 10 patterns of success in public relations (Heyman, 2004), and experience was one of the most distinct patterns in the study. However, the executives said that though years of experience count, the diversity of experiences count for even more. Diverse experiences were identified as a primary influence resource, an important consideration in hiring, and a favorable tipping point in the careers of more than one third of those interviewed. As summarized by one longtime corporate executive, "Experience is extremely valuable. I don't mean just years of experience, but rather a mix, a kind of portfolio of experiences that, taken together, provide you with skills, knowledge, even wisdom to practice successfully."

Diverse professional experiences help develop interpersonal, strategic, tactical, and problem-solving skills by exposing one to differing people, problems, and contexts in different organizations and even cultures. Collectively, these experiences create a repository of knowledge and practical solutions that can enhance performance and boost influence in political arenas.

Professional experience has close ties to performance record, which was rated as the third most valuable influence resource (mentioned by 53 professionals) in the combined results of the studies. One way to define successful professional experience is as a strong record of performance. If a professional has helped the organization successfully resolve problems and conflicts in the past, it's likely that others in the organization will have greater appreciation for this professional's recommendations in the future. As one female agency executive from

England said, "If you've been there and done it successfully, people will listen to you."

Another agency executive linked performance to trust and judgment: "When you have a good track record, people believe what you're saying. They trust your judgment, and let's face it, in this business if you don't have trust you will not make it."

Most would agree that experience counts in any profession, so the reality is that the experiences of different professions and professionals compete in political arenas. In corporations, for example, the experiences of public relations professionals often compete with the experiences of human resources or plant management personnel in employee communication decision making. They compete with the experiences of lawyers, marketers, and financial executives in crisis situations, and they compete with the experiences of virtually every other function or unit in the company when it comes to resource allocations. Given the importance of experience as an influence resource, and the diversity and pervasiveness of competing experiences in organizations, it falls on public relations leaders to continue to develop and mobilize this resource.

Relationships, Relationships, Relationships

It's no surprise that public relations professionals view relationships as important influence resources. Externally, the practice is all about communicating, interacting, and building relationships with a variety of external stakeholders, from media to government personnel. Internally, it's all about developing relationships with others inside the organization to get ahead, gain access to information and resources, play a role in strategic decision making, and help the organization do the right thing.

In both research projects, nearly half of those interviewed (75, or 46.3% of 162) said that relationships with others were among their most valuable influence resources, and one in six (27, or 16.7%) indicated that access to decision makers, achieved through relationships, was one of the most valuable influence resources. Proportionally, female professionals placed somewhat more value on relationships as an influence resource than did male professionals: 53 female and 49 male professionals said that relationships, or access to decision makers, were among their most important influence resources.

A number of those we interviewed emphasized the importance of relationships with superiors or others with key decision-making responsibilities. One female corporate executive perhaps best captured this view:

> In PR, you have to have the support of top executives ... and relationships
> [with top executives] are the critical component of influence. I can't think of
> any resource that's more important than these relationships. Expertise and
> good judgment, these count for a lot, too, in building up trust and credibil-
> ity, a good performance record. But it's relationships in the beginning, the
> middle, and the end.

Another corporate practitioner put it even more succinctly: "Ninety-
nine percent of your ability to influence is having a boss or executive
who supports you by pushing you up to the [decision-making] table."

Others described the value of superiors as mentors or sponsors,
whereas some highlighted the importance of coalitions with other organizational members and the development of peer and subordinate relationships—networks cutting across the organization—to gaining
influence and getting things done. One public relations director described it this way: "People who can help you out are not always at the
highest level; sometimes they are in the oddest places. We must look for
relationships and networks everywhere."

A handful of the professionals pointed to another type of relationship—cross-functional alliances—which can provide a more powerful
collective face and voice in decision making. One director of media relations for a large consumer company described it this way:

> With executive management, relationships are driven by performance
> record, experience, and organizational knowledge. And these relation-
> ships can be strengthened by cross-functional collaborations. When
> we—IR, HR, PR and Legal—present our collective thinking to the top
> three guys, we show a united front, never criticizing each other in public.
> So cross-functional relationships are very important in influencing deci-
> sion making.

As noted earlier, relationships also were identified as one of the most
important characteristics of success in the Success Interviews. Top executives in the study suggested that the relationships they developed provided them with more power than their titles or formal reporting
positions. This possibility is also supported to some extent in the combined data sets for the two studies. Only 39 of the 162 professionals we
interviewed (24.1%) indicated that their reporting position was one of
their most valuable influence resources: They rated five other power
sources as more important. This may mean that professionals value
these other influence resources more highly, or it might mean that some
professionals are disadvantaged by lower-level reporting relationships
that don't provide them with a great deal of formal authority.

Building and cultivating relationships requires time, willingness, access, and a number of skills, perhaps the most important being interpersonal communication skills. In the two studies, 24 professionals (14.8% of total) said that interpersonal communication skills were among their most valuable influence resources. This seems like a relatively low number when compared to the number of professionals who placed high value on relationships (75). However, some respondents might simply subsume interpersonal skills into relationship building and networking. In our view, there are close linkages between interpersonal communication skills, the development and maintenance of relationships, and the extent to which such relationships may translate into influence. The communication manager at a manufacturing plant in Sweden described such links in the following anecdote:

> Every day when I come to work, I take the long way around from the parking lot to my office just so I can walk through the factory floor. To me that's the best way to pick up the specialized language of the line and build trust with the workers. I have always been a believer in actions speaking louder than words, so I've become a trusted conduit between worker and management. I listen carefully to line workers, handle those things I can handle, and pass along those I can't, and always, always, always I get back to the worker with an answer.... On those issues [involving line workers] I feel strongly about, I will fight like hell with top executives.... I recall one day I was discussing with our GM the hourly wage increases for the coming year. He told me there might be a nickel an hour for the troops, and he asked me how I thought they would receive the news. I pointed out to him that his bonus for the year was $27 million [sic], and how did HE think the troops would react to a nickel increase? After a relatively brief discussion, he totally agreed with me. He increased the amount to the troops.... Why? Because I talked and listened to line workers every day, I had good relationships with them, and management knew and respected these relationships.

INFLUENCE RESOURCES IN SHORT SUPPLY

We also asked participants in the two studies to identify one resource they felt they needed more of—and found difficult to obtain—to increase their influence in organizational decision making. Some professionals named two resources, and the frequencies of their responses are presented in Table 4.5.

Responses of most of the professionals are captured in the first 12 resource influences listed in the table. Only one most-needed influence resource—access to, and relationships with top executives—was named by more than 20% of respondents (33, or 20.4%), suggesting that prac-

TABLE 4.5
Most-Needed PR Influence Resources—Combined Studies

Influence Resource	Success Study	Influence Study	Total
Access, relationships with top execs	18	15	33
Financial resources	18	8	26
Better measures for PR value	17	9	26
Stronger persuasion skills	10	7	17
People resources	8	8	16
Better executive perceptions of PR	5	9	14
Stronger PR team	4	10	14
More time	8	4	12
Political skills, knowledge	7	5	12
Higher level reporting position	7	4	11
Business, financial knowledge	4	6	10
Better reputation for profession	7	2	9
Creativity	4	0	4
Stronger PR leadership	0	3	3
Professional expertise	0	3	3
Others (all personal characteristics)	6	5	11
Totals	123	98	221

Note. $N = 162$.

titioners have a number of influence resource needs rather than one predominant need. However, the fact that the top resource need concerns relationships with top decision makers underscores the importance that professionals attach to relationships as influence resources.

Some professionals also noted that relationships with those at the top provide important opportunities to influence executives' perceptions about the role and value of public relations (14) and enhance the profession's image (9). One communication manager at a nonprofit organization put it this way:

> One deficient PR influence resource is managerial appreciation of, or understanding of, the use of the function. Currently, management looks at the communications function at a tactical level and doesn't see it as a strategic tool. Of course, that keeps us from getting the maximum value out of

it. We need to develop better relationships at the top and get some wins to illustrate our arguments.

Some professionals who cited management's lack of understanding and appreciation of the practice's role and value said the profession itself was partly to blame for this predicament. One longtime public affairs executive harshly criticized the profession for its complicity in the construction of its current image:

> We need better PR people and a better reputation. Not this organization, necessarily, but the reputation that PR people create. On the one hand, you have the flacks who feel they have to rush to the press with everything, and who tout their ability to know people, and to get stories placed, that sort of thing, all of which is very superficial. On the other hand, you have the [named PR leaders] of this world who write books boasting about how they solved all the problems of their clients. Look, executives … are not dummies. You're not going to sell them a bill of goods. And … they are not going to pay top dollar for someone to write a press release for them.

Structural resources to do the job—financial (26), personnel (16), and time resources (12)—represent other crucial influence needs that were mentioned collectively by one third of the professionals (54 of 162 participants). This finding is consistent with chronic complaints in the profession about controllable-resource shortages, as reflected in the following comments by a director of government affairs at a manufacturing company:

> Today, we're four times as large a company as we were 15 years ago, and we have global responsibilities … yet our resource base, our people and dollars in the function, have changed very little. Whenever I make this argument, I'm told to work smarter and harder, but there are certainly limits to that. In the end … the communications work we do has less value than other things people do in the company.

Overall, when we examine these resource needs in terms of categories of influence, a little less than half (96 of 221 mentions, or 43.4% of total) of these resources fall into the structural influence category. This includes financial, personnel, and time resources noted earlier; stronger PR teams and better professional leadership; higher level reporting positions; and, improved understanding and support of the public relations role by organizational executives who allocate resources and assign reporting positions.

Individual or personal influence resource needs, on the other hand, account for about one fourth (54, or 24.4%) of those mentioned in the interviews. This category includes stronger persuasive communication skills, political skills, business and financial knowledge, creativity, more education, and other personal characteristics. The emphasis given to structural influence resources over individual resources contrasts with earlier findings where about half of the professionals said their most valuable influence resources were individual resources, whereas only about 10% of them said that structural resources were among their most valuable.

In other words, the professionals we interviewed appear to value and use most often a variety of individual and relational influence resources, while drawing far less often from structural, systemic, and informational power sources. This may be due to lack of control the professionals exert over structural and systemic resources, less access to them, or less understanding of how to mobilize and use them. Nevertheless, practitioners recognize the need for such resources: Nearly half said they have great need for more structural resources to increase their influence. In addition, some identified the need for two systemic influence resources—better measures for PR value (26) and a better professional reputation (9). We believe that PR professionals can do more to develop and mobilize structural and systemic influence resources, and we address this opportunity in chapter 10.

Modest Differences by Gender and Organizational Type

The perspectives of female and male public relations practitioners regarding most-needed influence resources in both studies are presented in Table 4.6, which lists the 10 most frequently mentioned resources. Although these expressed needs are quite similar, there are several modest differences. Female professionals somewhat more often than male professionals said that access to, and relationships with key decision makers was the resource they needed more of to increase their influence. Professional women in the study also placed slightly more emphasis on financial and people resources, a stronger PR team, and higher level reporting positions. Male professionals cited the need for improved public relations measures somewhat more often than female professionals. Professional men also placed slightly more emphasis on time resources and enhanced political skills and knowledge.

Other slight differences were noted by organizational type. For example, most of the female professionals who said that relationships with

TABLE 4.6
Most-Needed PR Influence Resources by Gender—Combined Studies

Influence Resource	Success Study		Influence Study		Totals	
	F	M	F	M	F	M
Access, relationships with top execs	11	7	10	5	21	12
Financial resources	8	10	5	3	13	13
Better measures for PR value	5	12	2	7	7	19
Stronger persuasion skills	6	4	2	5	8	9
People resources	3	5	5	3	8	8
Better executive perception of PR	2	3	3	6	5	9
Stronger PR team	1	3	7	3	8	6
More time	2	6	1	3	3	9
Political skills, knowledge	2	5	1	4	3	9
Higher level reporting position	5	2	1	3	6	5

Note. N = 162.

key decision makers or financial and people resources were in short supply were employed in agency, nonprofit, and educational settings. On the other hand, nearly all of the men and women who indicated that better public relations measures and more political skills were needed worked in corporations or agencies. And with only one exception, those who said that enhanced executive understanding of the practice was a most-needed resource were corporate professionals.

CONSTRAINTS ON THE INFLUENCE OF PUBLIC RELATIONS PROFESSIONALS

We asked public relations professionals in the two studies to name two or three factors or realities in their organizations that limited or constrained their influence. Their answers are presented in Table 4.7, which suggests that five factors most often curb the power and influence of public relations professionals. Collectively, these five factors—executive perceptions of PR (mentioned by 79 of the 162 professionals surveyed), insufficient resources (45), reporting positions (27), weak PR teams (27), and culture for communication (25)—accounted for

TABLE 4.7
Constraints on PR Influence—Combined Studies

Constraints on Influence	Success Study		Influence Study		Both Studies		
	F	M	F	M	F	M	All
Executive perceptions of PR	21	28	11	19	32	47	79
Insufficient resources	7	15	12	11	19	26	45
Reporting position	9	7	4	7	13	14	27
Weak PR team	6	10	3	8	9	18	27
Culture for communication	3	4	7	11	10	15	25
Lack measures for PR value	6	7	1	3	7	10	17
Lack access to decision makers	4	4	5	2	9	6	15
Organizational politics, turfism	5	6	4	0	9	6	15
No seat at decision-making table	1	6	4	3	5	9	14
Poor image of PR profession	3	3	2	5	5	8	13
Weak PR leadership	2	1	2	4	4	5	9
Gender	0	0	3	0	3	0	3
Others	4	7	4	5	8	12	20
Totals	71	98	62	78	133	176	309

Note. $N = 162$.

nearly two thirds of all responses to the question (203 of 309 total mentions, or 65.7%).

Nearly half of the professionals (79, or 48.8%) said that a leading constraint on their influence was the perception of key decision makers regarding the role and value of public relations. In this longtime view, organizational leaders don't understand or appropriately value the role and contributions of public relations. As a result, the profession is seen as peripheral to the organization's success and is underfunded, underappreciated, and underutilized. One corporate director in the Success Interviews bluntly summarized this view: "Most executives just don't understand PR. They see it as free advertising, or as an ancillary or nice-to-do business function. They don't see how it drives business results. Until we can convince executives of the role PR needs to play in the business function, it will always be peripheral."

As noted earlier, opinions are divided about who's responsible for this situation. Some professionals place the blame squarely on organizational decision makers, whereas others point to the profession's own shortcomings and its checkered history. One agency director captured the sentiments of a number of those we interviewed who believe the profession has yet to earn credibility: "The perception of PR is very low in my opinion because we don't advocate strongly, and we don't earn our stripes, and we don't want to risk being unpopular and risk having our mistakes splattered all over the newspapers."

Some participants said that the publicity legacy of public relations created problems for both professionals and organizational decision makers. To the extent that practitioners themselves see and advocate public relations as the manufacture of buzz and publicity, so too will decision makers perceive the manufacture of these communication products as the primary and perhaps sole role of the practice. An agency executive summed up this view as follows: "I think the overall reputation of the craft as being spin doctors and publicists ... has limited public relations. It is the power of the media voice which has been a great thing for our industry, but the negative side of that is it has sort of pigeon holed us—that is all that we do."

Others suggested that increasing specialization in the field was a trap, as captured in this agency director's comment:

> We are our own worst enemy. We are out there insisting we need to specialize in, say, media relations. Maybe that makes sense at some point in your career, but it's such a limiting factor.... You can have a particular expertise but if you're doing just that, you're eventually going to be marginalized because people will only see you for that function and not for what a true communication professional can offer.... If you're just perceived as a press relations person, even if you're the best press relations person possible, it's still one dimensional.... We need to redefine who we are.... We need to make some changes.

Twenty-five participants said that "culture for communication" was an important limiting factor on their ability to exert influence and practice effective public relations, which is consistent with findings in the Excellence Studies (J. E. Grunig, 1992; L. A. Grunig et al., 2002). According to professionals in our studies, this factor is closely linked to executive perceptions of public relations. One PR director in the financial services industry defined this linkage: "By a culture for communication

I mean especially how the CEO views communication, how he perceives and values it, trusts it, believes in it, leads the way with it, and sets good examples, and so forth, and how the company's climate is supportive of, or restricts actual communication."

Another corporate practitioner elaborated on the powerful effects of organizational culture on both decisions and the decision-making process:

> The culture of an organization is probably far and away the strongest factor because the culture has everything to do with how decisions are made and what reality the organization accepts. Every organization has things that everybody in the room knows are real, but which cannot be mentioned in the conference room. That's where the culture starts to cut people off at the knees. The more parochial the culture, the more what happens in the conference room is going to be divorced from reality. So that [culture], I think, is the single most inhibiting factor in success in the organization.

Organizational culture directly bears on resource allocations, as well, as described by one communication VP:

> Culture is first—culture will drive the resources. It has to do with the kind of organization you are in, their orientation to the public, their understanding of what the communication function is about, what it can achieve. Going back to a former company I worked for, the guy who was president ... was famous for a statement, "The whale that surfaces first takes the harpoon," meaning stay below the surface of the water, try not to let anybody know you exist aside from your customers and people who buy stock.... With that kind of attitude, PR will never be an optimized function.

A number of practitioners described specific cases where the culture influenced communication decisions and outcomes. One agency executive, however, underscored the power of culture even when executives at the company he was advising knew that the existing culture was powerful and needed to be changed:

> I recently worked with a company that was obsessed with engineering and engineering safety because the products they made, if poorly made, could destroy the world. And they had an appropriately conservative and cautious culture. The kind of communications we were trying to do for them, which they saw other companies doing, was just too hard for them to emotionally embrace. They saw it, they understood it, and they saw the value of it, but they couldn't bring themselves to be that open because it went against other, more ingrained parts of their culture, which was to absolutely control everything.

Qualitative Differences by Gender and Organizational Type

The professionals we interviewed in the two studies—across gender, organizational type, and nationality—were consistent in naming executive perceptions of public relations and insufficient resources as the top two constraints on their influence. However, several slight or modest qualitative differences were noted regarding other constraints:

- Female practitioners mentioned their reporting position, lack of access to decision makers, and organizational politics as constraints slightly more often proportionally than did male practitioners.
- Nearly all of the non-American professionals (13 of 15) identified insufficient resources as a primary limitation on their influence.
- Most of those who named hierarchical position as a limitation work in corporate settings.
- Nearly all of the participants who identified weak public relations teams and leadership as limitations work in corporations or agencies.
- Participants in the Influence Interviews mentioned insufficient resources, culture for communication, and weak PR leadership as constraints somewhat more often than did those in the PR Success Interviews.
- Participants in the Success Interviews, most of whom were high-ranking executives, named organizational politics and the lack of public relations measures as constraints slightly more often than did those in the Influence Interviews.

WHEN ARE PR PROFESSIONALS MOST INFLUENTIAL?

We asked the 65 professionals who took part in the Influence Interviews to identify those situations or circumstances in which they felt they were most and least influential in decision making (Table 4.8). Nearly half of the professionals (28, or 43.1% of total) said they exerted most influence during crises. At such times, media attention may be focused sharply on an organization, and every decision and step the organization takes may be scrutinized and made visible in the court of public opinion. Why are public relations professionals at these moments suddenly sought out, listened to, and invited to take a seat at the table?

Strategic-contingency theorists provide one explanation. According to this approach, practitioners are granted more power during crisis situations because they possess something that is vital to the organization

TABLE 4.8
Situations Where PR Is Most Influential—Influence Study

Situation	F	M	Total
Crisis situations	13	15	28
Preparing communication messages, plans	6	7	13
Media relations programs	1	5	6
Employee communications programs	2	3	5
Working with smaller clients	1	2	3
When trusted (by the client)	2	0	2
When performance record backs up advice	1	1	2
Others	2	4	6
Totals	28	37	65

Note. N = 65.

at such moments—relevant professional (media and stakeholder) expertise and problem-solving knowledge that can help the organization cope successfully with environmental disturbances and uncertainties (Mintzberg, 1983). Environmental problems and uncertainties that threaten the stability and legitimacy of the organization help determine the distribution of power (Pfeffer, 1992; Salancik & Pfeffer, 1977).

Savvy professionals also scan the environment for other potential crises in order to head off such problems and to market the unit's problem-solving capabilities to garner resources and power. In this regard, the head of a public relations agency described the important responsibilities and opportunities that recent corporate accounting scandals present to professionals:

> Until a company has faced a difficult situation where the PR person has stepped forward and performed admirably, I think PR is looked at by a lot of executives as a kind of necessary evil. Maybe the current environment of malfeasance by so many corporations has made it easier to sell the value of PR. This current emphasis on greater transparency and candid disclosure actually provides a very good opportunity for PR professionals and the profession to step forward. The age of the CEO celebrity is over ... so maybe companies can focus on accurately positioning the organization and not focus on selling the celebrity of the CEO. This is probably an important moment for the profession.

One in five professionals (13 of 65) said they were most influential when crafting communication messages or developing communication plans. These professionals felt they were given a great deal of technical authority in their work after strategic decisions were taken by others. Eleven other professionals indicated they exerted most influence when managing the day-to-day activities of particular functions or units, that is, media relations programs (6) and employee communication programs (5). A handful of agency professionals said their greatest influence was achieved with smaller rather than larger client organizations and when clients knew and trusted them. Other professionals felt they were most influential when they were involved early in decision making, possessed good data to back up arguments, or worked with line or midlevel managers from other functions, rather than top executives.

On the other hand (Table 4.9), the professionals said they had far less influence in decision making that involved important strategic initiatives (18, or 27.7% of participants), when they were perceived as technicians by organizational leaders (13, or 20%), or when they dealt directly with the most senior executives in their organizations (11, or 16.9%).

A number of the professionals expressed frustration at being excluded from strategic decision-making discussions. These are familiar laments to practitioners. Others indicated that even when they are involved in strategic decision-making meetings they are involved as technicians, not as managers. The public relations director at a Canadian company perhaps best expressed this concern:

> I am often involved in meetings ... where major decisions are taken, but I often feel that they don't really want my input on the wisdom of such issues or decisions; they just want me to tell them how to best communicate their decisions to our employees. That's critical, of course, but I also think I have valuable advice about other matters. Is restructuring, for example, the only way to deal with the financial health of the organization? Must we periodically lay off hundreds of workers as a matter of course? I mean, if we do that, doesn't it mean that we've somehow failed? That whatever our last rationale was, just wasn't right?

DO PR PROFESSIONALS BELIEVE THEY HAVE ENOUGH INFLUENCE?

Finally, we asked participants in the Influence Study to tell us whether they have enough influence; that is, do they believe they influence organizational decisions and communications to the extent they should? We

TABLE 4.9
Situations Where PR Is Least Influential—Influence Study

Situation	F	M	Total
Strategic decision making	7	11	18
Perceived as technicians	8	5	13
Interactions with senior executives	4	7	11
Advocating social-responsibility programs	2	3	5
Involved late in decision making	2	2	4
Dealing with large clients	1	3	4
Budget discussions	1	1	2
Others	3	5	8
Totals	28	37	65

Note. N = 65.

left open the issue of to what extent that might be, and none of the participants asked us to clarify the question. The results are presented in Table 4.10.

We anticipated that the vast majority of the professionals would say "sometimes" given the many contingencies of the job, the diverse political arenas in which practitioners interact, the many influence resources they draw from, and the examples of both wins and losses they described in the interviews. However, only about one third (23, or 35.4%) of the respondents answered "yes and no," whereas one quarter (16, or 24.6%) said "yes" and 40% (26) said "no." In short, a majority of the professionals did not equivocate in their responses.

TABLE 4.10
Practitioner Beliefs About Their Influence—Influence Study

Answers	F	M	Total
Yes, I have enough influence	8	8	16
No, I don't have enough influence	7	19	26
Yes and No: Sometimes I have enough influence	13	10	23
Totals	28	37	65

Note. N = 65.

In addition, though the answers were more or less consistent according to organizational type and nationality, some gender differences emerged. Exactly three quarters (21 of 28) of the female professionals we interviewed said they always or sometimes influenced organizational communications and decisions to the extent they feel they should. Slightly less than half (18, or 48.6%) of the male professionals said they always or sometimes had enough influence.

This could mean that female professionals are more influential in practice than are male professionals. It also might mean that female professionals are simply more optimistic about their influence, or that professional women and men view or define successful influence in different ways. Perhaps female practitioners measure their influence by the quality of the relationships and mutual respect they develop with others, rather than as outright wins and losses in ongoing organizational conflicts (Bologh, 1990). Our data set is too small, and our discussions with practitioners too incomplete, to draw any conclusions in this regard. But the finding is nevertheless intriguing and worth more research.

We are also heartened by the finding that 16 of the 65 professional women and men in the study believe they virtually always influence organizational decisions and communications to the extent they should. Perhaps these practitioners are reflecting on their influence in a purely technical sense; that is, they always influence channel selection, message construction, or the development and implementation of communication plans. Some professionals in the two studies defined influence in exactly these ways. Or perhaps they are deceiving themselves, or "drinking too much of their own Kool-Aid," as one senior communication executive suggested:

> I don't have all the influence I need. I may think I'm doing a great job helping and influencing the organization, but in my heart of hearts maybe I admit to myself that I do spend a lot of time implementing and not a lot of time actually influencing or engaging in influencing decision makers. I think this is another one of those areas where we, as a profession, may be pretty good at thinking we are doing a better job than maybe we actually are. Maybe we're drinking too much of our own Kool-Aid.

Of course, these 16 individuals also may be highly influential professionals in their organizations. If this is the case, what can we learn from them or about them? Is their successful influence related to the type of organization for which they work? Do they define influence differently? Are they better educated? Do they have more experience? Do they mobilize and use different influence resources or tactics?

We went back into the data set to explore some of these issues. We discovered that the educational backgrounds of these individuals are quite diverse, as are the types of organizations they represent: corporations (7), agencies (4), nonprofits (3), educational institutions (1), and government agencies (1). However, they share in common a great deal of professional experience, and, with one exception, they all defined influence as holding a seat at the decision-making table and participating in strategic decision making.

In addition, they identified the same three most valuable influence resources: (a) relationships, which were highly prized by a number of participants in the study, (b) political and organizational knowledge, and (c) political will. The latter two resources were mentioned by relatively few study participants. Again, we can't draw any conclusions about these 16 professionals given the small sample size, but we come back to issues of political skill and will in chapter 9. These resources may be pivotal to gaining influence and getting things done inside modern organizations (Mintzberg, 1893; Pfeffer, 1992).

OBSERVATIONS ABOUT INFLUENCE RESOURCES IN PUBLIC RELATIONS

Mintzberg (1983) argued that the greatest source of power for public relations professionals is the system of expertise, or the particular communication skills and knowledge that practitioners can bring to the table. Professional expertise is clearly an important form of power, but in this chapter we identified a great number of individual, structural, relational, informational, and systemic influence resources that practitioners may be able to develop, mobilize, and use in power relations. According to the 162 professionals we interviewed, some of these influence resources are heavily used, whereas others appear to be underutilized or virtually unrecognized, which leads us to suggest the following three propositions regarding influence resources:

> **Proposition 9: Public relations professionals rely heavily on personal and relational influence resources for their power in practice.**

Overall, practitioners said they draw primarily from well-known individual or personal resources—for example, professional experience, expertise, and performance record—and secondarily from relationships, access to decision makers, and other relational influence resources. They may rely on individual and relational influence resources because they possess more of these resources, exert greater control over them, feel more comfortable with them, or have relied on them for so long that they have become internalized in practice. Because individual and relational resources also are widely used by others in organizations, they are likely to be deemed highly acceptable and legitimate influence resources. Furthermore, professional associations reinforce the primacy of such resources through myriad development programs and workshops.

Proposition 10: Structural power in public relations practice is in high demand and short supply.

Many of the professionals recognized the limitations of their influence resources. They particularly emphasized their need for more structural resources, that is, bigger budgets and more people, stronger PR teams, higher level reporting positions, and improved understanding and support for their work by the very organizational leaders who allocate resources and assign hierarchical positions. Deficiencies in controllable resources and hierarchical positions have long been contentious issues in the profession, and our research suggests that little has changed. Rightly or wrongly, many practitioners still believe that they are deliberately assigned lower level reporting positions and provided with fewer resources than other political influencer groups or functions in their organizations. This issue goes directly to the perceived legitimacy of the profession.

Slightly more than half of the participants (49 of 97) in the Success Interviews said that executive perceptions of the role and value of public relations limited their influence in practice. Findings in the Influence Interviews were similar. However, the sample in the Success Study consisted almost exclusively of seasoned and high-level public relations executives, many of whom report directly to CEOs or other top officials in their organizations and who sit at strategic decision-making tables. These professionals may be in the best positions to help organizational executives better understand the important role and value of public relations.

Yet, about half of these senior practitioners indicated that their organizational leaders still don't get it; they still don't understand that public relations can make a contribution and help organizations do the right thing. This disturbing finding suggests that everything the profession has done over the years to change these perceptions, all of the Alpha approaches that have been used, just haven't worked, or have worked only incrementally or in some organizations. We take this as some more qualitative evidence that new approaches to gaining influence in the profession are required.

What participants in the two studies appear to be saying, then, is that the limits on their influence are not largely circumscribed by their own capabilities, which in fact they earlier described as significant influence resources. Rather, their influence is constrained by other decision makers and influencers in the organization, *and* by the very structure of the organization itself, which is substantially defined by ongoing power relations and corresponding practices that serve to center or to marginalize particular individuals, units, and groups in the organization.

If this is the case, then public relations professionals must begin to push back more forcefully in political arenas against other influencers and prevailing organizational structures. And if this is not the case, if in fact structural constraints are also accompanied by some individual or relational resource deficiencies, then professionals need to identify what personal and relational resources must be further developed and strengthened even as they become more engaged in resistance activities in political arenas.

Proposition 11: Systemic influence resources are underutilized or underdeveloped in public relations practice.

Few professionals mentioned systemic influence resources, and this is an important oversight. Systemic influence resources offer increased opportunities for professional advocacy, dissent, and activist approaches at the association level. We suspect professionals also are aware of these opportunities but may not consider them to be viable given the structures and practices of their current professional associations. The practitioners we interviewed had a great deal to say about their associations in this regard, and we take a closer look at their comments and explore systemic influence resources in greater detail in chapter 10. In the next chapter, however, we turn our attention to the influence tactics that professionals use on the job.

CHAPTER 5

Alpha Approaches in Public Relations: The Use of Sanctioned Influence Tactics

> *I was able to be influential by building a strong relationship with executive officers of the firm, by insisting the emotion be taken out of the equation, by gaining trust, by developing clear strategy which was sold to them one on one, and by providing specific, well-developed execution plans.*
>
> —Agency executive with 30 years of experience

Success in public relations relies on political savvy perhaps as much as experience (Heyman, 2004). Knowing the organization, its players, and their predispositions, and knowing where the ultimate decision will be made and the most persuasive way to present a case are essential political skills, but there are many more. In daily practice, public relations professionals draw from a deep well of sanctioned influence tactics and strategies. Some of those sanctioned tactics are commonly used by many internal influencers; others are less common and riskier.

This chapter addresses the use of Alpha tactics by public relations professionals. Alpha approaches are commonly used influence tactics that are generally sanctioned or accepted in professional and organizational practice. They represent the first line of influence tactics. We explore more controversial Omega tactics in chapter 7.

IDENTIFYING AND CATEGORIZING INFLUENCE TACTICS

Though the choice of influence tactics is manifold, that set is limited by the personal style, beliefs, and habits of each professional. One professional told us, "I think the need for research is even more critical today in our work." Another said, "We had a nasty fight over what to do.... I think I was influential simply because I didn't back down." And yet someone else said, "Plain and simple, I used organizational politics." Though each of these exemplifies a source of personal influence, they also represent different styles for different people or in different situations. In short, influence tactics run on a continuum, perhaps several continua, from deferential to confrontational, from logic based to emotion based, from crisis driven to rote.

Beyond personal style and predisposition, there are other factors that affect the choice of strategies or tactics used to gain influence. These may include the relationship between the public relations professional and the target he or she intends to influence, the power differential (perceived or real) between the practitioner and his or her target, the opportunities for the professional to exhibit and exercise power, and more. A number of scholars in organizational studies have identified influence strategies and tactics (e.g., Falbe & Yukl, 1992; Farmer, Maslyn, Fedor, & Goodman, 1997; Kipnis & Schmidt, 1982; Waldron, 1999; Yukl & Tracey, 1992).

A seminal study in the use of influence tactics or, as the study's authors colloquially stated, "getting one's way," was conducted by Kipnis, Schmidt, and Wilkinson (1980). They found that the most common influence tactic was simply to explain the rationale for the request (17% of respondents), followed by a direct request (10%), or an exchange such as a compromise or calling in favors (8%). Less forthright tactics were also relatively common. Clandestine tactics such as manipulating information or cajoling the influence target accounted for 8% of responses. Personal negative actions such as slowing the job, expressing anger, or threatening accounted for 8% of responses (p. 442).

In a second phase of their study, Kipnis et al. (1980) conducted factor analysis on 58 items identified in the first phase. Their analysis yielded eight influence dimensions—ingratiation, rationality, assertiveness, sanctions, exchange, upward appeal, blocking, and coalitions. When attempting to influence superiors, Kipnis et al. found that rationality tactics were most common. Assertiveness and sanctions were used more for influencing subordinates than for influencing coworkers or superiors. Ingratiation, exchange, and upward appeals were used significantly more to influence subordinates and coworkers than they were to influence superiors. Blocking and coalitions were least commonly used influence tactics (p. 449).

Kipnis et al. (1980) concluded:

> The frequency with which each influence dimension was used related to the relative power of the respondents and targets of influence, the reasons for exercising influence, the resistance of the target person, the organizational status of respondents, organizational size, and whether the organization was unionized. (p. 440)

Yukl and Falbe (1990) extended the work done by Kipnis et al. (1980). Yukl and Falbe found that frequency of use of influence tactics, from most to least frequent, were consultation, rational persuasion, inspirational appeals, ingratiating tactics, coalition tactics, pressure tactics, upward appeals, and exchange tactics. They also found that there was substantial agreement between influence agents and targets regarding frequency of tactics (p. 139).

Falbe and Yukl (1992) subsequently worked at defining and testing conceptualizations of influence tactics. They used Kipnis and Schmidt's (1985) categories of "hard," "soft," or "rational" to determine the effectiveness of various tactics. Hard tactics include pressure and legitimating (appeals linked to organizational values, objectives, and policies) as well as some forms of coalitions, according to Falbe and Yukl. They identified ingratiation, consultation, inspirational appeals, and personal appeals as soft tactics.

Falbe and Yukl (1992) measured effect as "resistance," "compliance," or "commitment." Commitment was defined as when the influence target agrees with the action or decision and works diligently to carry it out. Compliance was defined as when the target apathetically carries out the action or decision, using minimal effort and no initiative. Resistance was defined as when the target is opposed and actively works against the action or decision.

Findings in a Falbe and Yukl (1992) study showed that rational persuasion was most common followed by hard tactics, but consultation and inspirational appeals (soft tactics) were most effective in gaining compliance or commitment. Pressure tactics were most commonly associated with an outcome of resistance. But hard tactics can gain compliance, especially if used with rational persuasion. Combining tactics often had an effect. Combining two soft tactics, for example, was more effective than combining two hard tactics. Combining either a hard or soft tactic with rational persuasion was more effective than any of the three by themselves.

Yukl and Tracey (1992) wrote that their assumption in building and testing a model of influence tactics use and direction was that influencers prefer "socially acceptable" tactics that are "feasible in terms of the agent's position and personal power in relation to the target, that are not costly (in terms of time, effort, loss of resources or alienation of the target), and that are likely to be effective for a particular objective given the anticipated level of resistance by the target" (p. 526).

Yukl and Tracey (1992) found that the most commonly used influence tactic by a subordinate on his or her superior was rational persuasion. Rational persuasion and inspirational appeal were found to be most effective in influencing superiors. They also determined "in general the most effective tactics were still rational persuasion, inspirational appeal, and consultation, and the least effective tactics were still coalition, pressure, and legitimating" (p. 532). ·

Farmer et al. (1997) affirmed earlier findings regarding upward influence attempts. They determined that rational tactics were the most often used tactics when subordinates were attempting to influence superiors. They noted that coalition tactics may be either hard or soft in their approach. Education, paired with other factors, was found as a predictor of tactical choices. Higher education and Machiavellianism (i.e., manipulating others to achieve one's goals) were significant predictors of use of hard strategies. Higher education, self-monitoring tendencies, and having external locus of controls were significant predictors of soft strategies. The authors surmised:

> Both high Mach[iavellian]s and better-educated individuals may be more adept at picking spots to selectively use hard or coercive forms of influence, and thus may be likely to wield it more often than others ... high Machs and well-educated people may simply be more self-confident in "pushing" for things that they want from their supervisors. (p. 35)

Farmer et al. (1997) also suggested that ability to communicate face-to-face had an impact on influence tactics. They found that rational persuasion was more frequently used when face-to-face interaction between supervisor and subordinate was limited. In short, the stable of influence tactics is diminished when face-to-face interaction is absent.

A review of influence research (Waldron, 1999) suggests consistency in definitions and findings related to upward influence. Waldron reviewed and critiqued communication literature as well as that within other disciplines. He found that nearly all research in the area "conceptualized upward influence ... as a deliberate attempt by a subordinate to select tactics that will bring about change in a more powerful target and facilitate achievement of a personal or organizational objective" (p. 253).

Waldron (1999) also found consistency among studies regarding upward influence tactics. He noted that work by Kipnis et al. (1980) serves as a seminal point for such research. Kipnis and Schmidt (1982) identified six tactical categories that have "persisted in the literature," according to Waldron (p. 258). Those categories are: rationality/reason, ingratiation, exchange/bargaining, assertiveness, coalition, and upward appeal (over the head of a superior). Subsequent research (Bahniuk, Dobos, & Hill, 1991) addressed the importance of connections with "mentors, peers, coaches, family members, and others" (Waldron, 1999, p. 270). "This work takes the notion of coalition-building tactics in the upward influence literature to a new level of specificity and expands it in ways that recognize the web of connections that facilitates or impedes upward influence efforts" (Waldron, 1999, p. 270).

Waldron (1999) summarized research findings related to power differences: "As followers become more powerful through position, expertise, information access, or other power bases, their tactical options increase and their tactics become more assertive, particularly when the influence attempt appears to be 'legitimate' from the organization's point of view" (p. 275).

Furthermore, goals of the influence attempt affect type of tactic (Waldron, 1999). His meta-analysis showed that for achieving personal goals soft tactics are more likely to be used, whereas organizational goals are more often to be pursued using hard tactics. Age, experience, roles, and political and cultural factors all influence tactics in upward influence. But, Waldron noted, "empirical research on upward influence rarely acknowledges the larger political forces in organizations that shape follower behavior" (p. 279). Waldron (1999) cited Senge (1990) as suggesting "upward influence might be not just an exercise in 'getting one's way' but also a process of exploring new ideas and questioning assumptions in dialogue with leaders and peers" (p. 286).

In summary, research on influence tactics, particularly upward influence tactics, suggests dominant tactics and an influence of education, position, and age on tactic choice. Rationality was the most common influence tactic. Hard tactics or multiple tactics, either hard or soft, are effective at gaining compliance. Inspirational appeals are effective with influencing superiors. Higher education predicts more willingness to use hard tactics and a greater diversity of tactics used. In addition, increased power tends to be accompanied by increased tactical options and greater assertiveness.

PLAYING BY THE "RULES": ALPHA TACTICS

Related to the subject of influence tactics and "playing by the rules" is the notion of compliance gaining in persuasive and organizational communication literature. Compliance gaining, as summarized by Gass and Seiter (2003), is "aimed at getting others to do something or act in a particular way" (p. 236). Compliance-gaining research mimics influence research in some ways. In 1967, Marwell and Schmitt identified 16 compliance-gaining tactics including categories such as promise, threat, positive or negative expertise, moral appeal, debt, esteem, and more.

Research in compliance gaining grew to analyze situational dimensions such as dominance, resistance relational consequences, apprehension, and others that would affect compliance-gaining strategies (Sillars, 1980). Power relationships have also been analyzed. Scholars have studied reward power, coercive power, and legitimate power, all of which have relevance to the study of public relations influence in organizations.

Gass and Seiter (2003) wrote:

> Each of us has a perceptual "threshold" that helps us make decisions about what strategies are acceptable and what strategies are not. Threatening someone, for example, may exceed the threshold, whereas promising something may not. Strategies that do not cross the threshold are more likely to be used. (p. 248)

As noted earlier, these "thresholds" vary from person to person, but most people have a strong desire to play by the rules established by their organization and society. More recent compliance-gaining research has focused on identifying influence goals. Gass and Seiter noted that "goals can help people define situations ... goals give meaning to situations, including situations that involve compliance gaining" (p. 251). Goals may range from seeking assistance to eliciting support to giving advice.

Categories of Sanctioned Influence Tactics

We noted that sanctioned influence tactics can be generally categorized in three ways—hard tactics, soft tactics, and rational tactics. These categories serve as the basis from which to explore some specific sanctioned influence tactics used by public relations professionals. Literature reveals many of the tactics within these categories (e.g., Farmer et al., 1997; Falbe & Yukl, 1992; Kipnis et al., 1980; Yukl & Falbe, 1990; Yukl & Tracey, 1992).

Hard tactics are generally assertive and straightforward. Tactics in this category include appeals to higher levels of authority, threatening, intimidation, overt coalition building, use of rewards or punishments, obstructing progress, manipulative exchange, frequent checking, persistent reminders, pressure, legitimating, and the like.

Soft tactics are indirect, at times clandestine. Soft tactics would include ingratiation, acting in a pseudodemocratic manner, cajoling or complimenting the target of the persuasion, promising a future payback (exchange), personal appeals, inspirational appeals, and more covert coalition building among others.

Rational tactics are reason based. These tactics would include showing expertise and credibility, logical arguments, and factual evidence or data.

What PR Pros Told Us About Influence Tactics

We asked practitioners in the Influence Study to describe a situation in which they had successfully exerted influence and to identify the tactics they used to do so. Table 5.1 lists respondents' influence tactics and groups those tactics in a modified version of Yukl and Falbe's (1990) typology of influence tactics. Most of the practitioners used multiple tactics in the situations they described, and some mentioned twice the same type of tactic, for example, coalition building. The situations practitioners described were diverse, including a variety of crises, budget and strategic plan reviews, communication content discussions, and tactical selections for product launches or special events.

The professionals said they most often used tactics of *rational persuasion* (30.98%, or 66 of 213 total mentions). This category included the use of data and research, case studies, relevant experience and expertise, and rational arguments. The use of *coalitions* was the second-largest combination of tactics (26.76%, or 57 mentions). Specific tactics in this category included building alliances with others and developing and using personal relationships. *Pressure* was the third-largest classification of tactics cited (13.61%, or 29 mentions); this refers to the use of persistence and assertiveness in advancing claims and arguments.

TABLE 5.1
Influence Tactics—Influence Study

Tactic	M	F	Total	% of Mentions
Rational persuasion	38	28	66	30.98
Coalition	27	30	57	26.76
Pressure	16	13	29	13.61
Inspirational appeal	12	7	19	8.92
Personal appeal	8	6	14	6.57
Legitimating	9	3	12	5.63
Consultation	4	8	12	5.63
Exchange	1	2	3	1.40
Ingratiation	1	0	1	1.00
Totals	116	97	213	

Note. N = 65.

Some modest gender differences appear evident when these results are assessed proportionally (two women equals about three men in the study). More professional women cited coalitions as an influence resource than did professional men. More female respondents also cited consultation as an influence tactic than did male respondents. On the other hand, somewhat more male respondents cited legitimating as a source of influence than did female respondents.

We also asked 97 public relations professionals in the PR Success Interviews to name the types of influence tactics they used and felt were most valuable in affecting organizational decisions (see Table 5.2). These seasoned professionals listed *rational arguments* far more often than any other tactic (39.75%, or 64 of 161 total mentions). The use of *pressure, coalitions,* and past *experiences* were the next most frequently mentioned influence tactics.

Modest gender differences also are evident in this study. When the results are assessed proportionally, somewhat more male executives than female executives cited the use of careful and thorough *strategic planning* itself as an influence tactic. However, more female executives than male executives said they used *pressure* tactics, past *experiences,* and *personal appeals.*

TABLE 5.2
Influence Tactics—PR Success Study

Tactic	M	F	Total	% of Mentions
Rational arguments	40	24	64	39.75
Pressure	7	9	16	9.94
Coalitions	7	6	13	8.10
Past experience	6	7	13	8.10
Consultation	5	5	10	6.21
Strategic planning	8	2	10	6.21
Personal appeal	2	7	9	5.60
Emotional appeal	6	2	8	4.97
Legitimating	5	2	7	4.35
Others	9	2	11	6.83
Total	95	66	161	

Note. $N = 97$.

As mentioned previously, Yukl and Tracey (1992) found that rational, inspirational, and consultative appeals were most effective, whereas co-alition, pressure, and legitimating were least effective, when dealing with a superior. Our findings paint a more complex picture. When we asked practitioners what tactics they used to successfully gain influence in a specific situation, rational arguments were mentioned most often in both studies. This affirms Yukl and Tracey's findings. However, pres-sure tactics and the use of coalitions were cited by professionals in both of our studies as the next most used and effective types of influence tac-tics. Both of these categories represent tactics that Yukl and Tracey found least effective. Among public relations practitioners, however, O'Neil (2003) found that tactics of rationality, coalitions, assertiveness, and ingratiation were predictors of organizational influence. Therefore, our findings appear to be relatively consistent with previous profession-specific research.

Rationality. Literature, anecdotes, and experience tell us that ratio-nality paired with a direct request is the default influence tactic for most public relations professionals. One professional, when asked what in-fluence tactics she used in obtaining influence in a situation simply said, "Being rational and spelling it out rather simply."

Sometimes rational arguments, like all messages, need to be tailored to the public to ensure effectiveness. One practitioner said of using rationality to affect executives' decisions:

> You use reason, experience, best practices, put in a framework of a business solution, not a communication solution. One of the fatal flaws that public relations executives will do is make the mistake of coming up with a communication solution when, in fact, an executive committee is seeking a management solution.

Another professional working in media relations in Washington noted, "We framed the analysis in a way that we knew the reporters we were sending this to would obviously call the U.S. Department of Agriculture, and we needed to lay it all out for them so they could ask the specific questions of the USDA."

A practitioner working within a church denomination explained the way he develops rational arguments for his particular audience, the denomination's board of directors: "One thing that's very important for church people is to give them a theological reason for doing something. They'll just accuse you of getting your nose into politics if you can't give them a theological background. A lot of times their argument may be that we should stay out of politics."

Rationality is mentioned most often, no doubt, because public relations practitioners are accustomed to framing ideas in a way that is palatable to specific audiences. Public relations professionals also understand the necessity of reason, data, and logical persuasion in their organizations, so rationality as an influence tactic is, understandably, the default mode.

Coalition and Alliance Building. Coalition building has been identified as both a hard and soft tactic, depending on how it is employed. As a hard tactic, coalition or alliance building is straightforward, open, and assertive. As a soft tactic, it consists of more clandestine work behind the scenes to quietly gather the support of others.

An example of coalition building as a straightforward tactic was provided by one of our respondents in the Influence Study. She simply requested the opportunity to sit in on steering committee meetings, assuring meeting conveners that she didn't need to have a voice at the meetings. She said, "Because of that, I have been to two or three years of meetings of people from all parts of the district who have influence on making decisions, and became a part of that community. And that's probably as big a factor as anything as far as having an inside influence automatically."

Another example of an influence tactic is to bring together external like-minded groups that can help increase the volume of the issue being addressed. One public relations practitioner working for an environmental group suggested this technique to build influence:

> We did involve a coalition of groups who had a stake in this, so it wasn't just our organization. We had both national and regional groups involved in the event. We were able to really take some pretty wonkish people (lawyers, Capitol Hill policy folks) and convince them that we had to convey this whole issue in a way that was going to be accessible to the average person.... We basically conceived the event and then put together the organizations and the people who were going to work on it. We organized conference calls and set up the entire teleconference instead of a press conference because we had people all over the country participating.

Another public relations manager at an international environmental group also noted the coalition building that happens openly and regularly between groups he works with:

> We actively, day in and day out, look for ways to assist each other, look for ways to cooperate, look for ways to provide support that they may not be able to afford otherwise, and at other times we can't afford. Whether it's access to reports or analysis of those reports or groups in countries where there's a language barrier for most of our staff, and groups will step up and say, "Hey, we will translate." But we really cooperate on the most basic levels.

Though anecdotal evidence from conversations with 162 public relations professionals in two studies revealed primarily what we would classify as hard or open tactics when it comes to coalition or alliance building, there are some examples of more clandestine or soft tactics in this influence category. One practitioner told us how he worked to "co-opt [a superior] through kind of an end run" when the superior hired a new employee to take some PR responsibility, in what the public relations professional perceived as a "pure power grab." He created a corporate advisory committee of which the new employee was only one of eight members.

Coalition building as a soft tactic acknowledges the political nature of organizations. Those who use coalition building as a soft tactic show confidence in their ability to read the political environment and quietly orchestrate a strategic and joint response by interested parties.

Assertiveness and Persistence. Pressure tactics were the third most cited approach in the Influence Study and the second most cited in the PR Success Study. A willingness to use pressure tactics is generally linked to length of tenure in an organization and education. Personality, as previously mentioned, also plays a role in the predilection to use pressure tactics such as assertiveness and persistence.

A practitioner in an agency explained how persistence paid off for both her agency and her client. Her case was an example of how a client didn't see an opportunity and had to be grudgingly convinced. The opportunity the practitioner saw was to get press coverage of a milestone in the organization's history and to reinvigorate a brand. She explained:

> We were planning to do a big celebration.... They said, "No, they didn't think it was a big opportunity." I said, "Are you kidding me? Of course it's a big opportunity. You'll get huge amounts of press, a chance to revitalize the brand, get it in front of a new audience, etc." They are not buying it. I did countless presentations to countless managers in the hierarchy, and they all said no, they couldn't get the funding, etc. It took me a year of preaching it and preaching it. Every time I saw a brand manager I said, "You can't cut me out.... You've got to do this." Finally I got one person who said, "Fine, I'll give you $50,000 to go do a program." I told them I'd start with $50,000 and make them a deal. If I spend the $50,000 wisely and start showing results right away, will you give me more as the program goes along? [The client] relented and said okay, I had a deal.... We started with $50,000, launched a campaign, and it took off like a skyrocket.... We got 1.1 billion impressions. Sales skyrocketed through the roof.... They kept giving me money all year long. And the result? What started as a $50,000 program became a million dollar PR program.... The moral of the story was I had to convince them they had a darling of a PR program on their hands.... It was only through constant badgering.

Hard tactics such as persistence and assertiveness may be used to force a program or thwart a planned course of action, but our interviews suggest that such tactics are not only relatively common, they're accepted by many practitioners as necessary weapons in the influence arsenal. Our interviews showed that even within this classification of tactics there are differing levels of intensity—from dismissing a superior's directive to persisting until a superior comes around to your point of view. In short, tactics—as logic would suggest—shift based on situation, urgency, personalities involved, and other variables.

Our List of Sanctioned Influence Tactics

Having reviewed literature that identifies a number of sanctioned influence tactics, we developed our own list based on conversations with 162 practitioners. We have defined sanctioned tactics as those that are generally acceptable within organizations, or Alpha approaches. Applying a metric to this definition leads to a list of eight influence tactics that appear to be commonly used by public relations practitioners. Clearly, professionals use many influence tactics, often in combination. Our research suggests, however, that rational arguments are used most often, followed by coalition building and pressure (see Table 5.3). These three categories account for nearly two thirds of all tactics mentioned by the professionals we interviewed (65.49%, or 245 of 374 total mentions).

OBSERVATIONS ABOUT ALPHA APPROACHES IN PUBLIC RELATIONS

Public relations professionals provided insights about their most common routes or Alpha approaches to gain influence in their organizations, leading us to make the following propositions:

Proposition 12: Rationality and coalitions are the first lines of influence for public relations professionals.

Practitioners most commonly employ rational arguments, whether or not the practitioners are senior. Both samples—the senior sample of the Success Interviews and the mixed sample of the Influence Interviews—ranked rationality above all other influence resources. Rational-

TABLE 5.3
Sanctioned Tactics—Combined Studies

Category	# of Mentions	% of Mentions
Rational arguments	130	34.75
Coalitions	70	18.71
Pressure	45	12.03
Inspirational appeal	27	7.21
Personal appeal	23	6.14
Consultation	22	5.88
Legitimating	19	5.08
Experience	13	3.48
Others	25	6.69
Totals	374	

ity accounted for close to one third of all mentions of influence tactics in both studies.

Coalition building was the second most mentioned among influence tactics in the combined studies, but made up more than one quarter of the influence mentions in the Influence Interviews and about one tenth of the mentions in the Success Interviews. This finding suggests that the most senior practitioners may not need to resort to tactics beyond rationality. They have ascended to their positions and earned the respect of decision makers.

> **Proposition 13: Practitioners use pressure tactics less often than rationality or coalitions and often reserve pressure for crucial ethical and legal issues confronting their organization.**

Beyond making rational arguments and building coalitions of the like-minded or those with common interests, practitioners noted a more assertive Alpha approach of applying pressure. Pressure was the second most mentioned influence tactic among the senior practitioners in the Success Interviews, and the third most mentioned tactic among those in the Influence Interviews. Although pressure was the second most mentioned tactic among Success Interview respondents, it ranked well behind rational arguments. About 10% of mentions in the Success Interviews referred to pressure, which includes assertiveness and persistence, as an influence-gaining behavior. In the Influence Interviews, nearly 14% of mentions referred to pressure, but that was a relatively distant third to coalition building at about 27%. In both cases, pressure is an acknowledged and employed means to influence, but it remains a far less common approach than making rational arguments.

Despite the fact that the number of mentions regarding pressure as an acceptable influence tactic were substantially fewer than other tactic categories, the finding is encouraging. It suggests an empowered and self-confident practitioner who, when necessary, might be willing to move from Alpha to Omega approaches in order to move an organization away from poor decisions or behavior. As results in the Dissent Survey suggest (chap. 8), pressure tactics may come into play especially in such decision-making moments.

BEYOND ALPHA APPROACHES

Reliance on common tactics is comfortable but may blind practitioners to other sources of influence that hold positive potential for career-minded professionals and ethical practice. Focusing so squarely on rational arguments as a means of influence, for example, may ignore the potential offered by consultation, inspirational appeals, or legitimating.

Because of the omnipresence of organizational politics, the variety of influence tactics available, and public relations' unique role as a profession that should be focused on both internal and external needs, practitioners need to embrace every tactic at their disposal to maximize efficacy and increase their influence in organizational decision making.

With respect to the ongoing and pervasive play of influence in organizations, Kipnis et al. (1980) wrote: "We would suggest that everyone is influencing everyone else in organizations, regardless of job titles. People seek benefits, information, satisfactory job performance, the chance to do better than others, to be left alone, cooperation, and many other outcomes too numerous to mention" (p. 451). We support this statement and believe public relations professionals should be given every strategic advantage to stand eye to eye with others in the dominant coalition, when it comes to having influence in organizational decision making.

In addition to developing and using a greater range of sanctioned influence tactics, it is important for professionals to consider other, more controversial approaches. Focusing solely on sanctioned tactics as a subject of research and a means of influence dismisses a potentially fertile field in both practice and scholarship. Admittedly, using unsanctioned tactics without due consideration of personal or institutional consequences would be foolhardy. But, we suggest that there are times when best practice and/or ethical practice of public relations invites, if not demands, the use of unsanctioned tactics to achieve an optimal result. We explore these more controversial approaches in chapter 7.

Before doing so, however, we present a comprehensive case study that demonstrates how practitioners in one company used multiple influence strategies and tactics to affect decision making regarding a major initiative in employee communication.

CHAPTER 6

The Communication Change Project at Whirlpool: Converting Power Into Performance

> *Continuous change is inevitable in a more competitive and global market. I believe that a well-thought-out communication plan, incorporating appropriate tools, is crucial to moving change quickly through an organization. New ways of thinking about communication can positively influence a company's success in today's and future business environments.*
>
> *—Kremer (1996, p. 10)*

We have argued that public relations professionals draw from five types of influence resources when they engage in power relations. They convert these resources into influence attempts in political arenas when they use data, rational persuasion, coalitions, consultation, pressure, personal appeals, and other approaches. Our research suggests that practitioners rely on individual and relational power sources and most often use rational persuasion and coalition approaches, though they use many tactics. In this chapter, we take a closer look at how these influence resources and tactics work together in practice.

We employ a traditional case study approach to develop and present a comprehensive review of a public relations project at Whirlpool Corporation. The case portrays how a team of professionals used a range of influence resources and tactics to develop, sell, and carry out a major internal communication change program during 1992–1995. Following a brief introduction to the company, the planning and implementation stages of the program are described, along with some of the issues and difficulties the public relations team experienced. Then the influence tactics used by the team are assessed, and some lessons and longer-term implications of power relations in practice are discussed.

WHIRLPOOL CORPORATION

Whirlpool was founded by the Upton brothers in 1911 in St. Joseph, Michigan, a small community on the southeastern shores of Lake Michigan. The company's first product was an electric wringer washing machine that Sears Roebuck & Company began to purchase and sell in 1916. Over the years the company added clothes dryers, refrigerators, freezers, ranges, dishwashers, and microwave ovens to its product line. Until the mid-1980s, Whirlpool manufactured and marketed its products primarily in the United States and Canada. The company was generally profitable in a competitive and cyclical industry characterized by narrow profit margins and an obsession with cost controls.

Under the leadership of Chairman and CEO David Whitwam, the company began an ambitious globalization program in the late 1980s. Whirlpool purchased a majority interest in the major-appliance division of N. V. Philips in Europe in 1989. Over the next few years the company purchased operations in Mexico and Latin America, and established operations or entered joint ventures in India, China, and several central and eastern European countries. By the end of the 1990s, Whirlpool's workforce had doubled to 68,000 employees, its annual revenues increased from $4 billion to $12 billion, and its Whirlpool-branded appliances became the best-selling brand in the global market. Today, the company manufactures appliances in 13 countries, maintains 50 manufacturing and technical research centers, and markets products in more than 170 countries.

Globalization produced many changes in the company, but none more dramatic than those in its culture. From the beginning, Whirlpool's culture had reflected the values and beliefs of its founders, that is, hard work, shared celebrations, job opportunities and promotion from within, the independent and autonomous character of each of its factories, and a top-down controlling orientation to getting things done. However, thousands of new employees in Europe, Latin America, and Asia brought their own ideas, values, approaches, and practices to the company in the early 1990s.

In addition, Whitwam hired a number of senior executives from outside the company, rather than promoting them from within. These executives also brought their own ideas and approaches, which frequently clashed with those of longtime Whirlpool managers and directors. At the same time, the company began to close or sell off some of its existing factories and operations in North America even as it was buying new businesses elsewhere in the world. In the first half of the 1990s, then, Whirlpool was growing rapidly and its culture was changing and churning, a situation not uncommon to hundreds of companies at the time.

THE EMPLOYEE COMMUNICATION INITIATIVE

Whitwam believed that effective employee communication was a priority for the company as it embarked on globalization, and several public relations executives were hired to address employee communication needs along with other responsibilities. The CEO's directive to the new PR leadership team was to build an internal-communication capability that would help empower the workforce, create a one-company culture, and leverage best practices and crucial information and communication across the global organization as rapidly and cost effectively as possible.

In 1991 the PR team began to meet informally with three consultants—selected because of their relevant experience and critical-thinking skills—to do some deep analysis of the internal-communication function. These free-flowing sessions were important in conceptualizing what employee communication might be and needed to be in light of the realities of globalization. To Whirlpool executives, these realities were that the company was changing rapidly and experiencing cultural difficulties. It nevertheless expected more of its employees. It had access to powerful technologies designed to improve the speed of responsiveness to situations that were themselves changing rapidly. Everywhere possible, the same work had to be done faster, better, and with fewer resources. In the minds of company executives, doing more with less and processing change ever faster were the twin requirements of the global competitive race.

In this context, what was the responsibility of the employee communication function? Who was it supposed to serve? What would it take to establish a world-class employee communication program that could truly help create an empowered workforce and one-company culture? In the end, these questions were not difficult to answer. The responsibility of the internal-communication function was to design, propose, implement, maintain, and improve the infrastructure—the communication pipelines—and to help keep the multidirectional pipelines filled with meaningful and credible information and communication that people needed to fulfill their new responsibilities.

The question of who the function served was almost academic. If the company was truly relying on its people to do more and to make more decisions on the job, then the communication function had to serve everyone in the organization, from the factory floor to the CEO's office. And one of the primary means for serving those needs globally was a technology-intensive process that "understood" the relationship between communication and business success, including the role played by employee morale in getting the work done and creating a one-company culture.

Stimulating this culture seemed possible only if internal communication was driven by a human responsibility to employees as well as a functional responsibility to Whirlpool's executive committee. In other words, the company could no longer afford distrust, poor morale, or anything that might cause employees to disbelieve important information, ignore it, resist it, or delay taking action on it. Viewed in terms of the pipeline metaphor, such powerful employee issues—and they were significant at Whirlpool—took on the appearance of a kind of sludge that stopped up the works, imperiled productivity, inhibited the exchange of ideas in the workplace, and fragmented the culture.

Seven Critical Employee Communication Issues

Throughout its analysis, the PR team and consultants were as concerned with "what's right and wrong today" as with "what's possible tomorrow." In early 1992, they initiated a number of research projects to ascertain and document the existing problems as well as the challenges presented by the new concepts that fueled a one-company culture. These projects included:

- A qualitative audit of 26 employee newsletters and magazines.
- Depth interviews with 32 Whirlpool communicators and communication suppliers.
- Depth interviews with the 28 highest ranking company executives.
- Focus groups with production employees and supervisors in seven factories.

- Analysis of employee opinion surveys (EOSs) conducted in 1990 and 1991 in North American operations.
- Benchmarking of eight companies regarding best practices in employee communications, for example, Malcolm Baldrige Quality Award winners Xerox, Milliken, Federal Express, and AT&T.

Analysis of the findings made it clear to the PR team that the power of employee communication was largely untapped at Whirlpool. In addition, the PR team identified seven critical issues, or barriers to success, in employee communication at the company (Berger, 1994, 1996a; "Corporate Profile," 1994; Moore, 1994):

1. **Outdated "Mental Models" of Communication**. Peter Senge (1990) argued that each of us has deeply held mental models, or internal images, that influence how we see and understand the world and how we act. Mental models tend to limit us to thinking in familiar and routine ways, which produce blind spots in our thinking, just like the blind spots in seeing through our human eye. As a result, if our mental model for something has too many blind spots, or is outdated or wrong, the actions and decisions we subsequently take based on this mental model are likely to be inadequate.

The Whirlpool research demonstrated that the mental model for internal communication held by most company executives *and* professional communicators was far more consistent with a 1950s business model than a globalization model. In the 1950s model, employee communication was seen more as: (a) a series of discrete activities and events rather than as a long-term strategic process, (b) separate from "real" business communications and not as a part of everyone's job, (c) the top-down transmission of messages and directives rather than a multidirectional flow of information, knowledge, and dialogue about matters of importance to the company, and (d) a low-technology function that relied heavily on print communications.

2. **A Serious Trust Issue**. EOSs indicated that Whirlpool employees did not have great trust in their management and frequently did not believe what they were told. On many questions, fewer than 30% of respondents could give any kind of affirmative opinion about management's credibility, respect for employees, or business judgment. Additional surveys of middle and senior managers confirmed that distrust was an issue at all levels. And the employee communication function also fared poorly in the surveys:

Three quarters of respondents said the corporate newsletter was neither valuable nor believable.

The causes of distrust were not hard to identify. The company was embarked on an ambitious change process, and periods of rapid change often give rise to fear and uncertainty. The changes included job cuts and other dislocations at Whirlpool, all of which produced human costs and emotions. The surveys also indicated that executives were almost invisible in the operations and that vital information about change wasn't being communicated. Employees perceived these two "absences" as sinister.

3. Companyspeak. This is the language of corporate euphemisms. It is often passive, faceless, and designed to prevent controversy rather than promote understanding. Companyspeak is usually seen by employees to be disguised language that masks a harsher underlying reality, and it chokes candor and breeds distrust, for example, the infamous "rightsizing," or "volume-related adjustments in production personnel." Based on the audit of publications and the interviews, the PR team concluded that companyspeak was widespread at Whirlpool, manifesting itself in false positives, 10-dollar terms for 10-cent meanings, and a pervasive underlying theme in communications of management's infallibility.

4. Fuzzy Communication Accountabilities. Benchmarking confirmed the importance of clear accountabilities and objectives for communications. At Whirlpool, however, managers had no specific accountabilities for communications. Executives said that professional communicators were accountable—sort of. They handled the writing and production but not most of the content and language. And no one seemed responsible for all of the day-to-day job interaction and communication that is at the heart of a healthy communication system. Underneath this surface problem lay another: Managers had no real access to, or requirement for communication training or development. Without knowledge of what was expected of them, and why, no approach to the accountabilities issue could be effective.

5. Communicator Skills and Training Needs. In the interviews, the professional communicators in operations across the company described themselves largely as communication technicians—newsletter writers, publishing coordinators, and expediters of emergency projects. They believed in this mental model as strongly as their managers did, and with good reasons. Most had little exposure to process thinking, strategic planning, or communication training programs of any kind. Most had been hired into entry-level positions by people other than communication professionals, and their performance expectations were related more to "budget and deadline" than to achieving meaningful long-term goals. The training requirement to prepare this team to help create a one-company culture was significant.

6. Quality and Consistency of Communication. Overall, employee communication in Whirlpool operations was found to be inconsistent, lacking discipline, and absent quality controls or measurement requirements. In part this reflected deficiencies in planning skills, lack of a common process language, and outdated mental models that didn't subject communication to any quality standards outside of local management dictates. A related problem was that factory communications professionals reported directly to HR directors and only on a dotted line to the public relations function. This organizational issue, combined with the lack of discipline, process management skills, and linkages to business goals, represented significant barriers to justifying and building a strong global communication infrastructure.

7. An Antiquated Communication Toolbox. Benchmarking confirmed the importance of technologies in speeding communication and reducing cycle times for understanding and change. Research at Whirlpool found that necessary communication pipelines at the company were deficient, missing, or obsolete. Newsletters were everywhere, but they varied in quality and were choked with companyspeak. An electronic-mail system did not reach all employees and could not distribute documents. The company had once investigated satellite television, but in the absence of a strategy to employ it for business benefit, the program had never been funded. Some factories in the United States had no capability to broadcast emergency information to all employees at the site. The company's communication toolbox needed a dramatic upgrade.

The PR team concluded that these critical issues were pervasive and embedded in longtime company communication practices as well as in the mental models for communication in the minds of executives and communication professionals alike. On the one hand, then, employee communication was doing exactly what management and communicators wanted it to: It was transmitting executive messages and information to employees with great frequency and urgency. On the other hand, a majority of employees weren't listening to the messages and didn't believe them when they did hear them. The PR team decided that incremental changes would not resolve these issues. Rather, massive, even revolutionary change was needed to update existing mental models and prevailing practices, and it would require a great deal of time and resources.

Political Intelligence and Influence Strategies

Throughout the summer and fall of 1992 the core PR team translated the research data and conceptual material into a proposal that could be presented to Whirlpool's executive committee, the primary strategic decision-making group in the company. In addition, the team regularly briefed the CEO on the project's status and shared its findings and ideas with other communications professionals in the company to gain their insights, contributions, and support. Some professionals were asked to provide additional information or ideas, or to further develop proposals and budgets. Others offered political counsel regarding executive committee members and other political players in the company who were likely to oppose the strategic proposal.

In addition to preparing the strategic proposal, the PR team considered two related issues. First, team members felt it was important to determine exactly what could be implemented successfully in the first year. They didn't want to overpropose and fail to meet their goals in what they imagined would be a critical period of evaluation by others. Thus, they opted for a two-stage approach: a short-term plan that would provide a necessary and manageable foundation for change, followed by a much larger plan and proposal for substantial investments in the communication infrastructure over a period of several years.

Second, the team conducted a political assessment of the company to increase its political intelligence and identify influence strategies to guide its short- and longer-term work. The political assessment drew heavily from interviews with 28 company executives and reviews of organizational charts, committee structures and practices, formal job descriptions, and historic resource allocations. The team also spoke with others in the function and organization to identify nonexecutive leaders and influencers. In this way, the PR team located key influencers and their perceptions of public relations, decision-making practices and processes in the company, and the needs and concerns of potential supporters and opponents. Following the assessment, the PR team selected five primary influence strategies:

1. Build alliances across the company to develop a critical mass of support for their ambitious and somewhat controversial proposals. They knew that some proposals would generate resistance because of

the nature of the concepts or the substantial budget requests accompanying them. The more support the PR team could build for its plans across functions, operations, and geographic boundaries, the greater was its chance for success.

2. Use pilot projects whenever possible to facilitate effective project management and produce visible or measurable results that, in turn, could be used as data to market subsequent proposals.

3. Overwhelm decision makers with data. Whirlpool was led by engineers, accountants, and marketing executives who relied heavily on numbers. The very nature of the company's business involved many numerical indicators, for example, product specifications, inventory turns, regulatory requirements for energy efficiency and safety standards, productivity targets, numbers of product defects and hours involved in product rework, volume of customer complaints, and so forth. The PR team's research suggested that the extensive use of data by communication professionals would be unprecedented and would likely capture and focus the attention of executives.

4. Frame strategic proposals and plans in language that would be most meaningful to executive decision makers and that was legitimated by the company's own business objectives, programs, and espoused values.

5. Stay the course. The team believed its proposals would encounter resistance and was not convinced that it could win the needed resources by relying exclusively on alliances, data, successful pilot projects, or framing approaches. Though these were crucial strategies, team members felt that the tipping point in their success might well be the extent to which they were committed to seeing the project through and their determination to remain strong advocates for communication change in the presence of other powerful political influencers. If the company was truly committed to creating an empowering employee communication program globally, then the PR team had to be prepared and committed to taking some risks and fighting at every turn to try to make this happen. In the end, they paired a highly professional approach with unflinching advocacy.

The Strategic Plan (Part I) and Presentation to the Executive Committee

In late 1992, the PR team presented its proposal to the executive committee and requested $1 million in new funding, roughly a 50% increase in the budget for employee communications. During the 2-hour session, the PR team drew heavily from its research data and seven critical issues to make the case for changing the company's antiquated communication mental model to a new one that was consistent with the corporation's new global objectives. They argued that employee communication was the single largest driver of quality and productivity improvements and competitive advantage in the company—but it was largely untapped and, in its current state, incapable of delivering on its promise.

The new model called for multidirectional and empowering communication, clear accountabilities, a process approach to communication planning and measurement, integration of communication into the business infrastructure, extensive training, and substantial investments in new technologies. Some specific components of the 2-year strategic plan included the following:

- Creation and implementation of a seven-step communication planning model worldwide, consistent with requirements of the company's quality program.
- Ten days of training for global employee communications professionals on the topics of mental models, strategic planning, use of feedback and measurement, and project management skills, among others.
- Elimination of two existing corporate employee publications and development of a new daily online employee newsletter and an innovative bimonthly management journal.
- Implementation of regularly scheduled employee meetings with divisional and corporate executives in all locations.
- Integration of employee communication issues and objectives into strategic planning in the businesses, and the requirement for all operations to develop strategic communication plans.
- Changing reporting relationships for the professional communicators from plant directors to the PR team.
- Funding to support the formation and work of three cross-functional and cross-cultural teams to carry out research and study regarding: (a) new communication and information technologies, (b) communication accountabilities, and (c) communication training requirements for company managers and supervisors (for inclusion in the company's developing management education curriculum).

The executive committee approved the $1 million budget request and all of the components except for the change in reporting relationships.

This request was tabled until divisional executives could be consulted. The PR team was directed to communicate its program to others in the company, provide regular progress updates, and demonstrate results before requesting additional funds. The PR team indicated it would return in 12 months to discuss the findings of the three research teams and outline proposals for communication technologies, accountabilities, and training requirements.

IMPLEMENTATION, MORE RESEARCH, AND A $20 MILLION PROPOSAL

The PR team took steps toward implementing every part of the plan in 1993, but first addressed the two items that would prove most visible and immediate in their impact: the bimonthly *Whirlpool Management Journal* (*WMJ*) and communicator training. The purpose of *WMJ* was to provide managers with a publication that was substantive, devoid of puffery, and written well rather than safely ("Corporate Profile," 1994; Moore, 1994). As CEO David Whitwam (1993) noted in his introductory letter to the new magazine:

> The purpose of *WMJ* is to help create an information-rich environment in which Whirlpool managers are free to question, think, debate, learn, and speak openly about matters of importance to our company.... Indeed, that will be the primary focus of our formal internal communication efforts in the future: to send a clear message that we want all of our people to use their minds to the best of their ability, and to express their ideas and opinions, even if this results in the surfacing of divergent views. (p. 2)

The format of *WMJ* included two principal sections: a "Point of View" section featuring a formal debate and supporting information about a question of relevance to the company, for example, employee morale, quality, productivity, sexual harassment, and globalization; and a series of shorter columns and features intended to provoke reader thinking and learning. The latter section included a regular column on "Companyspeak" usually written by experts on the topic, for example, Calvin Trilling and Edwin Newman, and intended to poke fun at such language. The debates featured company managers and executives and periodically outside experts.

The first communicator-training session included modules on mental models, the communication process model, and the new communication initiatives. The 2-day program was held with 15 U.S. communicators in Dayton, Ohio, and it concluded with a charge for the professionals to develop plans for changing the mental model of communication in their factories. Similar training was conducted with eight European communicators in Comerio, Italy, site of the European headquarters. Subsequent training sessions in Europe and the United States required the communicators to apply the communication process model to a real-life exercise. This exercise, which came to be called "The Monster," was a rigorous 36-hour experience designed to develop practice in using the quality-based planning model and to capture the full attention of the communicators, some of whom were slow to embrace the new initiatives. These sessions concluded with a call to redevelop their mental model plans for their own operations.

Following experiences with "The Monster," the communicators held a series of informal meetings among themselves where many of them decided that they had to overcome their resistance to the process model and other new initiatives, and they set to work on their mental model plans with new energy. All of the plans were presented at the first ever Global Communicator Conference held in July in Williamsburg, Virginia. That meeting included training regarding the use of communication feedback and measurement, as well as a section designed to help the communicators fight through management's standard excuses for not funding proposed communication plans.

The communication process model (Berger, 1996b) with which the communicators struggled was developed in 1992 in conformance with the company's existing quality program—the Whirlpool Excellence System—and in consultation with outside experts and the company's quality control managers. It was intended to discipline communication planning and provide a common language of process that could help alleviate language barriers in the global company. A primary reason the communicators resisted using the model was that they believed it required more work, and it did. The model mandated the definition of goals and measures that were tied closely to business goals and measures, and it required some research. No one disagreed that the planning that came out of the process was superior to previous planning approaches.

Progress was achieved in other areas as well. The PR team and employee communications professionals presented the new initiatives to units, functions, committees, and other decision-making bodies throughout the company. The online newsletter was quickly embraced and embedded as an expected fact of daily life at the company. A handful of top executives made time for regularly scheduled meetings with large groups of employees to discuss current issues and respond to employee concerns.

The Accountabilities task force, a cross-functional team of eight employees, developed a conceptual model of communication accountabilities based heavily on benchmarking research at leading companies. The model defined categories and constituencies for internal communication, as well as performance requirements. The team also proposed that employee communication responsibilities be incorporated into job descriptions and performance requirements for all supervisors and managers.

The Technology task force, which included 18 employees from diverse functions and countries, worked throughout the year to evaluate 13 promising technologies (Kremer, 1996). The team conducted benchmarking activities at 17 leading companies in six countries, including Apple Computer, British Coal, DuPont, Federal Express, Oticon, Union Pacific Railroad, and Vauxhall. As a basis for its comprehensive technology plan, the team identified specific communication problems and opportunities for improvement and then examined the 13 available technologies and their potential applications in solving problems or capitalizing on the opportunities.

Development of communication education courses for inclusion in Whirlpool's new management education program was turned over to human resource and organizational development specialists. These personnel had responsibility for the management education program and a new training center in Michigan. The PR team worked closely with HR management to assess specific communication needs and relevant content that would assist company supervisors and managers in becoming more proficient and effective communicators in their day-to-day interactions with employees.

Late in 1993, then, the three task forces had completed their research and developed specific proposals. Six days of training had been delivered to company communicators, and the communication process model was being used extensively if not always wholeheartedly in many company locations. Executives had become more visible and accessible to employees through increased town-hall meetings and briefing sessions. Information about the new communication approaches had been provided to many in the company. The question of changing communicator reporting relationships was unresolved: Factory and divisional managers were strongly opposed to the idea. The online newsletter had quickly become an important communication channel. And *WMJ*, which continued to draw favorable and unfavorable reactions among executives, received a 91% credibility rating in a year-end reader survey, the highest credibility rating ever earned by a corporate publication.

These developments were the backdrop at year's end for a second strategic presentation to Whirlpool's executive committee, where the PR team provided a detailed progress report and requested $20 million over 3 years to support new or expanded initiatives. These included additional communicator training funds, implementation of communication accountabilities company wide, and communication training for hundreds of line managers and supervisors, among others. However, the bulk of the budget request was for capital, operating, and staffing funds to support the expansion or acquisition and implementation of six information and communication technologies across the company—video bulletin board, business television, electronic mail, video conferencing, audio conferencing, and voice mail.

Drawing heavily from the technology team's detailed 250-page report (Whirlpool Corporation, 1993), the PR team argued that these technologies could help empower employees by facilitating the work of virtual and cross-cultural project teams. They also could provide real-time information, ensure more consistent communication, and dramatically enhance the reach and speed of communication throughout the global company. In effect, the technologies could provide a communication infrastructure—a set of electronic pipelines—that had the potential to dramatically reduce the cycle time for change.

Every new initiative the company introduced globally required time for employees to become aware of it, process it, understand it, accept it, and act on it. Productivity typically slipped during such change processes, so shortening the cycle time for change could yield productivity benefits faster. And given the many new initiatives and directions in the company's ambitious strategic plan, the potential benefits of this infrastructure were enormous.

Following several hours of questions and discussion, the executive committee approved the overall proposal and allocated $5.4 million for 1994 to support additional planning and the implementation of a series of pilot projects in operations worldwide. These projects would be used to test the six technologies in different locations and resolve any difficulties with them prior to full-scale implementation. Additional funding would be available in 1995–1996 to support continued rollout of the technologies, assuming that established metrics developed by the PR and project teams were satisfied through the pilot projects.

1994–1995: CONTINUING IMPLEMENTATION
AND SOME CRACKS IN THE WALL

The 2nd year of implementation is often the most difficult because the glamour of the new and different has worn off, and the challenge is to keep pushing the same ideas and practices into different parts and levels of the organization. This was very much the case with the 2nd full year of implementing the Whirlpool internal communication initiative in 1994.

WMJ and other new publications had to be "normalized," which included transferring most of the work for the publications in house from outside writers and contractors. Extensive work on a detailed technology implementation plan proceeded, and pilot projects for the six technologies were planned and carried out in a number of locations. Video bulletin board (VBB), for example, which delivers text and graphics via television monitors, was tested in two factories and in corporate headquarters. After initial resistance (managers thought the monitors were too expensive, and employees believed they were being spied on), VBB became a trusted channel for "breaking" company and world news and for local job and division information, employee recognition and accomplishments, and social information.

Training for the global communicators continued, focusing on project management and strategic planning skills required to help them implement and subsequently use the new technologies in their offices and factories. The communication accountabilities model was introduced and piloted successfully in five operations in the United States and Europe. Video-conferencing capabilities were expanded in Asia, Latin America, and Europe, and usage by global project teams rose sharply. The executive committee began to use this technology on a regular basis. Development work continued on communication training modules for supervisors and managers. The 2-day training program was completed in early 1995 and piloted later that year with 16 supervisors. The program consisted of four modules: organizational change and mental models, managerial communication accountabilities, listening and face-to-face communication skills, and QuickCom, a simple communication-planning approach (Whirlpool Corporation, 1995).

The Realities of Organizational Politics

For the PR team, project management skills and time were at a premium. The team had added only one professional to its staff since 1992, and the combination of ongoing work to support many other PR activities, along with project management requirements for the new initiatives, stretched the team nearly to the breaking point. In addition, virtually every pilot project was met with some resistance from local management, which historically had resisted most corporate communication initiatives. Though all of the pilot projects were eventually implemented, each required far more time and attention than planned. In this regard, members of the various communication task forces played important facilitation and advocacy roles, and the PR team's steadfast persistence proved crucial.

Political struggles multiplied in other areas of the company in 1994–1995, as well. The PR team had established itself as a legitimate player in company political arenas by virtue of winning one of the most coveted of corporate prizes: scarce financial resources. As a result, the PR team became a target for other political influencers, especially in corporate headquarters, who resented the resources flowing into communication initiatives and the favorable political attention the team had received. On the one hand, these high-level political influencers always openly expressed their support for enhanced global employee communications. On the other hand, they carried out a mostly discrete series of sniper attacks on PR team members and various aspects of the initiatives to try to derail them and redirect funding.

Sniping, a longtime practice in organizational politics, seeks to discredit other individuals or groups, or to plant doubts about their legitimacy. Sniping attacks at Whirlpool occurred in several ways. At opportune moments with the CEO or president, for example, the snipers would reveal that they had heard about some problems with one of the new technologies in such-and-such a plant—they didn't have any of the details—that was disrupting production and stirring up employee concerns. Or, the snipers might let it drop during an executive luncheon that they'd just learned that another company using VBB had abandoned the technology because it was already outdated. They hoped that Whirlpool wouldn't make the mistake of spending good money on bad or antiquated technology.

Some snipers also used cultural appeals, suggesting, for example, that the new initiatives, though important, had the unfortunate side effect of eliminating some other valuable, longtime communication activities and programs at the company, which was likely to dampen employee morale. Or, they pointed out that the company had embraced a number of changes historically, but it had always done so cautiously and deliberately. Although the new communication initiatives were important, weren't they being carried out too fast? Wasn't it still more important at Whirlpool to do things the right way rather than the fast way? And on and on and on.

Two incidents with *WMJ* during the year produced additional difficulties. In one instance, a lengthy story about a day in the life of a handful of production workers at a large manufacturing plant created a furor. In one passage in the story, the male and female employees in the group joked openly over lunch about "who was sleeping with whom." When the article appeared in *WMJ*, the production employees who participated in the story said it was the best portrayal of factory work they had seen, and they wanted extra copies of the journal. Plant directors, on the other hand, were furious. They felt the story portrayed their operations in very unflattering terms by including "lewd gossip and innuendo," and they gathered up copies of *WMJ* and burned them in a barrel behind the factory. This fueled more sniper attacks and led some executives to openly criticize the PR team and *WMJ*. The event also sent employees scrambling everywhere else in the organization to locate copies of the "offending" journal.

Another incident had a chilling effect on the participation of some directors and vice presidents in *WMJ* stories and debates. In one issue of the journal, a manufacturing vice president challenged the company's quality program and identified several shortcomings with it. That was his role in the debate. The VP's boss, however, was upset because he had publicly criticized the company's quality plan, and he dressed down the VP to such an extent that others in the area became aware of what was happening. Though the CEO subsequently supported the VP and his right to express concerns about quality or any other program, for that matter, news of the incident spread rapidly through the grapevine. For longtime Whirlpool directors and VPs, the incident only confirmed their suspicions that the company's culture hadn't really changed very much at all: It was still dangerous to one's career to challenge or speak out against the party line.

Challenges From Communicators

Perhaps the greatest difficulty with implementation of the new initiatives, however, was the communicator team itself. Though the majority of communicators actively supported the initiatives and eventually embedded them in their operations, roughly a third of the professionals continued to actively or passively resist the changes. They also were reluctant to take a bolder advocacy stance in their own operations, even though they believed the changes were necessary. This reluctance was linked to powerful local manufacturing cultures and to professional survival and self-interests, as one communicator candidly described his situation:

> Look, I think what you're trying to do is absolutely necessary, but the truth is, it only makes problems for me, and I don't want them. It took me a lot of years to get to this position. I make a decent salary, and I get along. People like me, and we socialize and get on in the community. I put out the newsletter, and I fight the fires. I'm pretty good at those things, and I get some recognition for my work. But trying to do all these changes in communication? Hell, my bosses don't want them. They just don't trust corporate, and they don't think they need the changes, and they don't want them. You see? So whenever I push for this new plan, or that new way of doing something, or some new technology, they let me have it, give me both barrels. Look, don't misunderstand, but my future isn't on your side. It's on their side.

The notion of going along, to get along, to get your share is nothing new and is widespread in some organizations (Jackall, 1988). At best, this communicator mental model for how things worked delayed project implementation at some Whirlpool locations; at worst, it prevented implementation in several locations and undermined the credibility of the new initiatives and the legitimacy of the profession. It also underscored the importance of a capable and committed professional team in effecting change of any kind.

THE SELECTION AND USE OF INFLUENCE TACTICS

In 1992, the PR team had identified a handful of strategies to guide its work, and throughout development and implementation of the communication initiatives the team used a variety of influence tactics to support these strategies. Eight influence tactics were used most often: data and rational arguments, coalitions and alliances, consultation with others, legitimacy linkages and appeals, framing approaches, exchanges with others, emotional and inspirational appeals, and persistence. Each of these tactics is briefly described in this section, and examples of their use are provided.

Data and Rational Arguments. The PR team relied heavily on data to "sell" its new initiatives for three reasons. First, previous PR teams at the company had not done so, and this positively differentiated the change efforts from past practices. Second, senior executives relied heavily on data in making decisions, or at least they did so in rejecting proposals that weren't data based. And third, the PR team believed that using significant amounts of data would strengthen their political profile. Getting over a longtime data hurdle for the function was seen as crucial.

The six research projects carried out by the team (as well as a number of subsequent research projects) provided a comprehensive data set unlike anything seen regarding employee communication at Whirlpool. In addition, the team ensured that all presentations incorporated data and case information, and each step in the initiative was subjected to measurement and evaluation, which in turn was reported to the senior executives. In effect, the data sets were the foundation "footings" for constructing the business case for the investments, and the central argument in the business case was that these initiatives would reduce the cycle time for processing and implementing change. This was an attractive and intuitive argument for the executives.

But even here the PR team believed more data were needed. The team was comfortable in making the argument and had gathered a number of examples to share, but was it possible to quantify the estimated savings in cycle time to Whirlpool? They turned to an economist at a nearby university, a friend of one of the team members. The economist collected information from the team and constructed a model that could be used to roughly estimate the productivity benefits for a 3-month and 6-month reduction in cycle times to process various change initiatives.

In this way, the PR team was able to estimate the productivity benefits of reducing the cycle time for the quality change process by 6 months—a cool $125 million. The team also provided the formula and contact information for the economist, and this one piece of data, legitimated to some extent by a credentialed economist, provided an important edge in selling the new initiatives. In Whirlpool's culture then, and given the accounting and manufacturing background of many of its executives, the use of data and rational arguments were necessary but not sufficient influence tactics to win resources and favorable decisions.

Coalitions and Alliances. The total number of professional communicators in the global company in 1992 was fewer than 50, most of whom held low-level management positions and were seen as communication technicians. To get things done and begin to build a critical mass of influence, the PR team needed to reach out to others across the organization to build alliances, working relationships, coalitions, project teams, consultation bodies, and so forth. The methodical development and cultivation of such relationships was a priority in the 1st year of the project.

Initially, the PR team reached out to communicators and various HR personnel to gather data and carry out the research projects. Subsequently, advisers from HR, legal, manufacturing, marketing, and other functions were recruited to review proposals and provide ideas and input. Cross-functional and cross-cultural project teams were established for virtually every aspect of the plan, including technology, accountability, training, and implementation teams. Alliances were created with a handful of respected directors and vice presidents in the company who provided candid input and feedback on *WMJ* and other publications. Small groups of staff and line managers from other functions were invited to participate in communicator-training sessions and conferences, and often they did. In these and other ways, the number of informed and supportive managers in the company increased 10-fold in 2 years and provided an important critical mass of support, especially during the implementation phase.

Consultation With Others. Consultation is one way of winning tacit support or agreement from other political influencers and is related to formation of alliances and coalitions. In this approach, the PR professionals actively sought out influential employees at diverse levels in the organization and consulted with them to obtain their ideas and feedback regarding communication plans or actions. They then used this feedback to adjust plans or approaches. Consultation sessions also helped to educate others about the new initiatives and to identify points of opposition and the specific communication needs of other influencers.

Consultation was used frequently and widely in 1992–1993 to build support for the communication initiatives and plans, to strengthen the plans themselves, and to uncover counterarguments that could then be preempted in political arenas. For example, one set of particularly valuable relationships was formed through consultation with several manufacturing supervisors who were rising young "stars" in the factory management ranks. Through consultation about communication technologies and accountabilities, these supervisors helped the PR team strengthen its plans and arguments, and they became advocates for trying out the new programs in their own operations. As stars in the company, they held strong platforms for championing the initiatives, and their support was invaluable. These and other stars were identified during the political assessment stage of plan development.

Legitimacy Linkages and Appeals. In a meeting with PR team members in early 1992, the CEO said that one of the major problems with past employee communication programs was that they weren't directly tied to business goals and drivers, that is, quality targets, productivity measures, market share objectives, and so forth. As a result, the CEO said, "In the eyes of many executives, employee communication programs are nice to do but of little real value to the business."

The PR team subsequently sought to legitimate and validate its proposals and work both internally and externally. For example, every component in the two strategic initiatives was closely tied to company objectives, from quality improvement scores to productivity issues. The communication process model was thoroughly grounded in the company's quality program and allowed communicators to talk "quality" with production managers. The PR team used the company's own process-mapping approach to refine some of the news distribution and environmental scanning processes it used, thereby saving time and money.

In addition, the overall objectives for the new initiatives were closely aligned with the company's statement of employee values and its new global vision. Capturing the feedback of other managers through consultation also helped the PR team ground its proposals in the actual work of the company. The use of benchmarking activities at leading companies, along with the PR team's involvement in a number of industry working groups regarding employee communication, provided the team with an aura of external legitimacy as well. Subsequent recognition and awards for many of the new initiatives provided further legitimacy for the communicators.

One other tactic provided a powerful stamp of authority for the communication work. The PR team employed a "chartering" process to launch the work of the major task forces responsible for technology, accountability, and education proposals. In this approach, the CEO or president participated in the initial task force meeting and formally spelled out the team's responsibilities, goals, deliverables, and deadlines. The executive also underscored the project's importance to the company's future and personally thanked team members for their participation.

Framing Approaches. The PR team consistently sought to frame their activities and presentations in terms that were most suitable for the particular audience at hand, but three frames of meaning were crucial to selling the program: *mental models, communication pipelines,* and *cycle time for change*. The discovery of mental models was serendipitous. The team had completed its research and was casting about for a way to discuss the gap between what communicators and executives thought communication was, and what it needed to be. One team member happened to purchase a copy of Peter Senge's book, *The Fifth Discipline* (1990), at an airport book store in his travels.

The book highlights the power of mental models in decision making, and all team members read the book and agreed that this was a powerful way of naming a central problem. Mental models provided a way of talking about the important gap the team had discovered, and yet doing so in a neutral way; that is, we all have mental models, and they all tend to get out of date. The term also provided a way to link the proposals to engineering by talking about outdated 1950 automobile models versus newer 1990 models, and then moving from automobiles to perceptions and mental models about employee communication. In fact, the term was understood and adapted in the company with little resistance.

Communication pipelines was designated to refer to the communication infrastructure. This was not a new term, nor perhaps the best term to describe the communications infrastructure at the company, but it was one that was readily understood by Whirlpool executives, many of whom were engineers. The image of new technologies as a set of pipelines conveying vital information to and from employees, or being stopped up with sludge in the form of companyspeak or employee distrust, was quickly grasped.

The term cycle time for change was selected out of the quality literature at the company, where it referred to production processes and the need to reduce the amount of time required to complete certain cycles in manufacturing, packaging, shipping, and so forth. The PR team felt that applying the term to employee communications offered two advantages. First, the term was legitimated in the company's existing quality program and manufacturing environments, so it had great currency. Second, the concept provided a way to highlight the substantial productivity-related costs of poor communication in global change processes, which were at the heart of Whirlpool's strategic plans. These potential costs were so great that the PR team was convinced they could capture executive attention with this argument.

Exchange. This tactic was used most often with peers and subordinates of the PR team and was often employed in conjunction with consultation. In exchange for the ideas and advice of peers in other functions, for example, PR team members would volunteer to help with communication tasks or issues, for instance, speech writing or preparation of materials for a functional meeting. The PR team also used exchange with the communicators. New computers were offered to all communicators for their help in project and planning teams. Their costs for participation in various conferences or training programs were reimbursed by corporate budgets in exchange for subsequent briefing sessions and written reports summarizing what they'd learned and how it applied to their work. And occasionally the PR executives exchanged their advocacy and support for the favored projects of others; for example, PR supported HR and its proposal for an educational conference center, for similar advocacy and support for PR's initiatives by other company executives.

Emotional and Inspirational Appeals.   These were used occasionally with professional communicators during training sessions and selectively with other audiences. The appeals were usually grounded in employee issues and concerns that had been expressed in interviews and focus group research and tape-recorded. Employee identities were protected, but their emotional calls for more candid communication, more advanced technologies, and more meaningful two-way communication channels were incorporated into strategic proposals and invoked in deliberations in various political arenas.

One set of emotional appeals was incorporated successfully into the PR team's strategic presentation and $20 million budget request to the executive committee in late 1993. During a rehearsal of the presentation, one team member said that something important was missing— the "power of the human face." The professional noted that the presentation was replete with impressive data and rational arguments, but it was "too much PR talking and not enough people in the field," especially field personnel who reported through the chain of command to members of the executive committee.

As a result, the PR team prepared a 4-minute video that concluded the strategic presentation. In the video, 11 mid- or upper-level executives who worked in factories or offices in six countries appeared on camera and explained in business and human terms why they needed the new technologies. Their colorful and inspirational testimonials were unscripted, and collectively they provided a powerful operational face that proved to be telling in the executive committee. In wrapping up committee discussion on the strategic proposal before a vote was taken, the CEO said, "Remember, it's not just our PR professionals telling us we need to make these changes. It's not just the results of the benchmarking work that's been done. It's our own people in Ohio and Italy and Canada and Germany and Sweden, the people who make it happen every day."

Persistence. This tactic was the glue that held together the PR team's many initiatives, activities, and proposals. And persistence was required virtually every day to get things going, to keep them going, and to fight off attacks and power thrusts that were intended to derail the initiatives. The team actively sought out meetings and forums to explain the strategic initiatives and advocate for them. Sometimes the PR professionals were welcome and sometimes grudgingly admitted, but they didn't back away from consistent professional advocacy for what they believed—and the research strongly suggested—were necessary and important steps to creating an empowering and communication rich environment. Each member of the global communicator group also was charged with similar advocacy efforts in their operations, and these charges were carried out to various extents. Over time, the strategic initiatives were explained and advocated in virtually every forum and arena in the global company.

In addition to sniping in some quarters, several operations resisted the initiatives by slowing down their implementation or by modifying the initiatives in order to "own" them. Occasionally the legitimacy of the team's work was directly challenged. Because the PR team enjoyed the general support of the CEO and president regarding the strategic proposals, it could turn to them for resolving direct challenges. However, the PR team also realized that high-level executive support is perishable and finite. Thus, appeals to the CEO and president were seldom used, and PR team members dealt with most direct challenges on their own. Sometimes exchange, consultation, or emotional tactics helped resolve such issues. But other times nothing worked, and in-your-face confrontations were the result. Professional persistence was perhaps most critical in these confrontations because they were all about power, the naked expression and display of power, and the extent to which influencers were willing to engage, commit, confront, and endure.

THE WHIRLPOOL PROJECT: IN RETROSPECT

In a letter to the editor of *WMJ* in 1993, an employee wrote that the magazine and other communication initiatives were the "catalyst for contagion," for spreading infectious change in employee communication thinking and practices in the company. For several years this was the case, but two developments during the 1995–1997 period altered the communication change program at the company. Whirlpool's economic growth slowed due to intense competition in many markets, slack demand for appliances, and a series of restructuring charges, among other factors. As a result, the company introduced cost controls that affected many areas, including the communication program. Rollout of the new technologies was delayed for a year, and training and project team activities were postponed. Though the budget cuts delayed progress and curbed some enthusiasm for the communication initiatives, they were not fatal.

A second development during this period was more telling. Three of the four senior PR team members left the company for attractive opportunities in other large organizations. In part, their achievements with the communication program at Whirlpool led to these new options. Departures of the senior professionals produced two crucial ruptures: a void in the PR leadership team itself, and a loss of strong, unrelenting advocacy for the change program at high levels in the company. These ruptures created space for other political influencers in the company to step in and try to redirect the communication program, and they did. Though some change initiatives continued and spread, others were delayed or eliminated, and the internal communication program lost its global momentum.

For example, *WMJ* was eliminated in late 1997 to reduce expenses. Though the magazine had developed an avid readership among low- and midlevel managers and especially managers outside of headquarters, some corporate executives had never become comfortable with its contents and candid approach. Several plant operations resisted virtually all of the change initiatives, whereas others curtailed activities once cost controls were announced. Two senior PR executives came and left the function in less than 2 years, and the public relations unit itself was weakened further when the government affairs unit was assigned to the legal department, and some of the responsibilities for employee communication reverted to human resources.

However, other aspects of the change program lived on. The process-planning model was integrated into most operations, and expectations were created throughout the company that communication plans would be based on research and include measurable objectives that were linked to business goals. Communication training for supervisors and managers was piloted in 1995, launched in early 1996, and subsequently integrated into the new management development curriculum at the company (Whirlpool Corporation, 1995). A handful of large operations aggressively embraced the initiatives and continued to implement them. And all of the technology recommendations, except for business television, were eventually implemented globally and have undergone several iterations since then.

Four Propositions Regarding Power Relations

The Whirlpool case provides some insights into the use of influence strategies and tactics by public relations professionals who sought to gain approval for and implement an ambitious communication change program. The case also highlights four aspects of power relations and practices that may be instructive to other public relations professionals, and these aspects are presented in the following four propositions:

> **Proposition 14: Power relations are ongoing in organizations, and hard-earned political achievements or victories are at best temporary and unstable.**

This is due, in part, to the diverse political arenas in organizations in which decisions may be contested. Inevitably, decisions in some arenas overlap or affect decisions made in other arenas; indeed, political influencers seek out alternative arenas for just such purposes. Achievements are also temporary because each of the phases in a political issue cycle— that is, development, proposal and decision making, implementation, and evaluation—is open to new or renewed influence attempts by other actors, and therefore no issue or project is ever safe from derailment.

In the Whirlpool case, some factory and plant directors used their authoritative and structural power to delay or altogether ignore implementation of the executive committee decisions. Other operational directors prioritized the communication initiatives "off" the active agenda in their own locally controlled political arenas, claiming that production deadlines and new product quality requirements didn't leave enough time or resources to support the initiatives. And in one operation, the implementation of a program was deliberately mishandled in order to produce a failure that could be reported as such, thereby freeing up the operation from accommodating other communication initiatives.

Achievements or gains also are temporary due to the very competitive nature of some political influencers, and the power relations process itself, which operates relentlessly around the clock. At Whirlpool, the communication change program was challenged directly or indirectly virtually every day somewhere in the organization through sniping, delaying, confrontation, or other tactics. Some challenges could be and were best ignored, but many had to be met. Thus, sustaining advocacy efforts and intensity over time in political arenas and throughout issue phases is demanding. This is not to suggest that such challenges are unique to public relations, but rather that they do exact a toll that must be considered in light of available resources and political willpower.

> **Proposition 15: Using a variety of influence tactics will yield better political results than relying too heavily on one or two favored approaches or tactics.**

Senge (1990) warned about the limitations of mental models, and these cautions also apply as well to mental models for influence tactics. The use of data played a key role for PR professionals at Whirlpool for two reasons: The previous PR teams had not generated or used substantive data, and Whirlpool executives relied on comprehensive data in much decision making. However, the data were necessary but not sufficient for winning resources. It was the use of data along with formation of coalitions, framing approaches, legitimacy appeals, consultation sessions, and other tactics that combined to produce political weight and influence. In addition, the Whirlpool PR leaders said that what favorably "tipped" their influence over time was their persistence, commitment, and political will.

The selection of influence tactics by the PR team grew out of their experience in working with others in the organization and their comprehensive political intelligence gathering and analysis. Subsequent tactical decisions were contingent on other political actors and their needs and favored approaches, the level and type of political arena, the issue cycle, timing, organizational culture, the relative financial health of the organization, the political skills of the PR professionals, the particular influence objective, and so forth. In this way, tactical selection and use are part science, part art, and sometimes the wisdom to concede or withdraw gracefully.

> **Proposition 16: The relative power and political success of the public relations function is dependent on the capacity, capabilities, and commitment of the entire team.**

At Whirlpool, one of the recurring problems with the change initiatives was the reluctance or unwillingness of some professional communicators to embrace the new approaches, even though the communicators readily agreed the changes were sorely needed and the right thing to do. In 1992, the senior PR team considered whether or not to try to replace some of the communicators, but this was never a realistic option. The communicators reported directly to plant managers, who had hired them. And given the controlling nature and power of local factory cultures, there was no guarantee that wholesale changes and the hiring of a new set of professional communicators would resolve the dilemma.

The PR leaders believed that through training experiences, increased skills, shared project work, and increased financial resources, local communicators would embrace the opportunity to empower employee communication in their local operations and thereby become more committed and forceful advocates and agents for change. But the PR executives were wrong, and their attempt to change communicator reporting relationships in late 1992 only exacerbated the situation with plant managers. Clearly, a committed, capable, and united communication team that speaks with one voice in political arenas possesses greater potential influence and implementation capability than does a single professional, or a divided team.

> **Proposition 17: The extent to which public relations may influence results in political arenas inside organizations is linked to the professional, managerial, and political skills— and especially to the political will—of the PR leaders(s) in the organization.**

Lauzen (1992) argued that public relations managers often possess more strategic power than they imagine and that PR departments can indeed become more powerful. She suggested that one key to this is that "the most senior practitioner in the organization must believe that PR is a powerful organizational function" (p. 77). Effectively, Lauzen was describing the kind of mental model that PR leaders must hold for the function; that is, to become more powerful you must see the function as powerful and actually believe that it can exert meaningful influence in decision making.

This is a different kind of mental model than that described by participants in the Most Important Issue in PR Survey we discussed in chapter 1. Nearly a third of the respondents in that survey said the top priority for PR was gaining a seat at the table. Why? Because power resides at the table, and, if PR professionals can only gain a seat at the table, they will gain the power they need to help the organization solve its problems and do the right thing. In this mental model, therefore, power is seen to be bestowed on or granted to professionals. Lauzen's model, however, suggests that power is already present in various sources and can be taken or acted on: PR leaders can increase their power by believing in the power of the function and its work, and then acting on these beliefs.

This is what the Whirlpool case suggests, too. The PR team there, new to the company and with few allies and even fewer resources in the beginning, was nevertheless able to research, develop, propose, win resources for, and partially implement a $21 million communication change program in a 3-year period. In retrospect, this seems an important accomplishment, one achieved in large part because of the leadership team's political influence skills, their belief that the change program was the right thing to do and could be done, and their tenacious political will in trying to make it happen.

CHAPTER 7

Omega Approaches in Public Relations: The Use of Unsanctioned Influence Tactics

> *There are times when you are working in, say, the political arena, where you do leak stories.... You can't just be sitting there playing totally by the book while somebody else is using all these tactics against you.... We don't like it necessarily, but we would be naive not to recognize it exists and to counter it.*
>
> —*An agency executive*

The Whirlpool case study and our interviews demonstrate that public relations practitioners use a variety of Alpha approaches, or sanctioned influence tactics, in power relations. Professionals also employ multiple tactics and base their choices on situational factors, past experience or practice, type and severity of issue, target(s) of influence, potential risks, and individual political intelligence and skills, among other factors.

But sometimes sound public relations counsel and Alpha approaches are not enough in power relations—they simply don't get the job done, and the organization makes an inappropriate choice or performs or communicates poorly. What do public relations professionals do in these crucial situations? What approaches do they take? Do they continue to doggedly advocate with decision makers, or do they back off, faithfully execute, and live to fight another day? Do they complain to fellow employees or family members about the organization's decision or action? Do they voice their concerns to professional colleagues or association members and solicit their support? Or do they update their résumés and search for work elsewhere?

In this chapter, we explore answers to these questions by examining the use of Omega approaches in public relations. Omega approaches refer to unsanctioned influence tactics that generally are not approved by the organization or validated by formal authority, organizational ideology, or professional codes and guidelines (Mintzberg, 1983). In public relations such tactics include leaking information to external publics, planting rumors in the grapevine, creating counternarratives in organizations, using professional activist approaches, and whistle-blowing, among others.

Omega approaches are virtually unexplored in the field, but that doesn't mean they aren't used in practice or worthy of study. These approaches represent other forms of influence that may be used in power relations and therefore they must be examined. In addition, some participants in the Power Relations Interviews (Berger, 2005), Influence Interviews, and Dissent Survey said they had used, or would be likely to use, these more controversial tactics if the organization made poor or inappropriate decisions. Virtually all of the participants in these research projects expressed opinions about Omega approaches. We examine the use of such tactics in this chapter. In the next chapter, we report on a comprehensive survey of more than 800 public relations practitioners and their perceptions about dissent practices.

BOAT ROCKING, WHISTLE-BLOWING, AND OTHER OMEGA APPROACHES

Omega approaches reflect organizational politics that "play outside the rules" and represent forms of illegitimate authority (Hay & Hartel, 2000; Porter et al., 1990). As a result, using these tactics challenges an individual's allegiance to the organization, represents significant career threats, poses difficult ethical dilemmas, and stirs controversy within professional ranks. Nevertheless, unsanctioned influence approaches may sometimes help organizations achieve their goals (Hay & Hartel, 2000) or stimulate needed changes to correct organizational deficiencies (Mintzberg, 1983).

In chapter 3, we characterized unsanctioned influence tactics as particular forms of employee dissent, or the expression of disagreement or contradictory opinions about one's organization in the workplace

(Kassing, 1997, 1998). Organizational members dissent for many reasons, including threats to job security, unhappiness with benefits or working conditions, disagreements with executive decisions, concerns about new job requirements or changes in organizational structure and strategy, and perceived injustices to themselves or others. Some members also dissent because they feel that dissent is an important part of their job, a matter of individual integrity, or a moral obligation on the way to trying to do the right thing. Members may decide not to dissent if they fear retaliation, believe they are powerless to effect change, or prefer avoidance over conflict strategies (Sprague & Ruud, 1988).

Redding (1985) differentiated between "boat rockers," employees who express dissatisfaction within organizations, and "whistle-blowers," individuals who protest their employer's decisions or actions outside the organization, often through media or government agencies. These two forms of dissent are unsanctioned influence tactics, though whistle-blowing is often deemed the most extreme approach and has received far more research attention in recent years (Colvin, 2002; Gong, 2000; Higginbottom, 2002; Lewis, 2002).

Sprague and Ruud (1988) examined boat-rocking incidents in high-tech companies in Silicon Valley to identify the situations that triggered employee dissent and the subsequent communication strategies that employees used to express their dissatisfaction. They found that antecedents to boat rocking were often related to personnel, organizational, and technical changes that employees felt were inappropriate. The employees interviewed, mostly engineers, said they dissented to maintain personal integrity and demonstrate concern for the company's integrity and welfare. They most often used blunt, face-to-face communication with supervisors to express their dissent, but they did so without much conscious strategy.

Rothschild and Miethe (1994) defined whistle-blowing as "the disclosure of illegal, unethical or harmful practices in the workplace to parties who might take action" (p. 254). They suggested that whistle-blowing was based on strong values and was frequently initiated by organizational members when they felt that organizational decisions and actions undermined personal or organizational values and ideals. Jubb (1999) went further in his definition of whistle-blowing to include any "illegality or other wrongdoing whether actual, suspected or anticipated" (p. 78). He argued that inactive observation by an employee in the face of illegal, immoral, or illegitimate activities by an organization should be viewed as neglectful behavior rather than a demonstration of loyalty.

Other researchers have categorized employee resistance or unsanctioned influence tactics as "open" or "hidden" (Caruth, Middlebrook, & Rachel, 1985), and "active" or "passive" (Hullman, 1995). Caruth et al. categorized complaining and sabotage as open forms of resistance, and spreading false rumors and doing minimum work as hidden forms of resistance. Hullman suggested that actively resisting includes such tactics as finding fault, ridiculing, and appealing to fears, whereas passively resisting refers to not following through on tasks, not implementing change, and allowing change to fail.

Manheim (2001) outlined many tactics that union members and other formal or informal groups of employees carry out to attempt to influence organizational discourse and subsequent decisions, practices, and policies. These approaches include strikes, picketing, boycotts, and demonstrations; work slowdowns, sabotage, or disruption of work processes and activities; intimidation and ridicule campaigns, symbolic rallies, and staged events to attract attention; formal litigation; stuffing suggestion boxes or established grievance machinery with complaints; and recruiting supporters in the community or other publics.

Manheim (2001) argued that availability of the Internet has increased the number of tactical resistance options and facilitated their application. Groups may now create countercompany Web sites to disseminate negative information about the organization, coordinate group communications, and mobilize member actions. They also may plant rumors or information in online chat rooms and discussion groups and pressure organizational executives through high-volume e-mail onslaughts.

In a study of 277 temporary workers, Tucker (1993) identified gossip, theft, noncooperation, resignation, collective action, formal and legal complaints, and violence, among other unsanctioned influence tactics. Morrill (1989) examined cases of executive conflict in a large corporation to determine how executives dealt with the conflict. He found that senior executives used a variety of approaches, including such unsanctioned tactics as making secret complaints to other executives or sabotaging others, for example, providing incomplete or inaccurate data or information for a meeting presentation.

The Power Relations Interviews

Through interviews with 21 corporate public relations executives, Berger (2005) identified three unsanctioned influence tactics used in the profession: information leaks, counterculture activities, and construction of alternative interpretations of official events or communications. The leaked information in the reported cases was not proprietary in nature but rather intended to correct or amend the company's officially released information on a topic. For example, one executive described how "corrected" information about a company's media campaign touting professional opportunities for minorities was passed on to a reporter:

> I didn't support the program because I felt it was a false campaign, another fashionable program of the month. So I gave some data to a reporter I'd known for a long time and encouraged him to contact an EEO official for more information. I'm embarrassed to say I did this through pay phones, real cloak-and-dagger stuff. The upshot was a critical story appeared, the company scaled back the program, but did hire two minority candidates. I can't say I'm proud of what I did, but I felt good about it. Does that make sense? (p. 20)

Counterculture actions refer to using the grapevine or other informal channels to initiate oppositional communications or to plant rumors and information. According to two of the executives in the study, such approaches can alert broader employee audiences to issues and concerns they might not otherwise be aware of. They also may spur management to "come clean" on organizational issues or decisions. In these ways, planting information in the grapevine can help set the company's formal communication agenda.

Many executives in the study also reported they often constructed and shared alternate interpretations of formal organizational communications and actions with their employees. They contended that shared interpretations helped employees understand what was actually occurring and stimulated team rapport and mutual understanding. This approach represents an unsanctioned tactic in that one tacit agreement among those in the dominant coalition, or senior-management ranks generally, is that members must mouth the party line, even if they don't agree with it. One executive described it this way:

> Championing a bad party line has always been difficult for me, especially with my own people. When they ask me what really happened in some meeting, or why the company made such-and-such a decision, I tell them flat out. We discuss the issue and what it really means and develop some common understanding. And then they go out and share this interpretation with their friends in the company, who tell others. The irony is, we do this even as we carry out the approved communication activities. (Berger, 2005, p. 21)

Unsanctioned Tactics in the Influence Interviews

To explore the use of unsanctioned influence tactics in the profession in greater depth, we posed two questions on the topic to the 65 public relations professionals who took part in the Influence Interviews. We first asked them whether they had ever felt so strongly about an organizational action or decision that they used approaches they might not normally use, such as planting stories or rumors in the grapevine, leaking information to outside publics, or whistle-blowing. We then asked participants if they knew other public relations professionals who had used such approaches. If the response to either question was affirmative, we asked the professional to describe the tactic(s) and the situation.

Many of the 65 professionals (50) indicated they had not and were not likely to use such tactics, believing them to be inappropriate or unethical in any situation. Two participants best reflected this dominant perspective. One communication manager at a nonprofit said, "I view all those things as unethical. If I felt that strongly about something, I would resign. What you are doing there is clearly wrong." A corporate public affairs director added that such tactics were career threatening: "Absolutely not. I think it's reprehensible. First of all, I think it's stupid. You end up shooting yourself in the foot and losing whatever influence you had. And second, it's unethical."

Several respondents said such approaches damaged the reputation of the profession, as well as that of individual professionals who engaged in them. One longtime corporate PR executive reflected this view of unsanctioned influence tactics:

> I don't know of anyone specifically who uses such tactics, but I sense it's all over. There are books written about it. If you are asked to do something in a company that is contrary to your value system, you don't do it. If that jeopardizes your employment, so be it. Some PR people don't have that constraint, which I think is part of the problem with PR generally.

Nevertheless, 15 practitioners (23.1% of total) said they had used these or other unsanctioned influence tactics. This group included six women and nine men who were distributed across the five types of organizations represented in the study: corporations (6), PR agencies (2), social-movement groups (3), nonprofits (2), and educational institutions (2). Six of the professionals were non–Americans. The unsanctioned influence tactics these professionals said they used are listed in Table 7.1.

TABLE 7.1

Unsanctioned Influence Tactics (Influence Interviews)

Participant ID	Unsanctioned Influence Tactic
01 M—Company	Leaked information about a report to a journalist
02 M—Company	Planted rumors in the grapevine (a few times)
03 F—Company	Fabricated employee quotes to capture attention of executives
04 M—Company	Planted tough questions for a town hall meeting with top executives
05 M—Education	Stonewalled the media and CEO to prevent implementing a poor decision
06 M—Education	Orchestrated aspects of a public hearing
07 F—Agency	Leaked information to the press about an event
08 M—SM	Leaked information to the press about an issue
09 F—Agency	Leaked information to the press about a company program
10 F—Nonprofit	Planted rumors in the grapevine (several times)
11 M—Company	Leaked information to the press about a plant strike
12 M—Company	Leaked personal information to the press about an executive
13 F—Nonprofit	Leaked information to the press about a product decision
14 M—SM	Leaked information to the press to damage legitimacy of a decision
15 F—SM	Leaked information to the media to pressure decision makers

Leaking Information. The tactic mentioned most often (nine practitioners) was leaking information to the press. According to the professionals, this approach was used to increase the profession's or function's own influence inside the organization or to pressure organizational decision makers to reconsider planned actions or decisions that practitioners felt were somehow inappropriate. One public affairs officer in a social-movement group described how using unconventional means like leaking information to the press or other outside publics can influence management's agenda and strengthen the PR function's role in decision making:

> Basically what you do with public affairs is when someone [an organizational executive] is reluctant, then you line up an audience to request something; it has to come from them because most organizations will re-

spond from a media desire to talk with them…. So if you're particularly sneaky as a media officer, PA strategist or crisis manager … then you bring in your press mates that want answers on something, and then they have to get back to the media. It's called reverse psychology, and I've only used it when I'm particularly desperate to get a result out of my team and they've been not cooperating because they've been too busy, couldn't see the point, or been in the bunker … it's an unconventional so-called strategy that is fairly common…. I find that unconventional tactics are often times the only way you can succeed. You know the reason is because … public affairs officers aren't given a formal inclusion or respect in top levels of organizations, so you sometimes have to resort to unconventional means to get the influence you require to make a difference.

Another public relations executive described how, when caught between the interests of his international branch office and those of an American parent company, he leaked information to the press because he thought it was the right thing to do for his branch office and his own reputation with the media:

I once leaked or confirmed some information about a report to a journalist. The journalist asked me about a possible product development deal with another company, related to a merger. I spoke with my management—the European branch of a big American company. I told them I thought we needed to confirm this [with the journalist] because otherwise the resulting story would be distorted and make us look bad, and it also would damage my and the branch's credibility with this influential reporter. So they said do it, but they didn't want to know and wouldn't know anything about it. So I did it, and American management was furious. They never found out what happened. I still think it was the right thing to do.

Though nine practitioners reported leaking information to the press, our analysis suggests that at least four of these reports are qualitatively different. In these responses, the goal of leaking information appears to have been to advance the organization's competitive interests or the professional's personal interests, rather than to influence organizational decision making or pressure decision makers. One public relations manager, for example, provided special services to the media and leaked personal information about the CEO in an attempt to garner favorable publicity: "During a process to enhance my CEO's image, I leaked private information to the press and supplied various services to the media also—a free book about my CEO, free lunches and dinners, and so forth." Another public relations director leaked information to journalists in an attempt to discredit striking members of a labor union: "When there was a strike by union workers for higher wages, I leaked false information about the union strike to the media to create a crisis atmosphere for the striking unions."

Two public relations agency professionals added two other perspectives about leaking information. One said that leaking information to the press is a relatively common practice that is acceptable *if* the client approves it:

> We've only done things similar to that [leaking information] with the client's approval, which is not the same thing. I don't believe we would ever do that behind the client's back. There's a big ethical issue in doing that.... There are times when you are working in, say, the political arena, where you do leak stories but the client totally approves.... In the political arena you almost have to do it. You can't just sit there playing totally by the book while somebody else is using all these tactics against you.

Another agency practitioner reported that information was sometimes leaked in order to advance one's career:

> Some of the people who work in Silicon Valley would do that. I know it's pretty much the MO in certain parts of the entertainment business, but not all.... When you're in a major PR agency and you're working your way up the ladder, a lot of folks will do some really unsavory things to get a better client, get assigned to a better account.

The Grapevine.   Apart from leaking information to the press, three other unsanctioned influence tactics were mentioned. Two PR professionals said they occasionally planted rumors or information in the organization's grapevine to attempt to influence decision making or to increase the visibility of significant issues among organizational members. For example, one professional used the grapevine to capture management's attention regarding a production problem that he felt the company needed to resolve:

> I planted some close but not quite accurate information about a product manufacturing problem. I smelled trouble coming with a potential recall, but I couldn't get anyone's attention. So I planted this rumor and then used content of the rumor as the basis of my argument to justify a close look at the product. I mean, I planted the rumor and waited for it a bit until it circulated, then I could point to the rumor in 2–3 different locations or sources by way of confirming there might be a problem. It worked.

A corporate executive reported that she fabricated employee quotations that were highly critical of company executives in order to successfully influence the manner in which a new executive was introduced into the company:

> There was a new VP who wanted to go out to the operations to meet everyone in the factories. But he didn't really want to meet them, just to be seen and say a few words and then fly out.... I knew this wouldn't work well with our people [in the factories]. Now, in trying to convince the new VP to do it differently—I did have some actual employee quotes [about such types of fly-in visits]—I invented two hyper critical ones that I thought would get attention. Well, they sure did. I know that's not the right thing to do, but it sure seems a small trade off to make when the final decision would have so much to do with the important first impression that this man would make with thousands of employees who were already somewhat jaded [about executives].

Planting Questions and Stonewalling. Two other professionals said that they planted tough questions with fellow employees for a town hall meeting, or with community residents in a public hearing, to increase the visibility of important issues and force their executives to acknowledge and respond to the issues. In another case, a university relations specialist tried a number of sanctioned influence approaches, all to no avail, to convince organizational decision makers not to participate in an on-site media tour and interviews with reporters from a well-known TV newsmagazine program. He was convinced that the university laboratory would be portrayed unfavorably, but the top university administrator was adamant that he could persuade the TV journalists to produce a highly favorable story.

In the end, the PR professional did what he thought was the right thing given the circumstances. He stonewalled the reporter by telling him that the administrator was more or less continuously unavailable. At the same time, he stonewalled the administrator; he told him that the TV journalists were having difficulty scheduling the visit because they were occupied with other stories. After several months the newsmagazine program abandoned the story and went on to produce a highly critical treatment of a similar program elsewhere.

Use Among Other Professionals. With respect to our second question, nearly half of the professionals (29, or 44.4%) said they knew other practitioners who had used unsanctioned influence tactics. Once again, many of the examples they reported focused on leaking information for competitive or personal advantage rather than for influencing organizational decisions or decision makers, as reflected in this comment:

"There are some people who use public relations which would be to, and it happens sometimes in Silicon Valley, to actually sandbag competition or to hurt a competitor, and that is planting negative information with reporters about a company. [Named company] does this a lot.... I think it's unethical."

Several professionals said such practices were problematic in intensely competitive industries, and one practitioner suggested that PR agencies played an important counterintelligence role in this environment:

> In our business, you might find that [leaking information] in areas where there is great competition.... For example, if a company has a new product ready for introduction, the competition may become afraid and do something in advance of the other person's new product hitting the market. Some companies like to steal the thunder from competitors by announcing something earlier, or to figure how to ride the coat tails of somebody else's news. The annals of business are full of such examples.... There's a lot of counter intelligence. That's just how it works. That's sort of what PR agencies do.

A half dozen of the professionals suggested that unsanctioned influence tactics were especially prevalent in the political arena, or in government affairs programs. One corporate VP of public relations explained the dilemma this way:

> Other professionals have done the kinds of things you mention. There are many who do it. It may be the worst on the political side of organizations, the government relations side, where you are dealing with people, with politicians, all of whom have huge amounts of paranoia. So the notion of guarding your relationships in this area, with these key decision makers, is paramount. If you think you are losing this relationship, you will do what you can to protect and guard it.

Though most professionals in this group were critical of unsanctioned tactics, a handful indicated that under certain conditions they would consider using such tactics to try to influence decision makers to do the right thing, or to communicate wrongdoings, albeit somewhat reluctantly. One new professional said: "I guess if I were in the tobacco industry, I might have considered doing what the whistle blower did. Or if I were in a company that was consciously polluting the air, I might consider it. In actuality, though, thinking about it is as far as I would go. If I were powerless to do anything about it above board, I would resign." A longtime agency professional went a bit further: "I can imagine a situation where I would have to resign because the client was doing something illegal. I can also imagine a situation where I would have to blow the whistle on a client. I can even imagine a situation where if I thought it was really in the best interest of society, then I might go off the record with the press."

For many professionals we interviewed, using Omega approaches is a last resort only, as this public relations director indicated: "I feel there's a place for that [unsanctioned influence tactics] if that's the only way. It obviously goes against the grain of a PR officer whose position is basically to keep the organization looking good. But if you feel strongly about something, it's not something you'd do lightly. I think you would try to use all other angles first."

Activist Advocates and Unsanctioned Tactics in the Dissent Survey

In chapter 2 we reported qualitative results of the Dissent Survey, focusing on how practitioners defined what it means in public relations "to do the right thing" when organizational leaders make an inappropriate decision. The responses of most participants were reflected in seven categories of advocacy (Table 2.3 in chap. 2) in which doing the right thing varied by the extent to which practitioners would advocate in this hypothetical situation, the types of advocacy approaches and tactics they were likely to employ, and the perspective from which they would advocate.

Activist advocates, one of seven categories or groups of respondents, indicated they would use sanctioned influence tactics in this scenario to try to influence decision makers to modify or reverse an inappropriate decision. However, if those conventional tactics failed, activist advocates said that they were prepared to use a variety of established internal approaches (e.g., compliance hot lines and governance committees) and more extreme outside or unsanctioned influence approaches (e.g., leaking information, alerting stakeholders, and whistle-blowing) to attempt to overturn the inappropriate decision or halt its implementation.

Of interest here is the type of influence tactics that activist advocates said they had or would use in such situations. In the Dissent Survey, 59 of the 707 professionals who responded to this question were categorized as activist advocates (37 women and 22 men). Some respondents mentioned several specific influence channels, and collectively the 59 professionals mentioned influence channels 68 times. Table 7.2 includes the frequencies of tactics mentioned by activist advocates in the Dissent Survey.

TABLE 7.2
Unsanctioned Influence Tactics (Dissent Survey)

Influence Tactics	F	M	Total
Notify authorities; blow the whistle on illegal activities	21	9	30
Alert, mobilize organizational members (grapevine)	4	6	10
Leak information to the press	4	4	8
Use internal channels (e.g., hot line, audit committee)	6	2	8
Alert, mobilize external stakeholders	4	2	6
Take "appropriate" measures to stop illegal activities	5	0	5
Sabotage implementation or communication of the decision	0	1	1
Totals	44	24	68

Whistle-Blowing.   Slightly more than half (30, or 50.8% of activist advocates) said they would notify authorities or resort to whistle-blowing if the decision was illegal or unethical. Two professionals said they had blown the whistle on such activities at previous employers. Five professionals indicated they would take all "appropriate" measures to stop illegal activities, which presumably might include whistle-blowing. Eight practitioners reported they would leak information to the press, whereas six others said they would alert and attempt to mobilize other external stakeholders (e.g., community leaders, stockholders, or customers) to pressure decision makers.

For some, the decision to notify authorities or other external stakeholders appears relatively clear-cut. One male public relations director said, "Are they [the decisions] illegal? Are they unethical? If so, then I would have to take the appropriate measures. If it's illegal, I'd approach the state attorney's office. If unethical, I'd approach the state's ethics oversight authority." A public affairs manager said she felt so strongly about this issue that she had already left one job because of it: "I've quit a job because I didn't believe in the ethics of management. I believe in confronting those making poor decisions and working to make them right. When an organization doesn't work to make it right, it's time to quit and blow the whistle."

For others in the activist group, however, whistle-blowing represents a more difficult dilemma, and this approach might be utilized only as a last resort after all other solutions have been tried, including leaving the job, as summarized in this comment:

> 1) I would confront management and explain why the decision is inappropriate; 2) explain the consequences in terms of legal, business and ethical outcomes (in that order); 3) use case studies of previously similar situations to explain the situation; 4) work with appropriate executives to find alternatives....; 5) If it is extremely unethical or dangerous, leave the company or resign from the client, and only then speak out publicly if there is a life-threatening danger to consumers.

A public relations VP described how he would first try to build a coalition among other senior executives before taking more drastic actions:

> I believe that if, after repeated attempts at persuasion, I could not convince the CEO that a proposed action was illegal, I would verify legal consequences of inaction, then work to find support among other members of the senior management team. Together, we would seek to petition the CEO for a change of decision. If this were not possible, I would contact a member of the Board. If that were unsuccessful, I would resign my position and then, only then, if warranted, I believe I would contact the appropriate agencies to report the impropriety.

Internal Channels. Eighteen professionals said they would use internal channels and mechanisms to the extent they could to try to overturn an inappropriate decision. Ten of these practitioners indicated they would use the grapevine or other informal channels to alert organizational members, form coalitions, and mobilize advocacy support efforts to resolve the issue internally. Eight respondents said they would use all "appropriate," organizational-sponsored channels and mechanisms to report illegal, unethical, or immoral decisions or actions, for example, employee hot lines, compliance committees, and audit committees. Professionals who say they would use such internal channels tend to draw the line there, as captured in this comment:

> I would use our appropriate methods of recourse, including using our compliance hot line, contacting the appropriate ethics/corporate governance/compliance officers, and even the chairman of the audit committee of the Board of Directors. I would not under any circumstances leak information or sabotage anyone, but rather would leave the organization in the worst-case scenario.

PROPOSITIONS REGARDING OMEGA APPROACHES

Omega approaches in public relations are virtually unexplored. Yet, they represent potential sources of power and forms of resistance in practice, and any discussion of public relations and power in organizations requires examination of both sanctioned and unsanctioned influence tactics. In this chapter, we drew from three research projects to assess professional reports and perceptions about unsanctioned influence tactics, which tactics public relations professionals use, and the extent to which they use them. Our qualitative analysis of these reports suggests five propositions regarding unsanctioned influence tactics in the profession:

> **Proposition 18: A small number of public relations professionals use unsanctioned influence tactics in their work to try to do the right thing or to further personal or organizational interests.**

Fewer than one in five professionals in each study reported using such approaches. In the Power Relations Interviews, many of the 21 executives said they often constructed alternate interpretations of formal organizational actions and communications with their employees. To what extent this approach is considered unsanctioned is not known, though we suspect the practice is widespread among many employees and functions in organizations today. Only four of the executives in the study indicated that they had leaked information, planted information in the grapevine, or used other unsanctioned approaches.

Eleven of the 65 professionals in the Influence Interviews reported that they had used unsanctioned influence approaches to try to influence organizational decisions or actions, whereas 4 other professionals leaked information to achieve other goals. In the Dissent Survey, 59 of the 707 professionals surveyed said they had used or would use unsanctioned approaches to try to change an inappropriate management decision.

Data in these three projects were self-reported and may therefore overstate or understate the actual use of unsanctioned influence tactics in public relations. In this regard, about twice as many professionals (29) in the Influence Interviews reported that they knew others in the practice who used such tactics as they themselves did (15). In addition, some respondents suggested that leaking information was a frequent tactic in certain industries and in political or government relations activities. On the other hand, the range of self-reported unsanctioned tactics was relatively consistent across the studies, ranging from about 10% to 20% of participants in each study.

> **Proposition 19: Public relations professionals select unsanctioned influence tactics from a range of options that are characterized by varying degrees of perceived severity of application and levels of self-conflict.**

Many of the professionals said that deciding whether to use Omega approaches was difficult and created personal dilemmas and self-conflict. We used this sense of dilemma to loosely organize the tactics reported in our studies into the following three groups:

- *Group I:* Unsanctioned tactics in this group produce relatively lower-level dilemmas for practitioners and appear to be used more widely than other tactics. Such tactics include: constructing alternate interpretations of formal decisions and actions, planting rumors or information in the grapevine, planting questions in meetings and hearings, fabricating quotations or other data to strengthen persuasive appeals, and bluntly confronting decision makers to express dissent. These tactics may not be sanctioned by the organization, but they appear to be used by a number of political actors in organizational politics.
- *Group II:* Use of tactics in this group appears to increase self-conflict for practitioners, rendering their selection and use more difficult and perhaps less frequent. Unsanctioned tactics here include: refusing to implement decisions, disrupting work processes (e.g., stonewalling), leaking information to the press for competitive or personal advantage, and alerting and mobilizing other organizational members regarding inappropriate actions or decisions.
- *Group III:* Professionals hold strong feelings about whether or not to use what they believe are the most extreme tactics in this group. These approaches include: whistle-blowing to authorities, sabotaging activities or communications, leaking information to the press about organizational matters, and alerting and mobilizing other external stakeholders regarding inappropriate actions or decisions. The use of these tactics was rarely reported by public relations professionals in our research.

> **Proposition 20: Public relations professionals hold strong but polar feelings about the appropriateness of whistle-blowing.**

The vast majority of professionals in our studies said that whistle-blowing was not the right thing to do under virtually any circumstances.

However, a small number of practitioners felt strongly otherwise; as a last recourse, whistle-blowing was exactly the right thing to do. Those who opposed whistle-blowing indicated that out of loyalty to the organization, or because of professional and personal ethics, it was simply not the right thing to do. A number said they would leave the organization if inappropriate decisions were made and simply walk away from the situation: They wouldn't be part of it, and they wouldn't report it.

This raises an important and unresolved question about professional responsibilities; that is, at what point do professional responsibilities end for trying to stop or correct what is perceived to be an organizational wrongdoing of some magnitude? For example, can public relations professionals justify walking away from a situation where consumers may be harmed, the quality of the environment may be jeopardized, or the safety or welfare of employees may be threatened? Walking away from such situations may help professionals protect their individual reputation and perhaps satisfy personal ethics, but it leaves open the question of responsibility to others.

> **Proposition 21: Leaking information is the most controversial and complex unsanctioned influence tactic in the public relations field.**

Many professionals in our research indicated that they were as strongly opposed to leaking information as to whistle-blowing. Others expressed discomfort with leaking information but subsequently described situations where they had done so because they felt it was the right thing to do under the circumstances to try to counteract an inappropriate organizational decision or action (e.g., the aforementioned European product deal and the media program falsely touting minority career opportunities).

However, professionals in our studies more often reported using information leaks to achieve other goals. A few practitioners reported that they leaked information to help the organization advance its competitive interests or to achieve self-interests. A few said they used this tactic to discredit other organizations or individuals. Several said they had to use this tactic because competitors did so. More indicated that the practice was all too common in certain industries or in government and political communication programs. In short, information is a powerful resource, and it appears that leaking information may be the most controversial and yet more widely used and multipurpose Omega approach in the field.

Proposition 22: Public relations professionals make decisions about whether or not to use unsanctioned influence tactics based on a wide array of factors, but the nature of the issue is a crucial factor.

Influencing factors include demographic variables such as age, gender, years of experience, type of organization or industry, and educational background. Our qualitative assessment of the three projects yielded no significant differences with respect to gender; we did not assess other demographic variables. Other factors include past practices, organizational loyalty, functional leadership, and career and personal advancement considerations. Individual, organizational, professional, and societal codes of ethics and standards are also important influencing factors, along with organizational and functional culture and professional courage.

According to professionals in the studies, one significant factor in their decisions to dissent or not, and the corresponding tactics they select for use, is the nature of the situation or issue itself, and the relative degree of "seriousness" of that issue in legal, ethical, and moral terms. We explore this contingency factor in depth in the next chapter where we report on a survey of more than 800 public relations professionals. Participants were asked to describe the tactics they would use to respond to a variety of inappropriate organizational decisions, ranging from inconvenient or irritating decisions to those that are illegal or unethical.

CHAPTER 8

The Use of Dissent
in Public Relations

> *I really think that assertiveness is the most important thing. I think you have to be able ... to say that "In my professional opinion and experience this is the right action to take and these will be the consequences of not taking that action." I think the more willing we are to step up and say these things, the more we will be heard. It really is a matter of influencing rather than demanding.... Ultimately, if you see your institution going in a completely wrong direction you may have to stand up and say that if we're going to do this, I can't be a party to this. And I'm not talking about illegal things, just wrongheaded things. Then you can quit.*
> *—University practitioner with 27 years of experience*

The preceding chapter introduced qualitative findings regarding Omega approaches from interviews with public relations practitioners from around the world. In this chapter, we report and analyze the findings from a survey of more than 800 practitioners from across the United States. We refer to this study as the Dissent Survey. Our exploration of influence required a study like the Dissent Survey to explore this particular form of resistance. This study represents the most comprehensive look yet at dissent practices and attitudes within the public relations profession. The goal of the Dissent Survey was to move into new territory related to understanding attitudes of public relations practitioners toward dissent, and accompanying behaviors or tactics, in the face of perceived organizational missteps or wrongdoing. We also wanted to learn how attitudes might vary by years of professional experience, type of organization, role, gender, and other demographics.

ORGANIZATIONAL DISSENT

Though there is a dearth of literature on the place of organizational dissent in public relations practice, there are some seminal studies from other fields of scholarship. We looked to these studies for dissent variables. Kipnis et al. (1980), for example, explored ways to influence others within an organization and identified eight influence dimensions—assertiveness, ingratiation, rationality, sanctions, exchange, upward appeals, blocking, and coalitions. These dimensions, by and large, fall under the category of acceptable means of influence muscle flexing, or Alpha approaches. Data from our interviews with professionals suggested that rational arguments, coalitions, and assertiveness (pressure) are the most common influence tactics.

The Kipnis et al. study (1980) informed our thinking about the range of influence tactics and our concepts of acceptable versus unacceptable, or perhaps more correctly common versus uncommon, means of expressing influence via dissent. Assertiveness is perceived based on both research and anecdotal evidence as a common and more acceptable means of expressing dissent; whereas blocking—or as we have characterized it, sabotaging—is a less common and less acceptable means of displaying dissent.

Schmidt and Kipnis (1984) found that subordinates most frequently employed influence tactics to sell ideas. In selling their ideas to superiors, employees were most likely to employ reason and coalition building. Whereas rationality is a common and accepted tactic, coalition building (or as we conceptualized it, agitating others to join in working against a decision) is less common and less accepted, according to findings from our qualitative research. These tactics were illustrated in the Whirlpool case study in chapter 6.

Schriemsheim and Hinkin (1990) tested and tightened the Kipnis et al. (1980) influence scale. Kipnis et al. had developed a scale using 27 variables to measure the eight aforementioned dimensions. Schriemsheim and Hinkin eliminated 12 of the Kipnis et al. variables and included 3 new ones in their development of an 18-item scale to measure six influence dimensions (ingratiation, exchange of benefits, rationality, assertiveness, upward appeal, and coalitions). Although these scales (Kipnis et al., 1980; Schriemsheim & Hinkin, 1990) inform our measures, we dug deeper because we were interested in focusing on active dissension as a means of influencing an outcome in a specific circumstance, such as illegal behavior by an organization.

In chapter 3, we introduced streams of organizational-dissent research by Kassing and colleagues, Redding, and others. Here we link those research streams to conceptualization of the Dissent Survey. Kassing (1997) defined "organizational dissent as a multi-step process that involves: feeling apart from one's organization (i.e., the experience of dissent), and (b) expressing disagreement or contradictory opinions about one's organization (i.e., the expression of dissent)" (p. 312). He proposed a model for conceptualizing dissent in which a triggering agent leads to a strategy selection.

Strategy selection relates to determining how one will express dissent and is moderated by individual influences such as value systems, relational influences such as quality of relationships with others in an organization, and organizational influences such as how employees identify with their organizations. Strategy selection leads finally to determining whether to engage in articulated, antagonistic/latent, or displaced dissent.

Articulated dissent is dissent shared with those in an organization who are empowered to change the organization's behavior. It is defined as "sharing concerns directly and openly with management, supervisors, and corporate officers" (Kassing, 1998, p. 190).

Antagonistic/latent dissent is dissent that is adversarial but designed to guard against retaliation. It is practiced by those who believe that their position in or relationship with the organization protects them from retaliation. Antagonistic/latent dissenters "dissent primarily about personal advantage issues ... and express their dissent whenever they believe a captive or influential audience exists" (Kassing, 1998, p. 190).

Displaced dissent is adversarial and likely to lead to retaliation. Displaced dissent is expressed "only to stakeholders who are clearly external" (Kassing, 1998, p. 191). Such audiences include family members, friends outside of work, and others in professional or trade associations. Displaced dissent constitutes an unarticulated disagreement, when disagreement is not accompanied by confrontation or challenge. Kassing introduced a 20-item dissent scale, which we used to measure tendency toward articulated, antagonistic/latent, and displaced dissent.

Redding (1985) took an activist approach regarding dissent. He pled for education that empowers students to become employees willing to dissent within their organizations, as appropriate. Redding envisioned a continuum "representing different degrees of 'badness' for managerial decisions" (p. 256). This range of situations wherein dissent might be appropriate ran on a spectrum as follows: clearly illegal, clearly immoral or unethical, psychopathic or insane, incredibly stupid, insensitive, inefficient or impractical, and irritating or annoying (p. 257). We used the points on this continuum as a means of suggesting scenarios or situations in which dissent might reasonably occur. Furthermore, we believed developing items based on Redding's continuum would provide substantial variance.

Work by a variety of other organizational scholars and consultants (e.g., Caruth et al., 1985; Hullman, 1995; Maurer, 1998; Recardo, 1995) were used to identify extreme examples of dissent. We developed the following six behavior categories based on this review of literature: (a) assertively confront management, (b) sabotage implementation of a decision, (c) agitate others to work against a decision, (d) leak information to external stakeholders, (e) use facts selectively in making a case against a decision, and (f) stand by and say nothing.

SURVEY DESIGN

Measures

Measures were constructed based on a review of the public relations and management literature related to roles, resistance, and upward dissent. Public relations roles literature (e.g., Broom & Dozier, 1986; Broom & G. D. Smith, 1979; L. Grunig et al., 2002) provides well-developed scales for measuring managerial and technician roles in public relations practice. These scales, as used in Grunig et al., were included in the Dissent Survey.

As mentioned earlier, the organizational-dissent scale developed by Kassing (1998) was used to measure tendencies toward articulated, antagonistic/latent, and displaced dissent. The continuum proposed by Redding (1985) served as the basis for six items measuring situations in which dissent is appropriate. Work by Caruth et al. (1985), Recardo (1995), Maurer (1998), and Hullman (1995) provided the foundation for developing six behaviors related to organizational dissent.

Finally, several demographic variables were included in the survey (see the Appendix for wording of survey measures). In the review of literature, four scales were analyzed and themes from those scales were selected to test. The goal was to arrive at appropriate dissent scales related to the public relations profession.

Sample

A random sample of PRSA members was constructed from the membership directory. A population of 5,252 PRSA members received an e-mail invitation to participate in the survey; 808 unique responses were collected giving a response rate of 15.4%.

What We Found

Demographics. Almost two thirds of our survey respondents were female (64.7%); 35.3% were male. Most respondents held a bachelor's degree (63%), one third held a master's degree (33.8%), and 3.1% held a doctorate.

Our sample was senior in terms of organizational reporting. More than one third (35.2%) reported directly to their organization's CEO, chairperson, or president. One quarter (25.2%) reported directly to a vice president. About 3 in 10 (29.9%) said they reported to a director. Most participants responded in the positive direction when asked how often (on a scale of 1 = Never to 7 = Always) they are directly involved in their organization's decision- and policy-making process ($M = 4.68$); but only 10% said they were always involved. Most of these practitioners are midcareer or less in terms of tenure in the profession—61.9% have been practicing public relations for 15 years or fewer; 38.6% have been in PR for fewer than 10 years. However, more than one in five (22.9%) participants have been in public relations for more than 20 years.

The highest percentage of respondents (33.6%) described themselves as corporate practitioners; 20.2% said they work in the nonprofit arena; 19.6% work in agencies; 14.7% work in government; and 12.0% work in education. Because e-mail addresses were randomly selected from the PRSA membership directory, some educators who are PRSA members were included among the respondents. By age, the largest percentage of respondents (27.7%) were in their 30s; 25.9% were in their 40s; 21.5% were younger than 30; 20.4% were in their 50s; and 4.5% were 60 or over.

Public Relations Roles. Sixteen items made up the professional-role scale. The scale used is that reported in L. A. Grunig et al. (2002). Confirmatory factor analysis was conducted to determine the fit of scale to the current sample of public relations professionals. The analysis yielded two factors—what have been commonly called the manager role and the technician role.

Based on the confirmatory factor analysis and acceptable alphas (.89 for the manager scale; .79 for the technician scale), the manager and technician scales were used as independent, demographic variables in subsequent analysis.

Inclination Toward Organizational Dissent. Kassing (1998) developed scales to measure predisposition to dissent. A confirmatory factor analysis was conducted after recoding reversed items. It duplicated Kassing's scales for articulated, antagonistic/latent, and displaced organizational dissent. Scale reliability was tested using Cronbach's alpha as the measure. The alphas for articulated (.67) and antagonistic/latent (.69) scales were marginal, but based on Kassing's previous development, the alphas were deemed within acceptable range. The alpha on the displaced dissent scale was .81.

Situations in Which Dissent Is Acceptable/Unacceptable. Based on Redding (1985), seven questionable organizational decision points were identified. The situations were conceptualized as, "When a decision is …":

- Clearly illegal.
- Clearly immoral or unethical, such as violating human rights.
- Psychopathic or insane and therefore dangerous.
- Incredibly stupid.
- Insensitive to human needs and feelings.
- Inefficient or impractical.
- Irritating or annoying.

Based on a review of literature, six categories of dissent tactics were defined as:

- Assertively confront management about the inappropriateness of the decision.
- Work to sabotage implementation of the decision.
- Agitate others to join you in arguing and working against the decision.
- Leak information to external stakeholders about the decision.
- Use facts selectively in making a case against the decision.
- Stand by and say nothing.

TABLE 8.1
**It Is Appropriate to Take Extreme Measures to Undermine
a Management Decision**

When the Decision Is	Never	2	3	4	5	6	Always	Mean
Illegal	11.4%	4.9%	4.0%	7.1%	13.1%	24.7%	34.8%	5.19
Immoral/ unethical	11.4	4.3	3.8	6.8	15.0	24.7	34.1	5.20
Psychopathic/ insane	10.4	3.5	4.0	8.1	12.5	18.5	42.9	5.36
Incredibly stupid	37.4	18.4	9.8	15.3	10.3	5.9	3.1	2.73
Insensitive	31.2	16.7	12.2	17.2	10.8	7.6	4.4	3.00
Inefficient/ impractical	45.3	20.1	9.7	10.5	6.9	4.4	3.1	2.39
Irritating/ annoying	61.0	18.3	7.0	7.4	4.1	1.1	1.1	1.83

When Do PR Practitioners Express Dissent? Respondents were asked when they believed it would be appropriate to take extreme measures, such as leaking information, to undermine a poor management decision (Table 8.1). The strongest dissent response was for decisions that were psychopathic or insane (42.9% would *always* dissent in such cases), illegal (34.8% would *always* dissent), or immoral or unethical (34.1% would *always* dissent). Of equal interest, more than 10% said they would *never* dissent under any of the aforementioned circumstances.

The public relations professionals were least willing to dissent with management decisions that were irritating or annoying (61.0% would *never* dissent in such cases), inefficient or impractical (45.3% would *never* dissent), incredibly stupid (37.4% would *never* dissent), or insensitive to human needs (31.2% would *never* dissent).

In response to the "When" research question, then, public relations professionals are most likely to dissent when a management decision is psychopathic, illegal, or immoral.

How Do PR Practitioners Express Dissent? Public relations professionals provided insight about both when and how they would express dissent when we asked them to consider specific responses to three specific scenarios. The most acceptable response to questionable management decisions was to assertively confront management. The mean response from practitioners to the question of whether they would assertively confront management in the face of an illegal decision was 6.34; in the face of an immoral or unethical decision the mean was 6.10; in the face of an inefficient or impractical decision the mean was 4.79 (see Table 8.2). All other responses had means below the scale midpoint; that is, the responses trended toward *never* rather than toward *always*. Assuming that the higher the mean the more acceptable the tactic, the ranking of dissent tactics from most to least acceptable was:

- Assertively confront management ($M = 5.74$).
- Use facts selectively ($M = 3.62$).
- Agitate others against ($M = 3.35$).
- Leak information ($M = 2.34$).
- Sabotage implementation ($M = 2.28$).
- Doing nothing ($M = 1.89$ reverse coded, $M = 5.11$).

In summary, practitioners indicated that it is almost always acceptable to assertively confront management regarding a poor decision; it is almost never acceptable to remain silent about a poor decision (Table 8.2).

Inefficient or Impractical Decisions.   In looking at the first specific situation, the most acceptable response to a management decision that is perceived as inefficient or impractical is to assertively confront management. The highest percentage of respondents said they would *never* leak information (72.1%), sabotage implementation (66.5%), agitate others

TABLE 8.2
Means of Responses × Situations

| | | Management Decision Is … | | |
| | | Immoral/ | Inefficient/ | |
Behavioral Response	Illegal	Unethical	Impractical	Combined
Assertively confront	6.34	6.10	4.79	5.74
Use facts selectively	3.90	3.74	3.22	3.62
Agitate others against	4.04	3.64	2.38	3.35
Leak information	2.92	2.60	1.51	2.34
Sabotage	2.83	2.52	1.50	2.28
Do nothing	1.58	1.72	2.41	1.89

against a decision (39.3%), or use facts selectively in arguing against an inefficient or impractical decision (32%). But most of these respondents also would not stand by and say nothing. More than one third (38.7%) said they would *never* stand by and say nothing when confronted with an inefficient or impractical management decision (Table 8.3).

In short, most practitioners would *never* leak information or sabotage implementation of a decision that is inefficient or impractical, but neither would they do nothing. Most would assertively confront management in the face of an inefficient decision.

Immoral or Unethical Decisions.   In the second specific scenario, more than half the respondents (51.2%) said they would *always* assertively confront management in the face of a decision that is immoral or unethical and that they would *never* stand by and do nothing (62.4%) (Table 8.4). When confronted with a management decision that is perceived as immoral or unethical, the highest percentage of respondents said they would *never* leak information to external publics (44.8%), sabotage implementation of the decision (44.6%), use facts selectively in arguing against the decision (28.4%), or agitate others to work against the decision (25.1%).

It again appears that the most acceptable tactic is to assertively confront management in the face of an immoral decision. Agitating others or using facts selectively are somewhat acceptable. Sabotage and leaking information are the least acceptable behaviors when dealing with an immoral decision.

TABLE 8.3
When a Management Decision Is Inefficient or Impractical
How Often Would You ...

Behavior	Never	2	3	4	5	6	Always	Mean
Assertively confront	5.1%	7.1%	6.5%	16.0%	27.0%	26.3%	12.0%	4.79
Sabotage	66.5	22.9	6.4	2.6	1.4	.1	.1	1.50
Agitate others against	39.3	25.5	11.0	11.1	8.9	3.3	.9	2.38
Leak information	72.1	15.4	5.5	4.5	1.8	.6	.1	1.51
Use facts selectively	32.0	15.0	10.0	12.9	10.5	11.8	7.9	3.22
Do nothing	38.7	22.7	12.2	17.3	4.6	4.0	.5	2.41

TABLE 8.4
When a Management Decision Is Immoral or Unethical
How Often Would You ...

Behavior	Never	2	3	4	5	6	Always	Mean
Assertively confront	1.1%	2.0%	1.4%	5.4%	12.9%	26.0%	51.2%	6.10
Sabotage	44.6	18.3	10.0	9.5	6.8	6.7	4.0	2.52
Agitate others against	25.1	14.1	7.3	13.6	15.5	13.7	10.7	3.64
Leak information	44.8	15.5	9.0	10.9	9.0	7.1	3.8	2.60
Use facts selectively	28.4	10.7	8.7	10.9	10.3	13.7	17.2	3.74
Do nothing	62.4	20.1	7.2	6.6	1.9	1.5	.4	1.72

Illegal Decisions. In the third situation, close to two thirds of respondents (62.4%) said they would *always* assertively confront management about a clearly illegal decision (Table 8.5). Even more (70.4%) said they would *never* stand by and say nothing in the face of an illegal decision. Still, the highest percentage of respondents would *never* sabotage implementation of an illegal decision (41.8%), leak information to

TABLE 8.5
When a Management Decision Is Clearly Illegal How Often Would You ...

Behavior	Never	2	3	4	5	6	Always	Mean
Assertively confront	1.0%	1.0%	1.0%	4.2%	8.2%	22.3%	62.4%	6.34
Sabotage	41.8	16.1	6.4	11.1	9.2	8.1	7.2	2.83
Agitate others against	23.6	10.4	6.9	11.0	12.3	17.5	18.3	4.04
Leak information	41.4	13.6	8.0	10.8	9.0	9.5	7.7	2.92
Use facts selectively	29.0	10.1	4.6	11.7	8.0	15.7	20.9	3.90
Do nothing	70.4	16.6	5.4	4.7	.9	1.0	1.0	1.56

external stakeholders about an illegal decision (41.4%), use facts selectively in making a case against an illegal decision (29%), or agitate others to work against an illegal decision (23.6%).

However, it appears that extreme tactics are more acceptable when trying to redress an illegal decision. Whereas 23.6% of respondents said they would *never* agitate others to work against an illegal decision, 18.3% said they would *always* agitate others in such a circumstance. Similarly, though 29% would *never* use facts selectively in arguing against an illegal decision, 20.9% would *always* use facts selectively in such circumstances.

When looking for trends in responses and circumstances, we find that it is *always* most appropriate to assertively confront management. The three highest means among the scenarios are to assertively confront management when faced with illegal decisions ($M = 6.34$), immoral or unethical decisions ($M = 6.10$), or inefficient or impractical decisions ($M = 4.79$). Next, responses are more situation-dependent.

TABLE 8.6
Means of Responses × Situation, Hierarchically

1.	Assertively confront management: illegal	6.34
2.	Assertively confront management: immoral/unethical	6.10
3.	Assertively confront management: inefficient/impractical	4.79
4.	Agitate others against: illegal	4.04
5.	Use facts selectively: illegal	3.90
6.	Use facts selectively: immoral/unethical	3.74
7.	Agitate others against: immoral/unethical	3.64
8.	Use facts selectively: inefficient/impractical	3.22
9.	Leak information: illegal	2.92
10.	Sabotage implementation: illegal	2.83
11.	Leak information: immoral/unethical	2.60
12.	Sabotage implementation: immoral/unethical	2.52
13.	Do nothing: inefficient/impractical	2.41
14.	Agitate others against: inefficient/impractical	2.38
15.	Do nothing: immoral/unethical	1.72
16.	Do nothing: illegal	1.56
17.	Leak information: inefficient/impractical	1.51
18.	Sabotage implementation: inefficient/impractical	1.50

When the situation is illegal or immoral, then agitating others to help or using facts selectively to make the case is acceptable. Respondents said it was unacceptable to dissent through leaking information or sabotage when a decision is simply inefficient or impractical (Table 8.6).

Factor Analysis to Develop Dissent Tactic Scales

Factor analysis of 25 survey items was conducted to develop dissent scales. Seven factors were identified for use as dissent scales. Dissent scales for public relations practitioners perform two functions. First, they allow us to determine the different demographic characteristics of those practitioners more or less likely to employ dissent tactics under certain scenarios. Second, because of the nascent nature of this line of study, they provide a means through which to continue this stream of inquiry in the future.

The first scale measures *nonthreatening management behavior* and includes four items: (a) when a decision is inefficient or impractical, (b) when a decision is irritating or annoying, (c) when a decision is incredibly stupid, and (d) when a decision is insensitive to human needs and feelings. These four items combine to measure attitudes toward management decisions that are perceived as unwise but nonthreatening. The higher the score, the more willing the respondent is to take an extreme measure to undermine management decisions that are nonthreatening. The scale has a Cronbach's alpha reliability measure of .93.

The second scale measures willingness to *agitate or sabotage* a decision and includes five items: (a) agitate others when a decision is immoral or unethical, (b) agitate others when a decision is illegal, (c) agitate others with a decision is inefficient or impractical, (d) sabotage a decision that is illegal, and (e) sabotage a decision that is immoral or unethical. These five items combine to measure extreme responses to extreme decisions. The higher the score, the more likely the respondent is to agitate others or work to sabotage a decision. The scale has a Cronbach's alpha reliability measure of .87.

The third scale measures willingness to *confront management* in the face of an extreme decision and includes three items: (a) assertively confront immoral or unethical decisions, (b) assertively confront illegal decisions, and (c) assertively confront inefficient or impractical decisions. These three items scale together to measure confrontation in response to illegal, immoral, or impractical decisions. The higher the score, the more likely the respondent is to assertively confront management. The scale has a Cronbach's alpha reliability measure of .80.

The fourth scale measures willingness to *stand by and do nothing* in the face of egregious (i.e., illegal, immoral, or impractical) decisions. The three items that combine in this scale are: Stand by and say nothing in the face of (a) inefficient or impractical, (b) immoral or unethical, or (c) illegal decisions. The lower the score, the less willing the respondent is to stand by and do nothing. The scale has a Cronbach's alpha reliability measure of .71.

The fifth scale measures a *serious threat* to the organization based on a management decision and includes three items: (a) when a decision is clearly immoral or unethical, (b) when a decision is clearly illegal, and (c) when a decision is psychopathic or insane. These three items combine to measure attitudes toward management decisions that are perceived as threatening. The higher the score, the more willing the respondent is to take an extreme measure to undermine threatening management decisions. The scale has a Cronbach's alpha reliability measure of .94.

The sixth scale measures *selective use of facts* in addressing (a) immoral or unethical, (b) illegal, or (c) inefficient or impractical decisions. The higher the score on this scale, the more willing respondents are to use facts selectively in making their case against a decision they believe is faulty. The scale has a Cronbach's alpha reliability measure of .94.

The seventh scale measures willingness to *leak information* to external stakeholders in the face of (a) illegal, (b) inefficient or impractical, or (c) immoral or unethical decisions. The higher the score on this scale, the more willing respondents are to leak information to external publics. The scale has a Cronbach's alpha reliability measure of .79.

Differences by Gender. A multivariate analyses of variance (MANOVA) was conducted using the aforementioned scales as dependent variables and gender as the independent variable. Analysis showed that men are significantly more likely to aggressively confront management in the face of a questionable decision than are women. There was a significant main effect between gender and the confrontation scale ($F = 11.84$; $df = 1$; $p < .001$).

In addition, women are more likely than men to selectively use facts in making their case against a decision they believe is wrongheaded. There is a significant main effect between gender and the selective facts scale as well ($F = 4.87$; $df = 1$; $p < .05$).

Differences by Manager Versus Technician. Using the aforementioned scales, significant relationships were discovered by public relations role. The higher a practitioner is on the manager role, the more likely he or she is willing to agitate others or sabotage a decision they believe is wrong. There was a significant main effect between managerial role and the agitate/sabotage scale ($F = 12.45$; $df = 1$; $p < .0001$).

Furthermore, the higher a practitioner is on the technician scale, the more likely he or she is willing to agitate others or sabotage a questionable decision. There was a significant main effect between technician role and the agitate/sabotage scale ($F = 4.49$; $df = 1$; $p < .05$).

These findings suggest that when a public relations practitioner strongly identifies him or herself as either a manager or a technician they are more likely to agitate or sabotage. Although this seems illogical at first blush, it suggests that both pure managers and pure technicians or specialists fall into the same category. Likely practitioners in both categories feel empowered by their position and specialty and are therefore more inclined to take a stand against what they perceive as an inappropriate decision.

Finally, the more likely a practitioner engages in managerial activities, the more likely he or she is to assertively confront management in the face of a misguided decision. There was a significant main effect between the manager role and the confrontation scale ($F = 60.43$; $df = 1$; $p < .0001$).

Differences by Type of Practice. Using the aforementioned scales, significant differences were found by area of practice. Analysis shows government practitioners are significantly less likely to selectively use facts than are agency practitioners ($p < .005$) or nonprofit practitioners ($p < .05$). There was a significant main effect between area of practice and the selective-facts scale ($F = 100.57$; $df = 4$; $p < .05$).

Practitioners in the nonprofit arena are significantly more likely to leak information to external groups than are corporate ($p < .005$) or agency ($p < .05$) practitioners. There was a significant main effect between area of practice and the leak scale ($F = 46.89$; $df = 4$; $p < .05$).

The fact that significant differences in both these scales occur within the nonprofit practitioner realm might be attributable to the type of person who is drawn to nonprofit work. Such practitioners might have a heightened moral sense and therefore be more inclined to actively work at correcting what they perceive as institutional wrongs.

Differences by Age. Four of the seven scales showed a significant difference by practitioner age. The nonthreatening scale ($F = 3.00$; $df = 4$; $p < .05$), confrontation scale ($F = 9.94$; $df = 4$; $p < .001$), do-nothing scale ($F = 4.37$; $df = 4$; $p < .005$), and selective-facts scale ($F = 12.13$; $df = 4$; $p < .001$) all showed significant difference by practitioner age.

Post hoc analyses were conducted to tease out the differences by age. On the nonthreatening scale, there was a significant difference between practitioners under age 30 and those in their 30s ($p < .01$). There also was a significant difference between practitioners in their 30s and those over 60 ($p < .01$). Finally, there was a significant difference between practitioners in their 40s and those over 60 ($p < .05$).

Practitioners over age 60 were more likely than practitioners in their 30s or 40s to believe intervention is acceptable in the face of non-threatening situations such as inefficient or impractical decisions, irritating or annoying decisions, stupid decisions, or insensitive decisions. Practitioners in their 30s were less likely than those younger than 30 to find intervention under such nonthreatening circumstances acceptable.

On the confrontation scale, practitioners younger than 30 were less likely than any other category—30s ($p < .0001$), 40s ($p < .0001$), 50s ($p < .0001$), or 60 and over ($p < .0001$)—to be willing to aggressively confront management in the face of a questionable decision. On the other end of the age spectrum, practitioners age 60 or over were more likely than practitioners younger than 30 ($p < .0001$), in their 30s ($p < .001$), or in their 40s ($p < .05$) to aggressively confront management about poor decisions.

On the do-nothing scale, practitioners younger than 30 were more willing to stand by and do nothing in the face of poor organizational decisions than practitioners in any other age category—30s ($p < .001$), 40s ($p < .05$), 50s ($p < .005$), or 60 and over ($p < .000$). Again, there was another significant difference on the other end of the age continuum. Practitioners age 60 or over were less likely than practitioners younger than 30 ($p < .000$), in their 30s ($p < .05$), or in their 40s ($p < .05$) to stand by and do nothing in the face of inefficient, immoral, or illegal decisions.

On the selective-facts scale, practitioners younger than 30 were more likely than any other age category—30s ($p < .01$), 40s ($p < .000$), 50s ($p < .000$), or 60 and over ($p < .001$)—to use facts selectively when making the case against illegal, immoral, or inefficient organizational decisions. Likewise, practitioners in their 30s were more likely to use facts selectively than practitioners in their 40s ($p < .005$), 50s ($p < .000$), or 60 and over ($p < .05$).

Differences by Professional Tenure.   The number of years that professionals practiced public relations had a significant influence on three of the scales. Confrontation ($F = 10.05$; $df = 5$; $p < .000$), doing nothing ($F = 4.23$; $df = 5$; $p < .001$), and using facts selectively ($F = 6.22$; $df = 5$; $p < .000$) all showed significant differences by professional tenure.

Practitioners who had been working in public relations for fewer than 10 years were less likely than every other category to aggressively confront management in the face of inappropriate decisions. They were significantly less likely than practitioners with 11 to 15 years' experience ($p < .000$), 16 to 20 years' experience ($p < .000$), 21 to 25 years' experience ($p < .002$), 26 to 30 years' experience ($p < .000$), or more than 30 years' experience ($p < .000$) to confront management about immoral, illegal, or inefficient decisions.

Practitioners with fewer than 10 years' experience also were significantly more likely than all but one other category to stand by and do nothing (10 to 15 years, $p < .005$; 16 to 20 years, $p < .005$; 26 to 30 years, $p < .01$; 30 years and over, $p < .005$).

New practitioners, those with fewer than 10 years' experience, also were significantly more likely than every other tenure category to use facts selectively when making a case against poor decisions. These junior practitioners were more likely than professionals with 10 to 15 years' experience ($p < .05$), 16 to 20 years' experience ($p < .000$), 21 to 25 years' experience ($p < .01$), 26 to 30 years' experience ($p < .000$), and more than 30 years' experience ($p < .05$) to use facts selectively in making a case against immoral, illegal, or inefficient decisions.

Professionals with 10 to 15 years' experience also were significantly more likely than those with 26 to 30 years' experience to use facts selectively in arguing against faulty decisions ($p < .05$).

Differences by Organizational Tenure.   The number of years that a practitioner worked for his or her present employer had a significant influence on only the confrontation scale ($F = 2.29$; $df = 5$; $p < .05$).

Post hoc analyses reveal that practitioners who have been with their organization for fewer than 10 years are significantly less likely to aggressively confront management than are those who have been employed with the organization for 16 to 20 years ($p < .005$). Professionals who have been with their organization for 16 to 20 years are significantly more likely to confront management than those who have been with the organization for 21 to 25 years ($p < .05$). This may suggest that when practitioners are just beginning with an organization, they are toeing the company line. Likewise, when they have been with an organization for 20+ years, they have bought in to the company line. There appears to be a dissent window between when practitioners have been with an organization long enough to be confident in asserting themselves in front of management, but they have not been there so long that they have fully embraced the corporate culture.

Predisposition Toward Dissent

Using the three levels of organizational dissent scales developed by Kassing (1998) (i.e., articulated, antagonistic/latent, and displaced predisposition toward organizational dissent), MANOVAs were conducted with gender, tenure with organization, tenure in the profession, age, and field of practice to determine if any of those variables influenced a predisposition toward dissent. There was no significant effect by gender or field of practice.

Predisposition by Age. Using the aforementioned Kassing (1998) scales, significant differences were found by age. There was a significant main effect between age and the articulated–dissent scale ($F = 4.04$; $df = 4$; $p < .005$), between age and the antagonistic/latent–dissent scale ($F = 6.17$; $df = 4$; $p < .000$), and between age and the displaced–dissent scale ($F = 2.93$; $df = 4$; $p < .05$). Post hoc analyses provide evidence of where within the age categories the significant differences arise.

On the articulated–dissent scale, practitioners under the age of 30 were significantly less likely to articulate dissent than any other age group. There was a significant difference between practitioners under age 30 and those in their 30s ($p < .001$), 40s ($p < .005$), 50s ($p < .01$), and 60 and over ($p < .005$). Younger practitioners are less likely to articulate their dissent compared to any other age category.

On the antagonistic/latent–dissent scale, practitioners under the age of 30 were significantly more likely to use antagonistic/latent dissent than every other age category. There was a significant difference between practitioners under age 30 and those in their 30s ($p < .05$), 40s ($p < .000$), 50s ($p < .000$), and age 60 and over ($p < .005$). In addition, practitioners in their 30s were significantly more likely than those in their 50s to express antagonistic/latent dissent ($p < .05$).

On the displaced–dissent scale, practitioners under age 30 were significantly more likely to displace dissent than were those in their 40s ($p < .05$) or 50s ($p < .01$). Additionally, practitioners in their 30s were significantly more likely to displace dissent than those in their 50s ($p < .05$).

Predisposition by Professional Tenure. There was a significant main effect between tenure within the profession and antagonistic/latent ($F = 7.13$; $df = 5$; $p < .000$) and displaced ($F = 2.99$; $df = 5$; $p < .05$) scales.

On the antagonistic/latent-dissent scale, practitioners who have been in the profession for fewer than 10 years were significantly more likely to use antagonistic/latent dissent than any other tenure category. Those with fewer than 10 years in the profession were significantly more likely than those with 10 to 15 years' experience ($p < .000$), 16 to 20 years' experience ($p < .000$), 21 to 25 years' experience ($p < .000$), 26 to 30 years' experience ($p < .001$), and more than 30 years' experience ($p < .000$).

On the displaced-dissent scale, newer practitioners again showed significantly more displaced dissent than their more senior peers. Those with fewer than 10 years' experience in the profession were significantly more likely than those with 16 to 20 years' experience ($p < .05$), 21 to 25 years' experience ($p < .005$), or 26 to 30 years' experience ($p < .01$) to exhibit displaced dissent.

Predisposition by Organizational Tenure. There was a significant main effect between tenure with an organization and antagonistic/latent dissent ($F = 2.47$; $df = 5$; $p < .05$).

Post hoc analyses showed how the significant difference was attributed. Practitioners who had fewer than 10 years with an organization were significantly more likely to use antagonistic/latent dissent than those with 16 to 20 years' tenure ($p < .05$) or 26 to 30 years' tenure ($p < .01$). Those with 10 to 15 years' experience with the same organization were significantly more likely than those with 26 to 30 years' experience ($p < .05$) to exhibit antagonistic/latent dissent.

Predictors of Dissent

Regression analyses were conducted with gender, age, tenure with organization, tenure in the profession, and manager/technician traits to investigate the relative influence of each variable on predisposition toward dissent.

On the articulated-dissent scale, the manager role is the most powerful predictor of predisposition toward dissent ($B = .327$, $p < .01$) followed by tenure in the profession ($B = .118$, $p < .01$) and technician role ($B = -.104$, $p < .05$). In short, the higher the manager role score, the longer the tenure in the profession and the lower the technician role score, the more willing the respondent is to articulate their dissent ($R^2 = .425$).

On the antagonistic/latent-dissent scale, manager role and tenure in the profession arose as significant predictors. Those who score high in manager role and have worked longer in the profession are less likely to express antagonistic/latent dissent ($B = -.183, p < .01, B = -.197, p < .01, R^2 = .364$ respectively).

On the displaced-dissent scale, manager role and age are negatively associated with displaced dissension ($B = .-075, p < .01, B = -.104, p < .01$, respectively). Female respondents are more predisposed to displaced dissent than male respondents ($B = -1.701, p < .01$). Those who have long worked in the profession are more predisposed to displaced dissent ($B = .112, p < .01$).

THE PROFILE STUDY

Following the Dissent Survey, we developed a Q-methodology study in an attempt to identify public relations practitioner types or profiles of practitioners with specific dissent tendencies.

Sample

A convenience sample of professional practitioners was developed. These practitioners were sent e-mail invitations to participate in an on-line Q-sort process. Fifty-one practitioners completed the study. Respondents included 29 women, 19 men, and 3 who did not provide complete demographic information.

By area of practice 16 respondents worked in agencies, 14 in corporations, 10 in nonprofits, 4 in education, 3 freelance, and 1 in health care. The sample was young, with 18 respondents in their 20s, 11 in their 30s, 8 in their 40s, 6 in their 50s, 3 in their 60s, and 1 over 69.

Twenty respondents were in the public relations profession for fewer than 5 years, 5 respondents were practitioners for between 5 and 10 years, 13 respondents had practiced for 11 to 20 years, 5 were practitioners for 21 to 30 years, and 5 were in practice for more than 30 years.

Twenty-four of the respondents had bachelor's degrees, 22 had master's degrees, and 1 had a juris doctorate. As for the course of study, 20 of the respondents majored in public relations, 9 in communication, 7 in English, 5 in journalism, 5 in political science, 3 in history, 2 in management, 2 in advertising, and 1 each in creative writing, engineering, marketing, and Spanish. Several of the respondents listed multiple majors.

Method

Based on findings from the Dissent Survey, 17 statements were developed and practitioners were asked to sort the statements along a continuum of most appropriate to most inappropriate public relations dissent response. Factor analysis of the statements revealed four types of public relations practitioners. Forty-four of the 51 practitioners loaded on the four factors, which are described next.

Dissent Profiles

Profile 1: The Balanced Practitioner. The Balanced Practitioner Profile is by far the largest factor with 25 practitioners split roughly evenly by gender—12 women and 13 men. This factor explains 37% of the variance in the population.

Respondents' areas of practice are education (two), agency (nine), corporate (six), nonprofit (six), and freelance (two). Eight practitioners in this factor have been practicing public relations for fewer than 5 years, one has been practicing between 5 and 10 years, six between 10 and 20 years, eight between 20 and 30 years, and two more than 30 years.

More of the practitioners in this factor have master's degrees (15) than bachelor's degrees (9). Five practitioners in this factor have degrees in communication, nine in public relations, two in advertising, three in history, four in English, four in journalism, two in political science, one in management, and one in Spanish. Some practitioners had multiple majors.

Eight of these practitioners were in their 20s, six in their 30s, four in their 40s, six in their 50s, and one in their 60s.

Demographically, this factor is varied. There are no discernible trends, beyond advanced education, that distinguish this factor.

Practitioners are distinguished by the statements they believe are most appropriate and most inappropriate (Table 8.7). Positive z-scores identify the statements these practitioners believe were most appropriate; negative scores identify those they believe are most inappropriate.

Seven statements were statistically different from the three other factors and thereby serve as a means of defining the Balanced Practitioner Profile. They are:

1. Most appropriate:
   - It's appropriate for PR pros to forcefully enlist the help of others to work against an immoral or unethical management decision (0.78).
   - PR pros should actively work to undermine impractical or inefficient management decisions (0.27).

- It's okay to use facts selectively in making your case if the goal is to derail an illegal management decision (0.04).
2. Most inappropriate:
   - When management makes an impractical or inefficient decision, it's acceptable to employ only supportive data in your argument against the decision (–0.11).
   - PR pros should stand by and do nothing when management is making an impractical or inefficient decision (–1.33).
   - PR pros should not interfere with management decisions even if those decisions are immoral or unethical (–1.37).
   - It's best to remain quiet when management is acting illegally (–2.02).

In summary, the Balanced Practitioner Profile is "balanced" because it spans experience, age, and area of practice. It is balanced because it spans circumstances under which dissent is appropriate (i.e., when a decision is illegal, immoral/unethical, impractical/inefficient). Furthermore, it is balanced because the acceptable dissent tactics run the spectrum (i.e., using facts selectively, enlisting the help of others, and undermining decisions).

Profile 2: The Internal Practitioner. The Internal Practitioner Profile consists of 11 respondents (2 men, 8 women, 1 nonresponse) and accounts for 18% of the variance in the population.

TABLE 8.7

Balanced Practitioner Profile

Statement	z-Score
PR pros should assertively confront management about illegal decisions.	1.94
The role of PR is to emphatically insist that management avoid acting in an immoral or unethical manner.	1.68
When faced with an impractical or inefficient management decision it is best to mobilize others to help argue or work against the decision.	0.91
PR pros should stand by and do nothing when management is making an impractical or inefficient decision.	–1.33
PR pros should not interfere with management decisions even if those decisions are immoral or unethical.	–1.37
It's best to remain quiet when management is acting illegally.	–2.02

Respondents' areas of practice are corporate (three), nonprofit (two), education (one), agency (three), and freelance (one). Five practitioners in this factor have been practicing public relations for fewer than 5 years, two have been practicing between 5 and 10 years, two between 10 and 20 years, and one more than 30 years.

Seven of the practitioners in this factor have bachelor's degrees; three have master's degrees. Five practitioners in the Internal Practitioner Profile have degrees in public relations, and one each in communication, English, political science, marketing, and engineering.

Four of these practitioners were in their 20s, three in their 30s, two in their 40s, and one in their 60s.

The statements that these practitioners believe are most appropriate and most inappropriate are noted in Table 8.8.

Only one statement served as a defining statement (i.e., statistically different from the other factors) for the Internal Practitioner Profile. It is most inappropriate:

- PR pros should offer internal private information to external stakeholders in order to squash an impractical or inefficient management plan. (−1.70)

TABLE 8.8
Internal Practitioner Profile

Statement	z-Score
PR pros should assertively confront management about illegal decisions.	1.89
The role of PR is to emphatically insist that management avoid acting in an immoral or unethical manner.	1.78
When management makes an impractical or inefficient decision, it's acceptable to employ only supportive data in your argument against the decision.	0.91
It's okay for PR pros to sabotage implementation of an immoral or unethical decision.	−0.93
The best way to fight an illegal management decision is to leak information to external audiences.	−1.31
It's okay to disclose confidential information to outsiders if the goal is to expose an immoral or unethical management decision.	−1.44
PR pros should offer internal private information to external stakeholders in order to squash an impractical or inefficient management plan.	−1.70

In short, the Internal Practitioner Profile represents practitioners who believe in asserting their opinions internally, but not sharing concerns or leaking information externally no matter the circumstances.

Profile 3: The Legal Practitioner. The Legal Practitioner Profile consists of five practitioners and accounts for 8% of the variance in the population. Three members of this factor were women, two were men.

Respondents' areas of practice are agency (two), nonprofit (two), and health care (one). Practitioners in the Legal Practitioner Profile have all been practicing public relations for 4 years or fewer.

Four of the practitioners in this factor have bachelor's degrees and one has a master's degree. Two have degrees in public relations, and one each in communication and creative writing. One practitioner had multiple majors. Four of the practitioners in this factor were in their 20s; one was in their 30s.

Practitioners in this factor were drawn to statements relating to behavior in the face of illegal decisions or actions (Table 8.9).

Six statements were defining statements for the Legal Practitioner Profile. That is, they were statistically different from the other factors. They are:

1. Most appropriate:
   - PR pros faced with management that is making an illegal decision should work to subvert implementation of the decision (2.43).
   - When faced with an impractical or inefficient management decision, it is best to mobilize others to help argue or work against the decision (1.78).
   - The role of PR is to emphatically insist that management avoid acting in an immoral or unethical manner (0.31).
2. Most inappropriate:
   - When management makes an impractical or inefficient decision, it's acceptable to employ only supportive data in your argument against the decision (–0.83).
   - PR pros should actively work to undermine impractical or inefficient management decisions (–1.22).
   - A good tactic to fight an illegal management decision is to agitate others to join in working against the decision (–1.28).

More than any of the other three profiles, this factor focused on how to deal with illegal behavior of organizational management. Practitio-

TABLE 8.9
Legal Practitioner Profile

Statement	z-Score
PR pros faced with management that is making an illegal decision should work to subvert implementation of the decision.	2.43
When faced with an impractical or inefficient management decision, it is best to mobilize others to help argue or work against the decision.	1.78
It's okay to use facts selectively in making your case if the goal is to derail an illegal management decision.	1.23
PR pros should actively work to undermine impractical or inefficient management decisions.	−1.22
A good tactic to fight an illegal management decision is to agitate others to join in working against the decision.	−1.28

ners in this factor were concerned with legal issues on both the most appropriate and most inappropriate ends of the spectrum. This profile therefore was labeled "The Legal Practitioner."

Profile 4: The Machiavellian Practitioner. The Machiavellian Practitioner Profile consists of three practitioners and accounts for 7% of the variance in the population. Two were women, one nonresponse. One of the respondents in this factor did not provide demographic material.

Their areas of practice are education (one) and corporate (one). Practitioners in this factor have been practicing public relations for fewer than 5 years (one) and between 10 and 20 years (one).

Practitioners in this factor have a master's degrees (one), and juris doctorate (one). They have degrees in public relations (one), law (one), English (one), and political science (one). Some practitioners had multiple majors.

Machiavellian Practitioners were 20 to 29 (1) and 40 to 49 (1).

Practitioners in the Machiavellian profile connected with statements that were more independent than collaborative (Table 8.10).

Five statements were defining statements for the Machiavellian Practitioner Profile. That is, they were statistically different from the other factors. They are:

1. Most appropriate
   • It's okay for PR pros to sabotage implementation of an immoral or unethical decision (1.98).

- PR pros should actively work to undermine impractical or in-efficient management decisions (1.45).
2. Most inappropriate:
  - When faced with an impractical or inefficient management decision, it is best to mobilize others to help argue or work against the decision (–0.31).
  - It's okay to use facts selectively in making your case if the goal is to derail an illegal management decision (–0.72).
  - The role of PR is to emphatically insist that management avoid acting in an immoral or unethical manner (–2.26).

The Machiavellian Practitioner is more likely to employ clandestine tactics than public tactics to achieve his or her desired outcome. They do not believe in the appropriateness of confrontation or collaboration, but do embrace sabotage.

PROPOSITIONS REGARDING DISSENT IN PUBLIC RELATIONS

Findings in the Dissent Survey and Profile Project suggest seven propositions regarding public relations professionals and forms of dissent:

Proposition 23: Dissent in public relations is situational but most often triggered by insane, illegal, or immoral decisions or actions.

TABLE 8.10
Machiavellian Practitioner Profile

Statement	z-Score
It's okay for PR pros to sabotage implementation of an immoral or unethical decision.	1.99
PR pros should actively work to undermine impractical or inefficient management decisions.	1.45
When management makes an impractical or inefficient decision, it's acceptable to employ only supportive data in your argument against the decision.	1.23
It's okay to disclose confidential information to outsiders if the goal is to expose an immoral or unethical management decision.	–0.91
It's appropriate for PR pros to forcefully enlist the help of others to work against an immoral or unethical management decision.	–0.94
The role of PR is to emphatically insist that management avoid acting in an immoral or unethical manner.	–2.26

When asked about willingness to engage in dissent activities, without citing specific activities, practitioners provided insight into their tolerance for poor organizational decisions. Practitioners were most inclined to dissent in the face of psychopathic or insane organizational decisions (42.9% said they would always dissent in that situation). Just more than one third said they would always dissent in the face of illegal (34.8%) or immoral/unethical (34.1%) decisions. But practitioners expressed much more tolerance for organizational decisions that were irritating or annoying (61.0% would never dissent), inefficient or impractical (45.3% would never dissent), incredibly stupid (37.4% would never dissent), or insensitive to human needs (31.2% would never dissent). Some professionals may be blindly loyal, too: more than 10% said they would never dissent, no matter the situation.

The three "I"s are situations in which dissent is most acceptable—insane, illegal, or immoral decisions. This finding suggests the trigger for dissent behavior among many public relations professionals is situations in which organizational decisions have the most potential for detrimental outcome, for both the organization and society. Analysis of these situations suggests an appropriate division by practitioners between loyalty to an organization and loyalty to society at large. When the decision is merely annoying, stupid, or insensitive, the organization may be harmed, but society is unlikely to be harmed and dissent is unlikely. But when the decision is one of the three "I"s, the organization and society may be harmed and dissent is more acceptable and likely.

> **Proposition 24: Public relations professionals embrace assertive behavior in the face of poor or inappropriate decisions in the organization.**

Among the dissent behaviors measured, assertively confronting management was the most accepted. On a scale in which 7 equals something they would always do, respondents said they would assertively confront management in the face of illegal decisions ($M = 6.34$), immoral or unethical decisions ($M = 6.10$), or inefficient or impractical decisions ($M = 4.79$). In all situations combined, assertively confronting management about its decision was the most acceptable response ($M = 5.74$). The next highest response was to use facts selectively ($M = 3.62$).

Within a dissent hierarchy, assertive behavior (persistent advocacy or pressure) is an Alpha approach. It is the first and most commonly acceptable dissent tactic. Understanding the general acceptance of this dissent behavior has pedagogical implications. This suggests the need to empower practitioners to engage in constructive conflict. Assertive confrontation can be addressed in classrooms and professional workshops. Such training would likely be embraced by practitioners and students because this is already a recognized and legitimate means of gaining influence in a contentious environment.

> ### Proposition 25: Practitioners prefer to express their dissent and deal with problems internally rather than with external audiences.

This proposition flows from the previous. Just as assertively confronting management is seen as the most appropriate dissent behavior, leaking information and sabotage are seen as the least appropriate behaviors. Nearly three quarters (72.1%) of respondents said they would never leak information in the face of inefficient or impractical decisions; 44.8% would never leak information in the face of immoral or unethical decisions; 41.4% would never leak information in the face of illegal decisions. Sabotage was also negated as an appropriate response. Two thirds (66.5%) said they would never sabotage an inefficient or impractical decision; 44.6% would never sabotage an immoral or unethical decision; 41.8% would never sabotage an illegal decision.

Together with the second proposition, these findings suggest that practitioners tend to prefer to keep their dissent behaviors aboveboard and inside the organization. They would prefer to confront rather than conspire. This finding affirms a strong need for political savvy when it comes to organizational activities. Because practitioners prefer to keep dissent in the organization, they need to understand just how to achieve political success without resorting to external or clandestine tactics.

> ### Proposition 26: Public relations specialists feel empowered to dissent, too.

As with previous research in public relations, this study found that being more managerial makes a difference. However, being higher on the technician scale also makes a difference. The findings suggest that being more managerial or more technician both lead to increased willingness to embrace specific dissent tactics. Practitioners who are higher on either the manager or technician scales are more willing to agitate others to help argue the case against a poor decision or to sabotage a poor decision.

These findings suggest the empowerment of specialists. Those practitioners who are higher on the technician scale are likely to be specialists in their particular area of practice (e.g., media relations, speech writing, event planning). Their expertise seems to provide them the same confidence as managers to engage in dissent behavior.

Another example that specialists are empowered to engage in specific dissent strategies is seen among nonprofit practitioners. Nonprofit practitioners were more inclined to selectively use facts to make their case than were government practitioners. Nonprofit practitioners were also more inclined to leak information than were corporate practitioners. Perhaps practitioners who are drawn to nonprofit practice are more engaged with the impact of their organization on society and are therefore more willing than other fields of practice to move beyond aggressive confrontation to express dissent through less commonly accepted tactics.

> **Proposition 27: When it comes to dissent, the age and tenure of public relations professionals count: They expand dissent options and spur expression of dissent.**

With increased age or tenure, dissent options are expanded. Older practitioners are more accepting of dissent responses to nonthreatening decisions. Practitioners under 30 years old are least willing to aggressively confront management. Practitioners over 60 years of age are more likely to aggressively confront management about questionable decisions. Younger practitioners are more willing to stand by and do nothing in the face of poor decisions. Older practitioners are less likely to do nothing. Younger practitioners (under 30) are more likely than other age categories to use facts selectively as a dissent mechanism.

Logic suggests that findings related to age and tenure would be linked. They were. Practitioners with fewer than 10 years of experience in public relations were less likely to aggressively confront management about a questionable decision, but they were more likely to use facts selectively.

Analysis of organizational tenure and its links to dissent provides insight into organizational culture. Our research suggests that early- and late-career practitioners—those practitioners who have been with an organization fewer than 15 years or more than 20 years—may be different from those who have been with an organization between 15 and 20 years. Midcareer practitioners, those who have been with an organization between 15 and 20 years, appear more likely to confront management in the throes of a bad decision than any other tenure category. This suggests there is a dissent window when it comes to organizational tenure.

Practitioners who are younger than 30 are less likely than other age categories to articulate dissent; they are more likely to express antagonistic dissent. These young practitioners are also more likely than other age categories to displace dissent.

The lack of will among young practitioners and early-career practitioners to rock the boat is understandable. They are working to curry favor with their superiors and build a career. They, therefore, do not want to make trouble through dissension. However, senior practitioners appear to understand the value of dissent to an organization, or to assume greater responsibility for dissent. Such dissent may keep an organization from making a decision that will affect its viability, at its most dramatic, or keep an organization from appearing foolish, at its least dramatic. Public relations educators and professional organizations can play a role in this regard by teaching students and new practitioners the value of dissent to an organization, as well as teaching appropriate dissent tactics in specific scenarios.

> **Proposition 28: Public relations managers and senior practitioners will articulate dissent rather than use antagonistic or displaced dissent approaches.**

When looking at predictors of dissent, we found that managers and longer-tenured practitioners were more willing to articulate dissent and less likely to use antagonistic/latent dissent. Managers and older practitioners were negatively associated with displaced dissent. In short, managers and long-tenured or older practitioners are willing to express their dissent to their superiors.

Again, age and status contribute to the confidence it takes to dissent with organizational decisions. Because managers and senior practitioners seem to see value in articulating dissent, they might mentor younger practitioners and nurture subordinates in appropriate ways to express dissent. For ethical practice of public relations, those who feel empowered to dissent owe it to others in the field to model and nurture dissent behaviors.

> **Proposition 29: Most practitioners are balanced or internal in their dissent approaches and use a variety of tactics to try to contain and resolve issues inside their organizations.**

Attempts to profile practitioners showed that most practitioners are balanced in their dissent approach. They endorse a variety of dissent tactics in a variety of circumstances. The second-largest number of practitioners is internal in its dissent approaches. These practitioners do not take concerns external, no matter what the situation, and they are opposed to leaking information to external stakeholders.

The findings that most practitioners either accept and practice a variety of tactics or prefer to deal with things internally are intuitive. The nature of the public relations profession is that of problem solving, which suggests the balanced approach to dissent. But, public relations is also a profession whose task is to advocate for a client or employer. Therefore, like the family that does not want to air its "dirty laundry," many practitioners prefer to protect the image of their organization by dealing with problems internally rather than externally.

Fewer practitioners were focused on legal issues when making dissent decisions. They were more willing to take a strong tack in the face of an illegal organizational decision. The fewest practitioners fell into a sort of Machiavellian category of dissent. Rather than dealing directly with management in an assertive way or enlisting the help of others, they prefer to go it alone. They are willing to sabotage, undermine, and use only supportive data in making their case against what they perceive to be a faulty organizational decision.

Dissent among public relations practitioners has been little explored and may be limited. However, findings from the Dissent Survey and Profile Study show the most common types of dissent among professionals and the circumstances under which dissent is most likely to be embraced. These studies also provide a means of conceptualizing categories of practitioner dissent and predictors of dissent.

As noted previously, effective dissent is often dependent on knowledge of organizational politics. We also believe that successful dissent is dependent on political will and political skill. These crucial influence variables are examined more closely in the next chapter.

CHAPTER 9

The Power of Political Will and Intelligence

> *Political power inevitably requires political will and political skill; in addition, it may draw upon privileged information or privileged access to those with any kind of power, and it may exploit in illegitimate ways the legitimate systems of influence.*
>
> —*Mintzberg (1983, p. 187)*

In discussing the importance of political willpower in the profession, a former public relations executive shared an anecdote about his first combat experience in Vietnam. He said his biggest surprise in the brief firefight was not the fear he felt nor a powerful adrenaline rush, but rather that some soldiers simply did not engage:

> At one moment during my first firefight, I remember taking a quick glance around me. Two men were balled up on the ground, trying to hide and not firing at all. Another was firing wildly with one hand while he kept his head down, turned away from the fight. I was amazed. Their lives, all our lives were on the line, yet they weren't fighting. They didn't fully engage.

The veteran went on to say that the willingness to engage was crucial in the profession, too, but it was often in short supply. In this chapter, we explore the place of political will and intelligence in public relations practice and analyze their interrelationships with power and influence. We draw from the interviews to illustrate practitioners' attitudes to-

199

ward political will and intelligence and suggest some ways to strengthen both in practice.

DO PUBLIC RELATIONS PRACTITIONERS LACK POLITICAL WILL?

Even the most cursory glance at scholarly or trade literature related to public relations practice reveals that the profession finds itself constantly having to elbow its way into decision-making circles. Furthermore, the profession is often seen as marginalized within organizations (e.g., Hon, 1997; Lauzen, 1992). To address these problems, scholars and professional leaders have called for public relations practitioners to become more managerial (e.g., Dozier et al., 1995; L. A. Grunig, 1992b; L. A. Grunig et al., 2002). Public relations educators are urged to teach students more strategic and managerial thinking and skills (e.g., Commission on Public Relations Education, 1999; Kruckeberg, 1998; Van Leuven, 1999; VanSlyke Turk, 1989).

With such a clear understanding of the need for empowerment in the profession, why is that power still so elusive? Is it a lack of political will? Is it a lack of political skill? Do public relations practitioners lack the will to convert power into political behavior and engage in power relations? For our purposes, we define political will as the internal fortitude, or biopower, needed to make use of political behavior. Political will is the willingness and discipline to assess the political environment and enlist influence tactics to achieve a goal.

Yukl, Guinan, and Sottolano (1995) found that managers generally "did not understand how to develop an effective influence strategy," and "most managers would benefit from formal training in how to diagnose their power relationships and how to use each type of influence tactic effectively" (p. 295). Public relations is not immune to this condition. There is evidence that some public relations professionals lack the political will and/or skill to have their voices heard.

A number of obstacles make it difficult for public relations professionals to muscle their way to the decision-making table (i.e., the dominant coalition). L. A. Grunig et al. (2002) outlined some difficulties public relations practitioners face in making their way into the dominant coalition. "The literature establishes that characteristics of practitioners themselves are a significant predictor of exclusion from the dominant coalition," they wrote (p. 149). They noted that individuals who lack business expertise, are naive about organizational politics, are passive, and have inadequate education, inadequate experience, or inadequate status within the organization, are less likely to be counted among an organization's decision makers.

Individuals have different skills and aptitudes for developing and using power, according to Pfeffer (1992). Nevertheless, he argued, success in organizations requires political knowledge, skill, and will, or knowing how to get things done and being willing to do them. Like L. A. Grunig et al. (2002), Pfeffer found that passivity among professionals is often a contributing factor to powerlessness.

Expanding the definition of acceptable organizational roles to include political behavior is another key to empowerment of the profession. How practitioners view the practice of public relations may limit their political will. As noted in chapter 1, McLaughlin (1972) argued for the advocacy role of public relations and cautioned against "the prevalent narrow concept of the role of public relations to be found among opinion leaders and public relations practitioners themselves" (p. 15).

Roadblocks to Political Engagement

If there is a lack of will to engage political skills, then it is essential to increase understanding regarding what may contribute to that lack of will. What may be real and perceived roadblocks to being politically engaged? First of all, "politics" is perceived by many as a dirty word. Political systems are viewed as illegitimate or, at best, "alegitimate," according to Mintzberg (1985). Therefore, political behavior "is neither formally authorized, widely accepted, nor officially certified" (p. 134). The first roadblock to overcome is the idea that political behavior is illegitimate. This point is illustrated later in the chapter. Many of the public relations practitioners we talked with distanced themselves from political behavior. But, Foucault (1988) was right. Political environments envelop us and to function successfully we must embrace that fact. Political behavior is embedded in the fabric of everyday life.

As noted in chapter 3, the dark vision of political behavior is demonstrated by Jackall (1988), who portrays the corporate environment as so political that individual survival and success become more important than meeting organizational goals. He described the corporation as a world in which rewards are more connected to self-promotion, patronage, or luck than to hard work. Such ignoble use of political skill and cynicism about organizational politics sullies political behavior and serves as a mental roadblock to its acceptance as a legitimate tool of the public relations professional. This requires a remapping of one's mental images of political behavior.

Our vision of political will is the polar opposite of Jackall's findings. Ours is one of employing political will and skills to be better and more effective public relations practitioners, that is, to work in the higher interests of practitioners' organizations and stakeholders. Far from the diabolical and self-serving label political behavior holds for many, political skill can actually be a more ethical and organization-focused means to serving organizations and publics.

Mintzberg (1983) made a persuasive case for the beneficial outcomes of political activity. He argued that politics help ensure the strongest survive and ascend to leadership; dissensus is created thereby exposing divergent issues, sides, and voices; organizational change is not unnecessarily blocked; and paths to decision making are open. If Mintzberg's view is accepted, then the perception of political activists as pariahs is dashed.

Beyond perceptual problems and out-dated mental maps that serve as roadblocks to engaging political will are common individual characteristics. There is a remarkable dearth of research regarding the personality traits of public relations practitioners, but some common characteristics arise anecdotally. The bridge-building and negotiating nature of public relations might suggest that many practitioners are conflict-averse. When faced with conflict, rather than engage it, many practitioners may choose avoidance. But this tendency toward bridge building and negotiating could be turned into political will. If relationship building is important, then public relations' leanings toward sensitivity and collaboration may be a motivator nudging practitioners in the direction of political behavior.

Several practitioners we talked with illustrated how attitudes toward gender also play out in organizational politics. One corporate practitioner explained how she overcame the problem through determination and political will. When asked about limits to influence in her work setting, she said:

> Being female, my gender, this is also a huge, huge issue. You cannot underestimate that, I mean, sometimes, it seemed like things happened every day, especially in the company where I was the only female executive. You might say something, in a meeting, for example, and they would look at you and say, "You're just being too sensitive." After about day five of that happening, I said, "You're right, I am. And it's a damn good thing I am because nobody else around here is. You guys could use some of that." It also manifested itself, not only in language, but in the way you were treated....
>
> They'd try to manifest it in the assignments, meetings, too. In meetings, I got myself known early on as someone who just invited herself to meet-

ings. And that caused a lot of consternation and resentment. I didn't wait on someone to tell me it was okay for me to attend a meeting, or to invite me to a meeting. In my view, PR is pervasive, and there wasn't a meeting going on anywhere about anything that didn't involve some aspect of PR, and I needed to know what was going on. So, I would just go.

Foucault (1988) noted that biopower, or internal strength, plays a role in whether an individual enacts political behavior. The practitioner just cited provides an illustration of political will leading to political behavior. The power of others, Foucault wrote, can be resisted. We can strategically attempt to modify the power of others through our own political behavior. Every power relationship, he argued, creates the opportunity or potential for resistance through biopower. Similarly, Holtzhausen and Voto (2002) contended that biopower, or the personal inner power found in self-knowledge and moral consciousness, is a positive form of power. They argued that power should be viewed as a positive force that is linked to inner strength. Weak biopower is a roadblock to political engagement.

Political behavior also may be constrained by a number of organizational factors. Waldron (1999) cited relationships between managers and employees, procedural structures, organizational culture and politics, job roles and stress, and external forces such as union or professional-community expectations as constraints to willingness or ability to manage upward.

The traditional roles of public relations practitioners may also be a limiting force. As noted in chapter 2, roles research is common in public relations scholarship. For nearly 30 years, public relations scholars have identified and developed two dominant roles for public relations practitioners—the technician and the manager (e.g., Broom & Dozier, 1986; Broom & G. D. Smith, 1979; Dozier, 1992; Dozier & Broom, 1995). The technician is generally seen as an order taker, whereas the manager is an order giver. The majority of public relations practitioners produce communication products and would, therefore, be labeled technicians. This leads to the view of public relations practitioners as production workers rather than influential strategists.

When public relations as a profession is seen as tactical rather than strategic, the potential as an agent of political change is limited. Allowing the profession to be defined as nonstrategic, regardless of the primary work product, is a collective failure and unnecessarily impedes political power among professionals. It may take individual political will to take a stand and overcome the pigeonholing of the profession by others in the organization. It also may require greater political will and increased political action on the part of professional associations.

Additional roadblocks to engagement in political behavior or conflict might simply include inexperience, lack of expertise, or uncertainty about how to proceed in engaging in a political situation. Because the profession often lacks clout, practitioners may believe the personal costs of political behavior are too high. Political behavior may risk job security, future promotion or assignments, and the like.

Bridges to Political Engagement

Despite the real and plentiful roadblocks to willingness to engage in political activity, we believe there are ways to build bridges to political will. What elements can encourage and embolden our political will to develop and enact our political skills? How and why should we develop an ability to embrace political conflict?

The first bridge to political engagement is increased experience and expertise. Waldron (1999) wrote: "As followers become more powerful through position, expertise, information access, or other power bases, their tactical options increase and their tactics become more assertive, particularly when the influence attempt appears to be 'legitimate' from the organization's point of view" (p. 275).

Longer work experience may increase political savvy, which may encourage influence behavior (Porter et al., 1990). Goals, job level and roles, age, power differences, and political and cultural factors all contribute to political will, according to Waldron. He also noted that changing organizational environments, an increase in the prevalence of work teams, flattening of organizations, and globalization are changing traditional ways of viewing leadership and may contribute to more involvement in decision making, which increases opportunities for political influence.

It is beneficial to view influence and political behavior as "not just an exercise in 'getting one's way' but also a process of exploring new ideas and questioning assumptions in dialogue with leaders and peers" (Waldron, 1999, p. 286). Asserting influence may have substantive and positive personal and organizational effects, according to Waldron. Rather than fearing political activity, it should be viewed as a process through which relationships are activated in order to improve organizational behavior and decision making. Therefore, another bridge to increased political will is understanding the positive and altruistic roles of political behavior.

Though many, including the authors, suggest that a lower position within the organization may serve as a roadblock to political will, Mechanic (1962) suggested that lower status is not necessarily detrimental to political influence and may be a bridge rather than a roadblock to political behavior. Because power is linked to dependence on one another within an organization, Mechanic argued that lower-level employees have substantial political influence, so much so that "organizations, in a sense, are continuously at the mercy of their lower participants" (p. 351).

Power in organizations flows through many channels and there are a multitude of ways to achieve it. Political influence can be enacted by lower-level employees by controlling access to information, people, and instrumentalities. Mechanic (1962) noted that factors affecting power include: specialization and expertise, levels of effort and interest in exercising power, personal attractiveness, use of coalitions, use of physical and social space, work and organizational rules, and more. In short, though role status and length of professional tenure may be viewed as roadblocks, Mechanic argued persuasively that they need not be.

Similarly, Holtzhausen and Voto (2002) suggested that membership in an organization's dominant coalition is not essential to being a successful public relations professional. In fact, such membership may actually co-opt practitioners and keep them from serving the needs of both the organization and its publics. Practitioners can build political power without authoritative power through the use of personal characteristics, relationship building, expertise, using access to powerful people, and building alliances at the micro level.

Though Mechanic (1962) and Holtzhausen and Voto (2002) provided a persuasive counter to the dominant theme in roles literature, Lauzen (1992) articulated the more common argument: Organizational position is empowering and may strengthen the will to take on political conflict. But even when lower-level practitioners *aspire* to management roles, they are more likely to enlist support for public relations activity as separate from other professional fields. In brief, when public relations practitioners are managers or aspire to management, there is a decreased likelihood of encroachment on the public relations role by other professions such as marketing, law, or human resources. Of course, decreased encroachment means empowerment for public relations.

Lauzen (1992) noted that:

> There are four keys to building powerful public relations departments.... 1. ... practitioners must aspire to the managerial role, 2. ... practitioners

must have the competencies necessary to enact the manager role, 3. The most senior practitioner in the organization must believe that public relations is a powerful organizational function, 4. … the most senior practitioners must enact the manager role. (p. 77)

Lauzen further suggested that political success in public relations is enhanced by centrality, substitutability, and ability to cope with uncertainty. Centrality is defined as a measure of the role the profession plays in organizational decision making. Substitutability is related to whether others in the organization can provide the same skills, products, or services. Ability to cope with uncertainty is simply the skill of dealing with the unpredictable. Lauzen wrote: "Public relations managers possess considerable strategic power. Such power is rooted in the manager's ability to increase centrality through participation in management decision making, and to reduce substitutability and uncertainty through the use of environmental scanning techniques" (p. 66).

Holtzhausen (2000) argued that political activity is enhanced by strong biopower, which increases the capacity for risk taking and arises from moral consciousness and self-knowledge. She suggested that public relations suffers from a narrow definition of the practice as "organizational communication management" (p. 93). From a postmodernist perspective, according to Holtzhausen, public relations is a politically charged profession. Public relations professionals are called upon to be organizational activists, challenging unjust views and behaviors by the organization and creating opportunities for dissent within the organization. "Public relations is about change or resistance to change," she wrote. "Public relations practitioners need to play an important role in activating and defining change in organizations and societies" (p. 110). In her view, public relations practitioners need to tap into their biopower in order to play the positive role of organizational activist.

Regardless of organizational position, if public relations practitioners understand their role as organizational activist and actualize their biopower, they have tremendous individual and collective political resources at their command. A. R. Cohen and Bradford (1989) identified an organizational resource that should be particularly useful to a profession whose days are spent building relationships and alliances. They wrote: "Too often organizational members fail to recognize just how much ability they have to influence others in the organization through mutually beneficial exchanges" (p. 5). In a profession that often defines itself as developing mutually beneficial relationships between an organization and its publics, surely internal relationships and alliances can be a bridge to political empowerment.

A. R. Cohen and Bradford (1989) provided a means for lower-level practitioners to engage their political will. They compared organizational relationships to currency that can be traded. Therefore, even if a practitioner does not hold a position of power, he or she can be politically productive by trading currency within the organization. Cohen and Bradford argued that effective organization exchanges arise out of seeing colleagues as allies rather than adversaries. When attempting to behave politically to benefit the organization, allies can be called upon and currencies exchanged.

A. R. Cohen and Bradford (1989) described several types of currencies that have potential for use in political situations: inspiration-related, task-related, position-related, relationship-related, and personal-related currencies. They argued that organizational actors often underestimate the range of currencies available to them. Identifying and using these currencies is another bridge to political empowerment. Building strategic alliances, engaging in exchange within the organization, and viewing colleagues as allies can be extremely helpful in accomplishing a political goal. More than that, because of the exchange nature of the organizational environment, such behavior can increase a practitioner's influence and build up currency for future political activities.

Finally, willingness to engage in political behavior may be situational and based on a view of the role of public relations. If the practitioner believes that the issue or conflict with which the organization is faced has the potential to hurt the organization or key publics, then she or he may be more likely to enact political power. This was evident in results in the Dissent Survey, where insane, illegal, and immoral decisions were powerful triggers for practitioner dissent.

If practitioners see the "emancipatory potential of public relations" as described by Holtzhausen and Voto (2002, p. 57), then political behavior will be seen as beneficial to the organization, key publics, and the practitioner. A key bridge to political will is an understanding by public relations practitioners that sometimes political activism can be the agent of positive change. Political activism can be a means of helping the organization do the right thing. But political activism is impossible without adopting political will

POLITICAL WILL IS USELESS WITHOUT POLITICAL INTELLIGENCE

After noting the roadblocks and bridges to political will, it must be acknowledged that political will is meaningless without political intelligence and skill. Political intelligence comes from understanding the political terrain within organizations, understanding where power bases exist or are perceived to exist, and how power is exercised. Mintzberg (1983) suggested that in addition to the political skills of persuasion, manipulation, and negotiation, political players "must have a special sense of how power flows ... where the formal and informal influence lies, which issues arouse attention, what friendships and rivalries exist, what the implicit and explicit rules of the organization are, and which of these can be broken and which evoked to win an issue" (p. 184). This is defined as mapping the political terrain.

Beyond reading the political map, political skills must be developed, according to Mintzberg (1983). He defined political skills as follows:

> [Political skills are] the ability to use the bases of power effectively—to convince those to whom one has access, to use one's resources, information and technical skills to their fullest in bargaining, to exercise formal power with a sensitivity to the feelings of others, to know where to concentrate one's energies, to sense what is possible, to organize the necessary alliances. (p. 26)

Pfeffer (1992) wrote that success in organizations requires understanding of the political terrain, that is, understanding how to get things done and being willing to do what it takes to achieve a meaningful end. Passivity is often a problem, but political knowledge is a power resource, according to Pfeffer. Mapping the political landscape, he said, involves understanding how power is distributed in the organization, understanding individuals and job categories that have power, knowing who benefits from organizational decisions and actions, who is consulted and when, who sits on key committees, and what power alliances exist.

"Political astuteness" is the term Spicer (1997) used for understanding the political environment in an organization. He wrote:

> The politically astute organizational member has knowledge of the formal and informal decision-making process: he or she knows how to use the system to his or her advantage. Knowledge of the process of decision making is grounded in being able to identify the key players and knowing their strengths, weaknesses, penchants, hidden agendas, personal likes and dislikes, and their degree of political astuteness. Political astuteness demands that one be aware of human nature, of the strengths and weaknesses of those with whom one interacts. (p. 145)

In review, the political map of an organization includes understanding when, how, and by whom decisions are made, who has influence and who can be influenced, recognizing your own power resources, identifying formal and informal alliances, and spotting the personal and collective goals and aspirations of key players in the situation or organization.

Linked to mapping the political terrain is understanding where power lies in the organization. Who holds the power and is the power real or perceived?

Williams and Wilson (1997) identified three types of power. *Perceived power* is that which is attributed to a person or group. *Participation power* refers to regular involvement in decision making across the organization by an individual or group. *Position power* is based on organization structure or reporting hierarchy. When identifying power centers within a political environment, this taxonomy serves as a useful means of parsing levels of power. Each type of power is real, but some are more legitimate and perhaps lasting (e.g., position power vs. perceived power).

Finally, understanding where power is exercised is essential to political intelligence. Central to the thesis of this chapter, power is found in political behavior. Such power is available at every level of an organization.

Understanding the type of power held by an individual, department, or alliance is essential to effective political mapping. Formal power, such as the power to make assignments and mete out rewards and punishments, is exercised by supervisors and management. But informal power is universally available and may be manifested in commonly accepted and unaccepted forms of dissent.

HEARD FROM THE PROFESSION: THE PLACE OF POLITICAL WILL, SKILL, AND INTELLIGENCE

We have previously cited data from the PR Success and Influence Interviews regarding sources of influence. Here we lift out and review some of the data that relate specifically to the use or lack of political will, skill, and intelligence. Political behavior was infrequently mentioned as an influence resource by respondents. In the Influence Interviews ($n = 65$), 16 practitioners said their greatest source of influence was political knowledge. Even fewer (seven) said risk taking or political will was their greatest source of influence. In the PR Success Interviews ($n = 97$), 18 respondents said their most valuable resource was political knowledge; 4 said that risk taking or political will was their most valuable influence resource.

In the combined studies ($n = 162$), 34 respondents said political knowledge was their most important influence resource. This response ranked political knowledge eighth in the PR Success Study and sixth in the Influence Study in terms of influence resources. The top two places in the studies went to relationships with others and professional experience with 75 mentions each. We argue that relationships with others might, at times, be political in nature. Individual definitions of political knowledge and political will may be varied and impact responses.

But, these findings empower the thesis of this chapter and much of the book—that public relations practitioners do not see political behavior as a legitimate and ethical means of influencing organizational activity and behavior. Many practitioners we talked with either did not think of political behavior as an empowering means to achieving a public relations outcome, or viewed political behavior with disdain.

In the combined studies, only 12 respondents cited political skills or knowledge as being a most-needed influence resource. But, respondents did not see politics as an impediment to their success either. Organizational politics and turfism were cited as a constraint on PR influence only 15 times.

Of those practitioners who said they valued political skills as an influence resource, this comment from an English agency practitioner was representative when asked what influence resources are most valuable: "Communications skills, particularly writing; and political awareness, or knowing what political effect your client's actions will have," he said. In his mind, tactics ranked before political strategy as an influence resource, illuminating the most common thinking among practitioners with whom we talked.

Others viewed political skills as relationship building. One corporate practitioner compared a large corporation to the U.S. Senate. "No senator can get anything done without the support of other senators," he said, metaphorically speaking.

Another practitioner from a U.S. government agency saw political knowledge as understanding the organization. He tackled organizational politics by assigning communications staff to sections of the organization, much like the news beat reporter. When asked about his most valuable influence resources, he said: "The knowledge of the organization, I tie that into the relationships.... We cover every center of the organization with specific individuals, and they know what they need to know, the people, they know it inside out. And so they bring their professional skills together with organizational knowledge."

Similarly, a corporate practitioner from the United States hailed relationships as important. Though using relationships is not inherently political, the range of categories he outlined could easily be developed into a powerful political network. He said his most valuable influence resource was as follows:

> Contacts, both inside and outside the company; people who know the most about a specific topic or are most knowledgeable about specific subject matter [are the most valuable influence]. Throughout my career, I have made it a personal priority to maintain a network of contacts, and I work very hard at it. These may include stakeholders such as management, and thought leaders, activists, advocacy groups, and a large number of people with whom I've worked over the years, etc. I've seen too many situations where a person will seek only the advice and counsel of internal contacts. That's fine as far as it goes, but if it's too internal, you're not going to get the full point of view on an issue. Good contacts are especially helpful if you don't have the necessary perspective on an issue but you know someone who does.

A female practitioner working for an activist organization in Australia put it more specifically and linked personal relationships and understanding of individual behavior to political outcome:

> Understanding organization politics is a separate influence resource, because if you're good at understanding how people operate you can figure that one out, although you need to start pretty quick smart when you join. I've always found that I've never had a real close, deep understanding of organization politics until I'm deep into the job (a month or two to figure it out).... Relationships with others, vital again ... because without that one you can't develop an understanding of organizational politics because you can't communicate properly with people and get them to share information with you in a friendly way.

Some practitioners acknowledged and embraced the value of political activity, but said they did not have enough political resources. When asked which influence resources she lacked, a corporate female practitioner from China said, "To me the political aspects of the job is a resource I could have more of, who you know.... Because people in an organization keep changing, that's a less reliable resource, but still important."

When a corporate practitioner from Canada was asked what additional influence resources were needed, she outlined the classic gap between being a good technical practitioner and being a strategic practitioner. She said:

> I wish I had more strategic thinkers and politically sharp members in my communication team. Don't get me wrong—I have a great group of people to work with. They have very strong and complementary skill sets—writing, editing, planning, understanding the Internet and other technologies, creative story ideas. I think they're experts. Being good at what they do, they're proud of that, and mostly content with that. I guess I wish a couple of them, at least, were more capable, or more interested in, the political and strategic management side of things in the company. I try to include a couple of training sessions each year to help in these areas, but it's not so much a lack of capability, I guess, as just a lack of interest. Or maybe they just see that as my role.

Other practitioners lamented the lack of political power of their position, or of those with whom they work, or the profession generally. A male corporate practitioner said:

> We have a weak vice president in charge of corporate communications. He's not highly regarded ... by senior executives. There are times ... when having another layer of stripes advocating on your behalf would be useful.... To rectify the situation, I work through cross-functional colleagues at a comparable level as the VP who are better regarded by most senior management. For example, I partner with the VP of Investor Relations. And with her, I can usually influence things that I couldn't do on my own.

A corporate practitioner from Sweden told us that he feels hamstrung by not being a card-carrying member of the dominant coalition. He said he maneuvers to overcome the exclusion: "I've learned to work around that to a great degree by developing solid relationships with people just below top staff level, for example, or someone who may not be at the top staff level, but has the ear of the top exec."

The profession generally lacks political willpower, according to one male practitioner at a U.S. agency. When asked what influence resources were lacking, he replied:

> [The profession lacks] personal or political will power. Is there enough of it in the profession? I don't think so. The issue is, is the PR executive or professional someone who has had enough wins or successes in their career, or do they just have the will, to go in and to deal with powerful decision makers, toe-to-toe, and to be comfortable and successful in doing it? How does the professional carry herself or himself in these types of tough or even confrontational situations?

A corporate professional in a technology business gave a more common reaction toward the idea of employing politics as an influence resource. He regarded politics as something to be avoided. He said his most valuable resources are, "performance record, organizational knowledge, and experience manifest through performance. All those are consistent with a place like this, which doesn't suffer wasted time, doesn't suffer fools, doesn't suffer gamesmanship and politics very well."

But some of the practitioners we talked with embraced political behavior and, in fact, cited it as a tactic they used to achieve success in a specific situation in which they helped influence their organization's decision. For instance, a corporate practitioner in the United States said he employed political tactics when he was faced with a vice president who made a new hire and assigned some of the respondents' responsibilities to the new executive. He said his most effective influence resources in that episode were as follows:

> Plain and simple, [they were] organizational politics. Knowing how things work in the company, who to approach, how to package and sell an idea or a solution, the language needed, etc. We assessed the situation when the new guy was hired. We couldn't see overturning the hiring decision, once it was done, but we thought we might co-opt him through a kind of end run.... The plan was co-option, and when we had it fleshed out, we went straight to the CEO with our idea and didn't wait to talk to the manufacturing VP about it. We did bounce the idea off two other directors who had some influence with the chairman. We armed ourselves with data about similar advisory boards in other companies, especially the company where our own CEO is a member of the board, and he's always telling everyone how well they do things in this other company. We picked up on that, and so we were able to make a strong case, get the CEO's endorsement, and then have him present the advisory board structure to the manufacturing VP and his new GR director.

A French corporate executive also cited his knowledge of organizational politics as an influence resource:

> It was a combination of tactics: knowledge of company politics, knowledge of how the company as a whole worked, understanding what the affiliate perspective was vis-à-vis headquarters, Europe and the world, my own professional communications expertise, market knowledge based on my facts rather than the affiliate's assumptions, and contacts ... contacts ... contacts ..., both at headquarters and within the affiliate.

Organizational factors serve as a limiting force on influence in a variety of ways. One practitioner from an agency cited organizational politics as a problem rather than a positive resource. When we asked her what in the organization impeded her influence, she said quickly:

> Corporate politics! That's what it is, all the time. There are silos within corporations, everybody has their own little fiefdom which they protect. To me this is what hinders overall corporate effectiveness. Period. And from a corporate communications standpoint, it totally hinders it. We deal with it all the time. They don't share information. The power of the corporation and the power of the job, their knowledge, their contacts, is their power within an organization and they guard it furiously instead of sharing. Being transparent, the more people talk to each other and share information, the better the ideas and the thinking. As a result, the better the business is. But I see it over and over and over again … the government people don't talk to the public affairs people, don't talk to the PR people, don't talk to the marketing people, don't talk to the internal communications people. You name it, they don't talk to each other. And it's all about power and politics, because they feel if they share it, they lose it. By far that's the biggest problem.

While talking does lead to better thinking, sometimes talking has to be forced through political will and skill.

Others also saw organizational politics as a limiting force. A practitioner working for government cited politics as an impediment to influence, but noted that her organization had worked around that problem: "We don't really have a lot of turf stuff in our organization because it's team based. The teams are designed to break that down. You are still going to have some people who are naturally that way, but they don't last too long around here in positions of leadership." A corporate practitioner from China said, "The politics boils down to who you know, who you trust, who has a certain agenda that may or may not be compatible with yours, how to get around certain people, and so forth." Though she noted that politics can be a limiting factor, this same practitioner said political skill was an influence resource she lacked.

A corporate practitioner noted that organizational politics, though problematic, do not have to be a roadblock to influence. "Each of the companies I worked for had different cultures, but once you figure out what the culture is, what the internal politics are, and the roles people play, they aren't limiting factors," he said.

We asked professionals what advice they would give new practitioners, and they both praised and ridiculed political behavior. A male practitioner from England lifted up political knowledge as a must-have asset for new practitioners: "You've got to emphasize the importance of gaining credibility and belief among your client or your company. You do this by showing a knowledge of the organization and its politics, which means you have to study, learn and understand it." Another practitioner from a nonprofit organization acknowledged the value of working together to achieve a goal, but negated the give-and-take that often is part of politicking:

> Don't advance the strategy or advance materials unless you're prepared to collaborate with the rest of your team on them…. There's a tremendous amount of influence when building consensus. You don't get any better influence than that. Learning how to do that is part skill and part intuition. It's something I think we all have the ability to do…. First, listen. Second, listen with an ear for building genuine consensus, not political consensus. And I would definitely make a distinction between them. And not trade-off consensus, but genuine consensus.

Discussions with public relations practitioners revealed that, generally, either they did not think of politics as an influence resource, or they thought of it in a negative manner. The final two illustrative quotations in this chapter demonstrate the spectrum of embracing and spurning political behavior.

When asked what public relations professionals could do to become more influential, a governmental agency practitioner showed disdain for political behavior:

> If we wanted to try empire building or play politics there are different things we could do. But, I think one of the reasons we're in a strong position is that we don't do those things, so we're trusted to do our role and we have credibility with others, that we're not just going to turn around and have ulterior motives and that kind of thing. I think that's pretty important.

Finally, a practitioner with an Australian activist organization seemed to embrace political will as a means to be included in decision making. When asked if she ever resorted to extreme influence tactics in her practice, she said:

> I find that unconventional tactics are oftentimes the only way you can succeed. You know the reason is because … public affairs officers aren't given a formal, inclusion or respect in top levels of organizations, so you sometimes have to resort to unconventional means to get the influence you require to make a difference.

So, from hours of conversation with public relations practitioners there was remarkably little talk about political skill as a positive influence resource. This is a cause of concern because when practitioners did talk about political behavior it was often as a roadblock to getting things done. If others in the organization are using political behavior as a means to advancing or curbing a cause, then we believe public relations practitioners should acknowledge and develop the power of political will and skill themselves.

PROPOSITIONS REGARDING POLITICAL INCLINATIONS IN PUBLIC RELATIONS

Data from practitioner interviews and a review of literature lead us to make two propositions:

Proposition 30: Relations of power in organizations are played out in the political behaviors of individuals and groups. Therefore, greater political will and skill among public relations practitioners can help empower the profession.

A modest fraction of 162 respondents said anything about political behavior. Those who did mention political behavior were inclined to refer to it as a detriment to influence. In addition, relatively few of the professionals mentioned political will or skill as influence resources they used. But, if the political will or skill of others can be a deterrent to public relations practice, then it follows that increased political will and skill in public relations professionals can help empower the practice. In short, these individual power sources can be mobilized and used in a positive and productive way.

Proposition 31: Relationship building, the key to successful public relations practice, is linked to political empowerment.

On one hand, professionals told us repeatedly in the interviews that relationships were one of their most crucial influence resources, especially those relationships with key decision makers. On the other hand, there was little talk about political will and political behavior. In our view, building alliances and coalitions, enlisting the help of others, and making arguments on behalf of various stakeholders are examples of political behaviors that are linked to or grounded in relationships. If relationship building is a strength of the profession, then political relationships can be nurtured to get things done in organizations and improve the standing of the profession in organizations and in society.

Whether they so name them, practitioners employ many other political behaviors on the job, for example, when they identify where the power lies related to a particular issue, assert their case with that power broker, inform unaware stakeholders of an issue, or bypass a roadblock in the organization to achieve an important goal. If practitioners can ac-knowledge that they already engage in types of political behavior, then perhaps they will begin to view organizational politics less as an impedi-ment, less as a dirty word, and more as a valuable tool for the advance-ment of ethical public relations. This acknowledgment alone could enhance political will among practitioners.

In the next chapter, we offer some specific suggestions for developing and nurturing political will and skill, and for strengthening other per-sonal, structural, and systemic sources of power.

CHAPTER 10

Breaking Out of the "Iron Cage" of Practice

> *We complain about not having more influence, but we don't or aren't will-*
> *ing to fight harder, to endure, to keep on trying to make changes. We too*
> *quickly become compliant in carrying out the role and practice as others*
> *would like us to, as we've always done. Or we play politics to maintain*
> *our position, status, benefits—not to try to influence organizational deci-*
> *sions and communications. So we need to try harder and be a little more*
> *courageous.*
>
> —Communications director at a power company

We live in a Golden Age of public relations according to some leaders in
the field (Elsasser, 2001), and the future of the profession appears limitless (D. J. Edelman, 2002). After all, practitioners today earn larger
salaries than ever before, more organizations invest resources in public
relations programs, and the ranks of trained professionals worldwide
continue to swell (Seitel, 2004). Professionals have at their disposal a
marvelous array of new technologies and channels that facilitate challenging work on an increasingly global scale. The scope of professional
training and networking opportunities is extensive, and association
conferences allow practitioners to wine and dine with business and political celebrities as they reaffirm the profession's importance and recognize achievements in the field.

At the same time, more colleges and universities offer more public relations courses and programs of study than ever before, the number of

undergraduate majors has never been higher, and there appears to be a shortage of qualified academics to meet the rising demand for education in the field. Also, despite some recent economic bumps, demand remains high for trained professionals who can help organizations communicate effectively in an increasingly noisy and message-cluttered world. Practitioners have become a driving force in a thriving industry of commercial and cultural message production that seems literally taken for granted in the construction of our daily world.

For others, however, all that glitters is not gold. It's unsettling that the profession still cites *defining itself and its relevancy* as one of its most important issues for the next decade (Gable, 2003). It's also no small irony that a profession so adept at constructing images for other individuals and organizations has failed to advance its own professional aura. Part of the problem is the high-profile media coverage devoted to any unethical practices in the profession, and there has been a "perfect storm of incidents" recently (Phair, 2005). Too many people still equate practitioners with shady publicists and spin masters who can always figure out a way to put a favorable twist on an unfavorable truth, or create a buzz about something inconsequential. Unfortunately, this "shine factor," a term used by several practitioners in the interviews, may be as alluring to some professionals as it is repelling to those outside the field.

Job dissatisfaction is also an issue. In one survey of nearly 800 practitioners representing diverse organizations and job levels, a majority said they were unhappy with their jobs and planned to leave their employer ("PR Pros," 2002). Lack of challenging work, poor company or professional leadership, and low salaries were the reasons cited most often for job dissatisfaction.

In addition, though practitioners are valued symbol producers and tacticians, there is scant empirical evidence to suggest that professionals today exert any more influence on strategic decision making than they ever have, or that they hold more power or are in better positions of power to advise and help organizations do the right things. Despite the extensive use of Alpha approaches in the past several decades, the profession is neither a serious power player nor represented in political power arenas in a number of organizations (Berger, 2005; L. A. Grunig et al., 2002).

Most of the professionals we interviewed acknowledged that power remains a crucial and contested issue in the field. Many also expressed concerns that the profession was at a crossroads in terms of its overall image and credibility. On any given day, they said, the future of the profession may appear golden and limitless, whereas the next day the reality and grind of daily practice are so discouraging that they contemplate finding a new job or career.

We explore these issues in this chapter and describe how the increasing rationalization of practice has both benefited and limited the profession, trapping it in a cage of paradoxes. We then summarize our descriptive theory of power relations and trace out a number of opportunities to increase influence in the profession at the individual, group, and association levels.

THE "IRON CAGE" OF PRACTICE

Through interviews we located and examined many individual, organizational, and professional factors that shape public relations, but developments and practices in the larger social system also influence and order the practice. Some of these are obvious, for example, the formulation of communication-related laws and regulations, the occurrence of professional or organizational misdeeds, political changes, the rise and fall of activist groups and social movements, the emergence and adaptation of new technologies, and wars and economic hard times, to name a few.

Other practices or forces are less visible, or perhaps so much a part of what we do, so taken for granted, that we are blind to them. One of the most powerful forces in this regard is what social theorist Max Weber called the "iron cage" in his provocative work, *The Protestant Ethic and the Spirit of Capitalism* (1958). This term refers to a technically ordered, increasingly rationalized and bureaucratized world that renders human work more efficient, focused, and productive. Weber theorized that the rise of large-scale organizations and enterprises in the last century was achieved in part through bureaucracy, a superior form of organization that orders and structures the actions of large groups of people to efficiently pursue and achieve organizational goals.

Bureaucracy rationalizes human actions by focusing individuals on: (a) the calculability (counting and quantifying) of their work products and assignments, (b) the efficiency of work processes themselves, and (c) the continual refinement of work practices and processes to eliminate waste and increase the similarity and predictability of operations from one location to another. Human actions are further rationalized through the development and use of professional specializations, which help manage complexities and control uncertainties, and the distribution of awards and power which are based on achievement of organizational goals and conformance to specified rules of conduct.

Weber (1958) believed that bureaucracy rationalization was a crucial spur to significant economic growth and spreading materialism and industrialism in the world. However, he concluded that this growth and wealth came with a high price: the diminution of human values, traditions, and individual spirit and potential. Thus, the iron cage represented a paradox of material advancements on the one hand, and constraints on human values and potential on the other.

Our world today bears many signs of bureaucracy rationalization, apart from traditional characteristics such as formalized job descriptions, professions and narrow specializations, chains of command, work rules, and so forth. Over the past two decades, for example, large organizations have regularly merged with and acquired other large organizations to grow even larger and increase profits. They accomplish this by spinning off jobs, eliminating duplicate functions, refining processes, leveraging materials buying power, reducing unit costs, and improving efficiencies in every part of the merged operations. Mergers and acquisitions represent a form of rapid, rationalized expansion.

"Hollow" corporations like Nike have so thoroughly rationalized manufacturing processes for their products—they purchase their athletic footwear from cheap labor outlets in other countries—that they now focus almost exclusively on manufacturing meaning and rationalizing the marketing and branding of products. Advertisers and other symbol production specialists manufacture symbols and logos and then infuse them with cultural meanings that inflate their true economic value (Goldman & Papson, 1998).

Organizations of all kinds routinely use new technologies to sort, process, batch, and continuously refine data sets to more precisely target and segment audiences for persuasive message appeals (Gandy, 1992). Technologies are more efficient, calculable, and predictable than human agents in these and related tasks.

The process of globalization itself is bureaucracy rationalization on a large scale that seeks to erase geographic, political, and cultural boundaries on the way to constructing, reaching, and servicing one vast, new global economic market more efficiently and profitably (T. L. Friedman, 2000).

This iron cage of bureaucracy rationalization shapes public relations practice, as well. We see it in the alignment of individual performance goals with functional goals and overall organizational objectives, and in the corresponding linkages between the attainment of these interrelated goals and individual compensation incentives. We see it in formal plans that specify measurable objectives, in reports that calculate the economic contribution of the function, in process maps and quality indicators that demonstrate efficiencies and refinements, and in established reporting relationships and protocols for interactions. We see it in professional-training programs and university courses and programs that underscore the importance of technical communication skills, production efficiencies, and measures.

Public relations professionals participate in bureaucracy rationalization when they refine and dehumanize message contents in editorial reviews, systematically produce reports and analyses that rationalize their value, develop unit missions and visions that order and direct their work lives, allocate scarce resources in the most cost-effective manner, and carry out research to refine messages, target publics, select best channels, and evaluate outcomes—all in the interests of achieving organizational goals and needs in the most efficient and effective manner.

Practitioners perpetuate bureaucracy rationalization in public relations practice when they try to do more and more with less and less, work smarter not harder, continuously raise the performance bar, treat the production and distribution of information as if it were a meaningful communication act in itself, and support talking and writing the talk rather than walking it.

Practitioners advance bureaucracy rationalization in public relations when they develop precise measures to legitimate and value their work and when they make strategic choices based on the economic value added calculus of prospective solutions. They do so when they spread this managerial and administrative ideology by taking up its vocabulary and internalizing and applying its thinking in their professional and social lives.

In these and many other ways, public relations practitioners reinforce and perpetuate an iron cage of professional practice. Because they are part of this system, and in some part responsible for its construction, they find themselves trapped inside it and forced to conform to its rules for action. The pressures for conformance with the organization and its needs and goals are insistent and powerful. So professionals usually comply, and in successfully and effectively complying they may contribute to organizational success, reap personal rewards, and advance their professional careers and standing in organizations.

One of the unspoken reasons that the vast majority of professionals we interviewed said that they serve the organization first and foremost is because they do and they must as a result of the very real pressures for conformance created by bureaucracy rationalization and manifested in organizational and professional cultures and structures. The belief in organizational service is nurtured and reinforced at virtually every turn in the workplace—in socialization processes, job descriptions, individual and unit performance objectives, the contents of formal communications, performance reviews, rewards and advancements, resource allocations, and the process efficiencies and continuous improvements dictated in productivity and quality programs.

In many cases, of course, compliance is exactly the right thing to do. Professionals do need to provide information to stakeholders and meet media deadlines. They do require formal plans and research to help organizations stay focused and deliver their messages to various stakeholders. They must prepare rational arguments to advise and counsel executives about stakeholder needs and the risks and benefits of particular decisions or courses of actions with respect to these publics. They want to work efficiently and cost effectively, achieve success, and be recognized as valuable contributors to the organization.

It's their job, after all, to produce communication materials and carry out strategic programs and campaigns that present and position their organizations in the world because they do compete for attention and action in a busy and cluttered market place. How else does an organization present, differentiate, sustain, and attempt to make meaning of itself in the modern world if not through such communication acts?

But though compliance is often what professionals do, and often absolutely the right thing to do, some professionals occasionally accept the risks of nonconformance and say *no,* or *wait a minute,* or ask *why,* or speculate *what if,* or demand *what about others?* In certain situations, some professionals sometimes resist—they push back against the formidable powers of organizational decision makers and bureaucracy rationalization to advocate other solutions and possibilities that may be more humanely rather than economically or technically oriented, or that otherwise represent the right things to do. Some public relations professionals choose to resist, and in doing so they draw from power resources, they select and use a variety of influence tactics, and they exert their will and engage in power relations in organizational political arenas.

A DESCRIPTIVE THEORY OF POWER RELATIONS AND INFLUENCE OPPORTUNITIES

In this book, we have focused on power relations and described a number of ways in which public relations professionals can increase their influence in practice. Gaining influence is necessary to stand eye to eye with others in political venues when important decisions are being shaped and constructed through power relations. Power, at least in a latent form, is ever present, and power relations are virtually inescapable at the individual, group, organizational, and social system levels.

At the highest level the country's founding document, the Constitution, is a prescriptive for power relations in terms of how we are governed. The authors were so concerned with power in its many forms in the political system that they specified how power should be allocated and separated among institutions so that no single one predominated, so that appropriate checks and balances were built into ascribed power relations to prevent abuse and protect individuals.

Power also is formally and structurally assigned in organizations through charter, that is, the legal and administrative specification of policies and hierarchical positions, the designation of accountabilities, and the construction of various power-holding and decision-making committees and groups, protocols, and practices. Public relations practitioners often see their own power deficiencies reflected largely in these very structural forms—no seat at the table, lower-level reporting relationships, and limited resources. However, structural power is only one type of power in organizations, and power relations also are generated and infused by other individual, relational, informational, and systemic power sources, each of which may be developed and mobilized for use.

In our model of power relations, we argued that public relations practices are defined and structured through systems of power-over, power-with, and power-to relations. These relations have their roots in social and organizational forces; they are driven by various internal and external influencers who interact in myriad political arenas to try to shape and produce favored political outcomes in the forms of problem definitions, decisions, actions, resource allocations, communications, and ideologies.

To compete effectively in political arenas, influencers draw from a wide range of individual, structural, relational, informational, and systemic power resources. They convert these resources into Alpha and Omega influence tactics and strategies, selected according to the nature of the issue or problem, the target(s) of influence, the strength of opponents, available resources, the prospective costs of winning or losing, and their own levels of political skill, will, and intelligence, among other factors.

Our research suggests that Alpha approaches are frequently and widely used, perhaps because they best conform to bureaucracy rationalization. These tactics include rational persuasion, coalitions, pressure approaches, inspirational and emotional appeals, legitimation, exchange, consultation, and ingratiation. Omega approaches are riskier and more controversial and are used far less often by fewer practitioners, generally when sanctioned tactics have failed to produce the desired outcome in more problematic legal or ethical situations. Such approaches include boat rocking, refusing to implement changes, allowing changes to fail, planting rumors in the grapevine, leaking information to outside publics, constructing alternative interpretations of formal actions and communications, fabricating data to support a favored position, and whistle-blowing.

HOW CAN PR PROFESSIONALS GAIN INFLUENCE?

To get things done in organizations, then, and especially to help get the right things done, public relations professionals must better understand power relations. They also must recognize, develop, and mobilize more diverse influence resources even as others do so. Above all, they must enhance their political skills and intelligence and possess the will to engage in the many political arenas in which power relations are enacted. Most of the professionals we interviewed expressed concerns about power relations and their corresponding deficiencies. They indicated that the presence or absence of power affected the practice of public relations in many ways in their organizations, and accepting and understanding that reality was a necessary first step in becoming more influential.

A handful of practitioners disagreed. They said that public relations wasn't or shouldn't be concerned with power or persuasion; rather, public relations was about helping people to dialogue, negotiate, compromise, and accept and understand the point of view of others in order to take the right decisions. We agree that this is an important set of professional goals. But the process of "helping" others to get there and to arrive at such positions inevitably involves advancing arguments, countering arguments, overcoming uncertainties or deeply held attitudes and beliefs, and making persuasive appeals to try to convince others that these very approaches are the right ones. Calling *influence*, *persuasion*, or *power* by other names, or refusing to acknowledge them, neither negates their presence nor their use in and around the practice of public relations.

If power is present and important in practice, how can professionals become more influential? What approaches can they take? What can the profession and academia do? We have partially answered these questions through numerous quotations and examples in the book that reflect the insights and suggestions of professionals we interviewed. In the next few sections, we offer a number of additional ideas. We return first to professionals in the Influence Interviews and then share some of our own recommendations for strengthening personal, structural, and systemic resources.

We directly posed the aforementioned questions to the 65 professionals in the Influence Interviews, and their responses are presented in Table 10.1. Many practitioners named several approaches or factors that might increase their influence in organizations, and overall more than 35 wide-ranging approaches were cited.

Personal Influence Resources

Nearly all of the professionals mentioned strengthening personal or individual resources. For example, slightly more than one quarter of the practitioners (18 of 65) said that consistent high performance led to

TABLE 10.1
How PR Professionals Gain Influence

Approach	F	M	Total
Demonstrate high performance	10	8	18
Develop measures for PR value	6	6	12
Obtain more PR education	6	5	11
Develop more, better relationships	3	8	11
Strengthen political will, skills	6	5	11
Sell practice better to executives	4	6	10
Strengthen PR leadership	3	5	8
Obtain more business education	2	5	7
Strengthen PRSA	2	4	6
Enforce ethics in practice	3	3	6
Improve professional image	2	2	4
Obtain more organizational knowledge	0	3	3
Improve technical skills	0	3	3
Others (fewer than three responses)	7	16	23
Total	54	79	133

Note. N = 65.

greater influence. High performance was described as producing tangible results, delivering high-quality products and services, achieving project goals, and helping the organization successfully solve problems.

This approach reflects a bureaucracy-rationalization orientation as well as a strongly held cultural belief associated with the American dream: One can get ahead and be successful through hard work, perseverance, and accomplishments. In short, good work gets rewarded, and one of the rewards may be more influence. This belief is supported in the PR Success Study (Heyman, 2004), where PR executives said that high performance was a crucial factor in their own professional success. L. A. Grunig et al. (2002) also found that an excellent performance record and problem-solving capabilities helped gain entry to the dominant coalition.

Other approaches linked to increasing personal influence include obtaining more public relations (11) and business (7) education, strengthening political will and skills (11), selling the practice more effectively to executives (10), obtaining more organizational knowledge (3), and improving technical skills (3). The comments of two professionals captured the strong feelings of those who argued that practitioners needed to improve their political will and engage more forcefully and passionately in organizational decision making. One communication director for a large power company said:

> Biggest thing in my opinion: we give up too easily. We complain about not having more influence, but we don't or aren't willing to fight harder, to endure, to keep on trying to make changes. We too quickly become compliant in carrying out the role and practice as others would like us to do them, as we've always done. Or we play politics to maintain our position, status, benefits—not to try to influence organizational decisions and communications. So we need to try harder and be a little more courageous.... It's up to us largely, and we need to be a little tougher, have a little more staying power, cut down on the shine factor.

Another high-level executive linked passion for the work and courage on the job:

> We know too many people who have invested 25–35 years in the profession, who've done well and made money and so forth, but who've never really felt passionate about their work and were not able or willing to effectively engage, or had the courage to engage. We don't hear a lot about courage in the profession, but that doesn't mean it's not important. In my view it's a critical resource in short supply. Look, today jobs are rented. They are not forever. They are for less and less time, actually. So, at some

point the lease is up, whether it's a professional choice or an organizational choice. The key issue, then, is what contribution have you made, what have you accomplished, during the life of the lease?

Systemic Influence Opportunities

Individual capabilities and resources are not distributed equally, however, and practitioners point to other types of influence opportunities. Eleven professionals said that relational resources were the answer—more influence could be gained by developing new or better relationships with key decision makers. Only one professional identified a structural resource—a higher level reporting position—and no one named informational resources.

The second most prominent group of answers described systemic influence resources that are often located within professional standards, practices, and associations. These include developing measures to document the value of public relations (12), strengthening leadership within the profession (8), strengthening PRSA (6), enforcing codes of ethics in practice (6), and improving the image of the profession (4). Systemic resources represent potential influence for individual practitioners and the profession, but practitioners contend such resources are underdeveloped, especially measures to document and validate the practice.

Measurement in the Practice.   Many believe that measures are the Holy Grail in the profession because they would validate the contributions the profession makes to organizations in the same way that other organizational functions or professions are valued, for example, sales, production and manufacturing, distribution, and so forth. Once legitimated in this way, the soft science of public relations would become a harder science, thereby helping PR professionals gain entry to dominant coalitions, become more valued counselors and problem solvers, and obtain increased resources. This line of thinking is quite consistent with bureaucracy rationalization; that is, the increased rationalization of the profession through documented measures of its value will increase its worth to the organization and thereby enhance its stature and perhaps structural power.

However, there's another side to the measurement issue. We imagine that any established measure(s) for public relations would reduce to some type of numerical economic value, for example, a dollar indicator, reputation index measure, or return on investment percentage. Let's assume, for example, that the profession has documented the average return on investment by PR in organizations is more than 100% annually, or that effective PR programs contribute as much as 50% of the value of an organization's public image.

On the one hand, possessing such measures lends clout to the function in making claims about its value and need for resources. On the other hand, within increasingly rationalized organizations today, measures of value and performance are not fixed endpoints but rather moving targets. Measures not only indicate and assign value, but also represent a baseline or benchmark against which all future work is assessed. This means that the public relations function would likely be required to continuously improve against the baseline, just as sales personnel are expected to increase sales annually, production workers to reduce quality defects, and so forth.

Can public relations improve continuously on its baseline measures and increase its value to the organization? Moreover, if PR becomes valued and measurable in some manner, does this "accounting" aspect of the practice further open the door for encroachment into the profession's managerial ranks by accountants, sales managers, marketers, or others who may be considered more experienced counters and quantifiers? We don't know, so although we believe that improved and reliable measures are important to the profession, we also believe that associated issues need to be more closely examined.

Strong Leadership. Eight participants in the Influence Interviews said that stronger professional leadership would increase influence in the profession. They referred to leadership in two senses. First, several practitioners indicated the profession itself required more charismatic, nationally recognized leaders who could strengthen the profession's image, as captured in this PR director's comment: "Maybe we have to do something significant or unusual, something that would attract attention to us in an intense but positive way. Or maybe we just need some powerful, highly ethical, charismatic leaders to focus attention on what we do."

Several others called for improved development and educational opportunities for senior professionals. One agency practitioner said that PRSA should "develop workshops or courses aimed at a higher level of professional leaders. The few workshops I've attended are intended for younger, entry-level professionals. Influence, for example, would make an excellent topic for an advanced seminar."

Strong Professional Associations. Some practitioners also called for stronger professional associations to enhance the practice. They lauded

PRSA for its developmental courses and networking opportunities for young professionals but criticized the association for not providing more substantive professional programs and support. One agency director said, "I believe our associations are good networks of other professionals, and they're kind of fun to attend to socialize, but they're relatively inconsequential beyond that." A public affairs manager echoed this sentiment: "PRSA has some great conferences, but they don't really deal with things like influence. Or maybe they wouldn't call it that. They are more flash than substance."

Several professionals tried to explain why associations found it difficult to provide more powerful leadership, as reflected in this comment:

> As far as PRSA is concerned, there are a couple of reasons for their relative inaction.... Turnover at headquarters is so high, and that's not where the pressure [for action] comes from. The pressure comes from the membership, and I'm not really sure what they want. PRSA has Jim Carville and Mary Matalin speaking at the national convention, and everybody's walking around starstruck. Better the membership should go learn something rather than be entertained.

A number of practitioners suggested ways to enhance the professional value of PRSA and other associations. A corporate public relations director suggested that existing professional associations needed to compete less and collaborate more to advance the practice:

> I think PR groups like PRSA, Arthur Page, and all of those, they need to identify their own specialty on what they are going to be adding to the profession and focus on that and not worry so much about who's on what turf. And so, maybe Arthur Page is going to be all about leadership, or whatever. PRSA is going to be all about building interest in the profession and training young people for the first job or two. And then the PR Institute does measurement. Let's divide and conquer the issues that have been hampering us from moving forward and tackle things that we each are able to bring to the table.

Education. Professionals also said that public relations educators can play a role in increasing influence in the profession. One agency leader said that public relations classes needed to open up the topic of organizational politics in practice:

> Educators could do the profession a great service by helping to prepare professionals for the politics they will confront in organizations. Can you name a course in the university that's about organizational influences in PR

or GR? This seems so central to me, influence, and yet it's invisible in professional meetings and education.

Another practitioner said that educators could do more outreach programs with decision makers in organizations: "Expert PR educators can do more outreach into executive suites in corporations.... This may sound odd, but aren't intelligent academics as well equipped as any group to speak to PR, its role and value, its history, its problem-solving capabilities?"

Several professionals called for increased collaboration between academics and practitioners to jointly tackle problems in the field, as reflected in this comment by an agency executive:

> I think the best solution is a collaborative approach by universities and professional organizations to provide deep professional knowledge and experience combined with excellent research. And a path in developing critical thinking among professionals is probably the best solution. I think a series of leadership institutes should be developed in which you bring professors together with high-level professionals in teaching professionals how to be leaders and how to develop strategic decision making. So you need to develop the thinking, you need to teach knowledge based on experience. And you need to teach people both a research and academic understanding of the profession. We need leadership institutes, and we don't have them now.

MORE IMPLICATIONS FOR PRACTICE

Our research findings suggest some other opportunities for gaining influence in practice. At the individual level, professionals can benefit from developing, mobilizing, and using a larger number of influence resources and tactics. Practitioners told us that they favor and most often draw from relational and especially personal influence resources, that is, professional experience, expertise, and performance record. This is not surprising because these resources directly reflect our specialized system of expertise (Mintzberg, 1983), and they are often more controllable. Professionals are relatively free to develop technical and interpersonal skills, establish and nurture relationships, and expand their capabilities through ongoing experience and performance. Indeed, many organizations encourage and support professional-development programs, which are consistent with bureaucracy-rationalization approaches.

Similarly, practitioners told us that they most often used sanctioned influence tactics and relied most heavily on rational arguments and coalitions to attempt influence. Other tactics like legitimation, consultation, and personal and inspirational appeals were used far less often, though some professionals provided vivid examples of their successful application. Reliance on rational arguments and coalitions is common because they are comfortable and widely accepted influence tactics. In addition, bureaucracy rationalization is driven by rational data, deliberations, and decision making.

Political Intelligence, Skill, and Will

By relying on a few influence resources or tactics, however, professionals neglect other potentially powerful resources and tactics. For example, as we saw in chapter 9, relatively few professionals in the interviews acknowledged the importance of political intelligence, skill, and will in gaining and exerting influence, though nearly all said that power was a central issue in the practice and within their organizations. Understanding how power works in organizations, then, and how things get done, where they get done, and who's engaged in getting them done, are forms of political intelligence that seem crucial to successful influence attempts.

Likewise, the development and use of political skills—for example, persuasion and advocacy capabilities, the selection of appropriate influence tactics, and the polished execution of those tactics in political arenas—help professionals gain influence and become perceived as serious, legitimate participants in organizational decision making. Skillful political activity also helps compensate for weak structural resources or other power deficiencies (Brass & Burkhardt, 1993) and increases the number of tactical options available for use (Waldron, 1999). Yet, the processes and mechanics of sharpening political intelligence, and developing and refining political skills, receive limited attention in professional-development and educational programs, perhaps because these approaches are not consistent with bureaucracy rationalization.

We suspect that political will is one of the most important individual resources in power relations, though we know relatively little about it in practice. The Whirlpool case study underscored the importance of sustained political will by a handful of public relations managers in the company's communication change program. It may be that political will sharpens and increases with years of professional experience and the accumulation of organizational savvy (Waldron, 1999).

Results from the Dissent Survey provide some support for this possibility. Older practitioners, those with more than 10 years of experience, and those with longer organizational tenure were significantly more likely than younger, less experienced practitioners to articulate dissent and to confront management about immoral, illegal, or inefficient decisions. Less experienced practitioners were far less likely to engage and more likely to do nothing than older, more experienced professionals when management made poor or inefficient decisions.

In our view, the issues of political will and courage in public relations warrant a good deal more academic research and professional attention. Stronger political willpower is needed in public relations at the individual level and at the professional-association level to help organizations do the right things and advance the profession and its image. The profession requires more leaders and managers who will when necessary say *no*, or *wait a minute*, or ask *why*, or speculate *what if*, or demand *what about others?* We also need to know more about the role that political will plays in successful influence and how the profession can distill more political will out of educational and professional development programs.

The Public Relations Team

Some structural influence resources also appear to be underdeveloped or underutilized in practice. Professionals may increase their influence by making better use of such controllable resources as physical space, technologies, and especially, the public relations team. Few of the professionals (10 of 162 interviewed) identified the PR team itself as a most valuable influence resource, whereas slightly more practitioners (16) said that a larger or more capable team was a most-needed influence resource. Several practitioners said their teams were so dysfunctional that they turned to those in other functions or other organizations for professional support.

Clearly, a cohesive and developed professional unit that speaks with one voice can be an important source of power (Pfeffer, 1992). It will fare better in the competition for resources and gain perceived power. A cohesive unit facilitates joint actions and communications and reduces turnover, conflicts, and costs (Pfeffer, 1992). In addition, it seems possible that the collective performance record of team members, and the extent to which the team itself is perceived as crucial to problem solving, may lead to greater PR participation in political arenas and to increased structural power.

Some public relations leaders develop strong teams through individual development programs, team-building exercises and experiences, the distribution of new assignments to develop intrateam relationships, and similar approaches. Successful leaders also may use a team-first concept, wherein they work diligently to cultivate a shared vision, communicate candidly with team members, practice empowerment within the function, and set positive examples for professional behavior and ethical practice.

The process of developing team capabilities also provides opportunities for encoding political intelligence and other forms of knowledge into the function. One corporate public relations director described how he requires every new professional entering the unit to complete a comprehensive written and oral report on power in the company—how it is distributed among individuals and committees, what types of power are present in the organization, the strength and weaknesses of the PR unit with respect to power, where untapped power resources may reside, and so forth. The director used this process to underscore the importance of political intelligence and power relations in the organization and to assess the research capabilities, presentation skills, and relative "political nature" of new hires.

Another public affairs executive related how she included discussion of organizational politics or power relations at virtually every staff meeting. The agenda item might deal with a current issue in the organization or a hypothetical situation. Staff members analyze the issue and then develop possible solutions for it. They assess the likely needs and perspectives of other political influencers in the organization, the probable influence approaches of others, the ethical implications of various solutions, and the counterarguments or most effective approaches that the public relations unit might use.

According to the executive, these exercises are an easy way to stimulate discussion about power relations. In addition, because the exercises are included on most staff meeting agendas, they highlight the importance of influence in the organization and the need to continuously take the perspective of others who are involved in decision making. This executive believes that professionals have more influence than they recognize and often just don't know how to skillfully use it.

Shared Experience

Given the importance of experience as an influence resource, it also falls on public relations leaders to develop and mobilize this resource among team members. The professionals we interviewed provided a number of practical suggestions for sharing experience within the work team, including the following:

- Take inventory of the types of experiences held by unit members and identify areas for development.
- Periodically devote a unit meeting to sharing unusual or valuable professional and political experiences by team members. Analyze each story (experience) in detail and discuss learnings.
- Document and detail significant professional experiences of unit members so that such learnings may be shared with others who join the unit.
- Distribute new assignments to increase the diversity of experiences of team members.
- Include experience-building requirements into individual development plans or performance requirements.
- Routinely ask a unit member to accompany you to meetings or events that you might normally attend alone, for example, a budget review session, a financial analyst presentation, a meeting with local community officials, and so forth.

Systemic Resource Development

Systemic resources—and especially professional associations—represent potentially rich sources of power that appear to be underutilized or underdeveloped. In fact, the profession is blessed with a plethora of associations, institutes, societies, councils, foundations, and centers of varying sizes and missions that provide resources and carry out a variety of PR-related projects. In the United States alone these include the Arthur W. Page Society, Council of Communication Management, Council of Public Relations Firms, Global Public Affairs Institute, International Association of Business Communicators, International Public Relations Association, National Black Public Relations Society, National School Public Relations Association, Public Affairs Council, Public Relations Society of America, and Women Executives in Public Relations, among others.

Some institutes and centers are linked to academic institutions and focus on public relations and communication research initiatives that support the profession, teachers and students, and service. These include the Arthur W. Page Center (Penn State University), Betsy Plank Center for Public Relations Studies (University of Alabama), Center for Corporate Citizenship (Boston College), Corporate Communication Institute (Fairleigh Dickinson University), and Institute for Public Relations (University of Florida).

Given the number and range of professional organizations, it's surprising that fewer than perhaps one third of the estimated 200,000 public relations professionals in the United States (Seitel, 2004) belong to any association. A far smaller number are actively engaged in organizational activities or advancement. Associations compete with each other for new members and for professional attention, and their various missions and initiatives sometimes align, overlap, or conflict with each other. Nevertheless, the presence of multiple organizations is a sign of a growing profession and represents a set of systemic power resources that may help enhance the profession and increase its capabilities to help organizations do the right thing.

Within their existing structures and programs, such organizations might do a great deal more to help professionals understand the interrelationships among power relations, organizational decision making, and doing the right thing. Utilizing current forums and meeting venues, associations might offer workshops or round tables that develop greater insights into power relations, political intelligence, and the types of influence tactics and resources that may be developed and mobilized for use in practice.

Leadership Development. The Institute for Public Relations, the Arthur W. Page Society, PRSA, and other organizations currently offer some leadership development programs, but collectively they reach only a small number of leaders in the field. As several executives pointed out, the creation of more institutes that are dedicated to strengthening leadership in the discipline seems crucial to overall advancement of the profession.

The influence and effects of leadership—good and bad—cannot be overstated. Hundreds of books have documented the importance of leaders and leadership roles, and we only need to reflect on current leaders in business, government, the military, and other organizations and institutions in society to realize how the words and deeds of individual leaders make crucial differences in the extent to which we accord them and their organizations legitimacy, credibility, and respect. So, too, the future of the profession is closely tied to what its leaders know and don't know, say and don't say, and do and don't do. Encroachment into public relations management, decision dilemmas regarding doing the right things in practice, and the legitimacy and credibility of the profession are nothing if not central leadership issues.

The Value of Case Studies.   Associations now provide a wealth of information to members, but there are nevertheless opportunities for further developing informational influence resources. Case studies are a good example. Many teachers use cases in public relations courses to enhance learning by providing insights into what happened in practice: Cases help link the classroom to the practice field. Case studies also are used extensively in association training and development programs, and each year our associations recognize and honor successful practice cases through competitive awards programs.

However, most published and documented award-winning public relations cases are punctuated by what Pauly and Hutchison (2001) called "strategic silences." These important silences refer to the absence of information about decision-making difficulties, process problems, and power and structural disadvantages that public relations personnel likely confronted in the campaign or case. Absent such information or context, most cases appear as well-planned, seamless, and efficiently executed accounts of reality.

Of course, the reality inside most public relations projects is messier; things are seldom seamless, organizational politics intrude, and people disagree about what to do, who should do it, and what resources should be brought to bear. These and other in-case difficulties and experiences can provide powerful learning opportunities in both the classroom and the practice field though reflection, critical thinking, and discussion. Highly successful as well as thoroughly flawed and failed experiences characterize our rapidly changing, complex, and often messy world of work. Including some of the behind-the-scenes exigencies of practice in case studies would enhance these prevalent teaching and learning tools and provide a more accurate historical record of our professional experiences.

Association Outreach and Collaboration.   Outreach programs to CEOs and other key organizational decision makers have been little used to date. Some of the larger associations, that is, IABC and PRSA, often include in their conference programs a CEO presenter who speaks to the importance of public relations or exemplifies the practice in some way. Trade publications also periodically feature interviews with organizational leaders "who get it" about public relations. But there are many leaders who still don't get it or only pay lip service to the practice. This provides opportunities for various outreach initiatives to key executives and decision makers:

- Market CEO stories and cases that demonstrate and endorse the value of the practice.
- Obtain speaker slots for public relations leaders on the agendas of executive conferences, for example, Business Roundtable, Conference Board, and Chamber of Commerce.
- Deliver presentations in executive suites regarding the role and value of public relations. As several practitioners suggested, these briefing teams might include professional and academic leaders and be linked to a current issue, for example, corporations and trust issues. They provide a way of delivering third-party support to in-house professionals.
- Provide organizational decision makers with periodic reports of specific public relations initiatives that produced results and helped organizations solve problems. Such tightly focused mini cases could become one element in a series of ongoing communications between the profession and decision makers.

Perhaps these and related initiatives could be taken up by PRSA's College of Fellows, a group of highly successful and seasoned PR leaders who now play a largely ceremonial role in PRSA.

One promising outreach initiative is production and distribution of a book by the Arthur W. Page Society (Koten, 2004), *Building Trust—Leading CEOs Speak Out: How They Create It, Strengthen It, Sustain It*. The book is a collection of essay responses by 23 chief executive officers to corporate scandals and wrongdoings that have tarnished the image and reduced public trust of business early in the new century. The CEO-authors respond to this issue by sharing their views on the importance of integrity in business and outlining a blueprint for companies to follow to help create a sense of openness, honesty, and trust among stakeholders. The book represents association outreach at the highest levels and reflects close collaboration among Arthur W. Page Society officials, corporate public relations and communication officers, and chief executives of the companies.

Collaborative rather than competitive efforts among professional organizations provide other opportunities for strengthening and advancing the profession. Two more recent examples highlight this potential:

- The Global Alliance for Public Relations and Communication Management (www.globalpr.org) consists of 60 member organizations that represent more than 150,000 practitioners (Molleda, 2004). The alliance was launched in 2000 to unify, advance, and strengthen the profession globally and to create a forum for professional associations to share information and resources and facilitate joint efforts in addressing universal issues such as accreditation and professional standards. One of the alliance's first initiatives was development of a protocol to standardize by 2005 the various codes of ethics in the profession ("Worldwide Standard," 2003). The protocol outlines minimum requirements for ethical codes and emphasizes that professionals must be responsible to publics and broader society, as well as to their employers and clients.

- The Public Relations Coalition is a partnership of 19 leading U.S.-based associations and organizations that represent more than 50,000 public relations and communications professionals. In 2003, the coalition produced and distributed to organizational executives, public relations professionals, and academics a white paper titled, "Restoring Trust in Business: Models for Action" (Public Relations Coalition, 2003). The white paper urged American corporations to embrace ethical principles, develop processes to ensure transparency and disclosure, and elevate trust and ethics to the highest levels of corporate governance. The document also included guidelines for developing measures of trust.

Association Activism. Increased activism provides other opportunities for professional and academic associations to strengthen professional visibility and put papers and words into public action. Derina Holtzhausen (2000; Holtzhausen & Voto, 2002) has argued that individual public relations professionals need to play the role of activists to drive needed changes in organizational practices, processes, structures, and culture. She identified a number of individual and relational influence resources that practitioners could draw from in this role. Holtzhausen didn't mention systemic resources like professional associations, but we believe that the tens of thousands of practitioners, teachers, and students who are now members in our various associations constitute a potentially large and influential activist community.

By adopting more activist approaches on a national level, these organizations may reinforce and strengthen the power of individual practitioners and enhance the profession's image. Activist approaches would combine advocacy with action to change or initiate some policy, practice, or situation related to the profession. One approach, for example, might be to increase the public voice and profile of PRSA or other professional associations in the light of deplorable public relations practices or organizational wrongdoings.

As a first step, an association could establish a public relations review board that would examine alleged wrongdoings in depth and publicly report its findings. An activist professional association would use such situations to publicly denounce professional wrongdoing, pressure its members, and call for greater social accountability and transparency within the increasingly larger social, economic, and political organizations that populate our world.

An activist association would routinely provide its perspective on current issues to media outlets and advocate directly with organizational leaders on these issues through a variety of communication channels. (We note that PRSA is increasingly following this approach through its Advocacy Alert System to members and its communications with national media outlets.)

An activist association would engage in the public policymaking process through issues management approaches or civil disobedience tactics—member marches, sit-ins, demonstrations—to lobby enthusiastically and in the glare of media spotlights for greater organizational transparency or empowerment, or to call attention to positive social-responsibility programs and exemplary organizational actions.

An activist association would also take a tougher stance on wrongdoings within its own ranks. If associations are unwilling to police their own professional membership, then codes of ethics and practice lose their teeth, and enforcement of such codes is abdicated to others outside the profession.

A recent incident (Gaschen, 2004) provides an opportunity to reflect on proactive versus activist approaches in the profession. In April 2004, the mayor of Los Angeles directed city departments to halt the use of outside PR firms. The action was taken as a result of an investigation by the *Los Angeles Times* that revealed that Fleishman-Hillard, one of the country's largest PR agencies, had apparently benefited from close ties to city government. The agency reportedly had made political contributions of more than $130,000—and provided pro-bono services and fund-raising support to the mayor—during a period when it had won more than $20 million in new business from various city departments. Just prior to the mayor's announcement, Fleishman-Hillard tried to end the controversy by replacing its office manager in Los Angeles and terminating its contracts with city government.

Other PR agencies and professionals in the region were concerned about damage to the profession's image, and PRSA leaders convened a meeting of some independent professionals and agency representatives to address the problem. The group quickly issued a media statement regarding the action, prepared a letter for the mayor, and by-lined an op–ed for the *Los Angeles Times*. The group also offered to develop standards for PR request for proposals (RFPs) and outlined longer-term plans to prepare materials to demonstrate the value of public relations, meet with city officials, involve affinity marketing groups in supporting actions, and become involved in relevant town hall meetings, among other activities. In short, individual professionals came together and collectively developed a rational and proactive approach to deal with an image crisis, a joint initiative that some described as the first of its kind among competing agencies.

Some also might describe this as an activist approach, but the way area and national professionals framed the issue, and the types of actions they may not have taken, suggest otherwise. The statement and initial comments by the professionals argued that the mayor's action was a short-sighted solution that unfairly singled out one profession of many that served the city and its departments. This frame suggests that the punishment didn't fit the crime and/or that it should have been applied equally to other professions in the region that might be guilty of similar violations.

This approach begs two questions: Was the profession equally critical of the public relations agency and actual practice that precipitated the crisis? And did the professionals develop action plans to try to prevent similar practices within its ranks in the future? Based on Gaschen's (2004) article, we just don't know, though PRSA and other associations did subsequently convene an ethics summit in early 2005 to discuss this and other ethical incidents. But if the profession didn't condemn such practices and attempt preventive measures, then at least in the public's mind these "absences" may have been seen to tacitly endorse the practice. An activist approach also would have been concerned with defending the profession's image, but it first would have condemned the actual practice and policed its own ranks.

BREAKING OUT OF THE IRON CAGE, CHASING OTHER POSSIBILITIES

The diverse professionals whose voices punctuate this book have grounded our study of power and influence in practice fields in corporations, agencies, nonprofit organizations, educational and religious institutions, and social-movement groups. Their stories and shared experiences highlighted some common issues and perceptions about public relations. Many share concerns about the profession's image and a continuing shortage of power in practice. Many rely on similar power resources in their work—personal and relational resources—and tend to use similar influence tactics inside their organizations—rational arguments, coalitions, and pressure approaches. Even more, however, the practitioners spoke to some compelling differences that divide and conflict the profession.

They expressed strong and diverse views about their roles and those of professional associations. Many said they serve their organization first, but a number added that they felt they needed to better serve other publics and even society at large: They just weren't sure how to do so, or how to do so without jeopardizing their careers. In addition, though virtually all of the professionals agreed that advocacy was a central job requirement, they were sharply divided in the Dissent Survey in terms of the extent to which advocacy is appropriate, and the types of dissent that should be practiced, when confronted with inappropriate management decisions.

By examining dissent practices and other Omega approaches, we learned that professionals also hold a wide range of views about what the right thing means in practice, and how far they might go in defense of doing the right thing. At one end, a small number of practitioners said they would unquestioningly follow their marching orders and not dissent in virtually any situation, no matter how egregious. At the other end, a small number said exactly the opposite: They would use any number of unsanctioned influence tactics, including whistle-blowing and leaking information, to try to halt or expose illegal and unethical decisions or actions.

The majority of professionals between these endpoints said they would not stand by and do nothing, nor were they ever likely to use Omega approaches. They said that doing the right thing means following established codes of ethics and advancing rational arguments to attempt to persuade organizational leaders to take a more appropriate decision.

Such differences may simply reflect the wide range of professionals included in our samples. It also may be that differences like these are common in other professions, or characteristic of a growing, evolving profession. Alternatively, such differences may reflect an essential dissonance in the field, or a set of powerful paradoxes within which the profession appears trapped:

- On one hand, professionals are the voices of organizations to the world; on the other, they must advocate inside organizations in the interests of external publics whose needs may very well conflict with the goals of their parent organization.

- Professionals are required to possess the technical skills to manufacture and distribute communication products and services for organizations, and, at the same time, they must command a strong managerial perspective and corresponding set of political and strategic capabilities to advocate forcefully in decision making.
- Practitioners must participate effectively in ongoing power relations with other influencers in the dominant coalition, but these very influencers shape the practice of public relations by controlling access to the dominant coalition, limiting structural resources, and just refusing to get it about public relations.
- Professionals believe that power is one of the most important issues in the field—they all want a seat at the table—yet they seldom address power in their association forums and appear uneasy with its corresponding vocabularies of resistance, dissent, and activism.

These paradoxes mirror the essential paradox in Weber's iron cage: Driven to calculable efficiencies and performance requirements in the overriding service to their organizations, professionals lose touch with or sight of the larger potential and promise of the field that is wrapped so deeply within layers of practice—to help organizations do the right things.

The Role of Resistance in Doing the Right Thing

Conceptualizing a resistance role for public relations has provided a way to abstract power relations out of practice and closely examine them in terms of influence resources, tactics, and decision-making arenas. This approach also allowed us to explore some related subfields that often lie within the shadows of power studies—unsanctioned influence tactics, forms of dissent, and professional activism. A resistance role may be seen as an additional role in public relations, or as another dimension of the managerial role. In either case, the role underscores the need for professionals to understand power relations, develop and draw from a wide range of influence resources and tactics, and cultivate a political will sufficient to engage in decision making in the many contested political arenas that exist inside most organizations.

A number of practitioners expressed uneasiness with our vocabulary of resistance. They told us that terms like *unsanctioned* tactics, *dissent*, and *activism* were inappropriate in a profession that defines itself in terms of productive relationships with others inside and outside organizations. Some suggested softer phrases such as *forms of advocacy*, and *professional mobilization* or *development*. Perhaps the larger issue was an unexpressed concern that seeing, expressing, and enacting the profession in terms of power and resistance is impractical and could ultimately prove damaging to individual professionals, as well as to the profession itself.

We have argued the opposite: Professionals need to become more powerful and influential in order to best help their organizations, advance the profession, and change executive and public perceptions of the role and value of the practice. Traditional advocacy efforts and Alpha approaches have produced inconsistent advances for the profession. If public relations is to become more influential, professionals must better understand the practice in terms of power relations and relationships that already exist, common as oxygen, in most organizations. They must scrutinize and cultivate their professional power resources and identify those that are underutilized or that need further development. They must consciously mobilize and bring to bear in political arenas a wider range of influence strategies and tactics, sanctioned and unsanctioned. And above all, professionals must develop stronger individual and professional political will to engage in power relations.

Some might suggest that this is an argument for subversion, but we are not advocating attempts to undermine organizations or organizational leaders. Nor are we suggesting that public relations professionals have all the answers or possess some superior moral compass. The profession's checkered history clearly suggests otherwise. Rather, we have reflected on the public relations profession "outside" of a more traditional Alpha perspective. The administrative and managerial ideologies of expertise and efficiency that underlie this perspective have obscured to some extent the essential power-rootedness of practice and a corresponding purpose and potential of practice—to try to help organizations do the right things.

The Right Things in Practice

We have referred to this normative framework for practice throughout the book. As professionals in our research have demonstrated, doing the right thing is easier said than done. Clear differences of opinion exist regarding what the right thing means in practice in given circumstances.

In our view, doing the right thing in the profession of public relations must work at several levels.

At the most basic level, and this is one thing about which most professionals agree, doing the right thing means:

- Serving organizations professionally, effectively, and honestly.
- Following existing laws and regulations.
- Conducting practice within the frameworks of prevailing ethical codes and guidelines at the organizational, professional, and societal levels.

At another level, many professionals also appear to agree that doing the right thing means:

- Advocating for power-with relations that incorporate the voices and points of view of others inside and outside the organization who are not present in political arenas but who are nevertheless affected by political outcomes determined in those arenas.

Professionals differ, however, with respect to the extent they are willing to advocate, and the types of approaches they are likely to use, in these relations of power. Individual decisions grow increasingly difficult as the nature of the decision moves from one that is impractical, inefficient, or insensitive, to one that may be illegal, unethical, or immoral.

We have added another, more political level at which doing the right thing in practice also means:

- Resisting or pushing back against the many forces that constrain the practice and seek to limit it to a technical niche function.
- Working actively to try to change organizational structures, policies, practices, and processes that prevent or impede power-with relations.
- Developing and mobilizing additional personal, relational, structural, informational, and especially systemic influence resources to strengthen the overall profession at the individual, team, and association levels.

Doing the right thing is tied to individual decision making. Many decisions are easy, undertaken with little conscious effort because they are simply part of practice or because they closely follow the established laws and rules of the profession and the land. Other decisions are far more complex and difficult. Should we, for example, use the grapevine as a channel to "correct" an inaccurate but formal account of organizational events or actions? Should we do so if the outcome is to make an organization more accountable for candor in its formal communications? Is this the time, or is there ever a right time, to leak information to outside publics? Should we blow the whistle on illegal or unethical activities? Should we stage professional demonstrations to protest the misuse of communications by other professionals or organizations?

As Gass and Seiter (2003) suggested, each of these and other situations represent a line in the sand or a threshold that we confront: "Each of us has a perceptual 'threshold' that helps us make decisions about what strategies are acceptable and what strategies are not.... Strategies that do not cross the threshold are more likely to be used" (p. 248). These thresholds vary from person to person, but most people have a strong desire to play by the rules established by their organization, profession, and society.

This makes it even more difficult to cross over some thresholds or boundaries that constrain the practice. At the least, however, we need to deliberate these boundaries to determine whether they may be outdated, inappropriate, or artificially constructed or imposed. We cannot do so without considering the power relations that flow in and around the practice and shape what we do, how we do it, who we are, and how others see us. Breathing into practice a dose of power considerations may help us imagine some other potentials and possibilities for the profession. Or it may even inspire us to say *no* or *wait a minute* more often or with more conviction, or ask *why*, or speculate *what if*, or demand *what about others*, on the way to trying to do the right thing.

In the end, doing the right thing is about expressing and living values. We conclude with a brief public relations manifesto, which reflects professional values and beliefs associated with a resistance role in public relations.

CHAPTER 11

A Public Relations Manifesto

> *PR professionals must help shape the image of their work: too often they are perceived as prevaricators and hustlers, spinners with little integrity who work in a world of fluff. I think the image of a PR professional should be a strategic thinker with a wide range of knowledge going well beyond PR who can talk in concrete terms and who embraces integrity.*
>
> *—Agency practitioner with 30 years of experience*

HEAR THIS:

I am not a flack, a shill, a barker, a hustler, or a spinner.

I do not stonewall, distort language, construct false images, or blindly follow directions in the interests of my organization or its leaders.

I am a public relations professional, and what I do is serve my organization, society, and profession as a communicator, professional, advocate, and activist.

I believe in public relations and its potential to help organizations make good choices and do the right things in a dynamic, often turbulent world. This is the core of practice. Everything else I do, from writing to media relations to strategic counsel, is wrapped in layers of practice around this fundamental belief.

I understand that our global world is increasingly populated by large economic and political organizations that touch and shape our public and private lives through their words and actions. Small and regional organizations can have dramatic impact on their levels. Given their considerable powers, I believe organizations bear obligations for doing the right thing even as they are driven to sustain themselves, compete, and grow. My job is to help my organization balance these needs and its social responsibilities.

I am a communicator, and my organization needs my skills. In a cluttered world of organizational signs and symbols, there is little more crucial than our words and actions, our communications and interactions with all the individuals, groups, and other organizations with which we are connected and interdependent. Through communications we gain or lose trust, build or destroy relationships, include or exclude others, unite or divide. We make meanings through communication, which is the real bottom line in an organization.

I will help my organization present itself to the world, capture attention and recognition, and acquire social legitimacy. I have the necessary technical skills to do so: I can write, edit, plan, program, place, produce, and evaluate communications.

I also possess managerial skills that are valuable in strategic decision making. I can help my organization resolve difficult issues, make tough strategic choices, and deal with uncertainties—all of which embody important communication implications. My voice counts when strategic decisions are on the line, and I will express it.

I am a professional and therefore responsible for excellence on the job in all that I do. There are no shortcuts to good work and high performance, and I will work and lead by example. I accept responsibility for my own actions and decisions—I will not blame others for them—and will follow prevailing laws, regulations, and organizational and professional codes of conduct.

I am an advocate, and my organization and society require advocacy. I will advocate to the best of my abilities for my organization with its diverse publics. I also will stand up for the rights, interests, and welfare of others who may not be present in decision-making arenas but who are nevertheless affected by my organization's decisions and actions. I will advocate, too, for policies and practices in my organization that promote open dialogue, greater transparency, shared decision making, and an empowering culture.

I am an activist, and my organization and profession need me to carry out this role. I believe public relations has the power to influence organizational decisions, actions, and communications, but must work to do so in practice. The profession will be weak if we believe it is weak. It will be weak if we practice it in that manner. Thus, I will develop my power resources and advance my political knowledge and skills.

Power relations shape what I do and what the organization does and says, and I must possess the will to engage in these relations. I will resist inappropriate or poor decisions in the organization and push back on the forces that constrain my ability to help my organization do the right thing.

I also will be an activist for and within the profession. Activism grows out of imagining or dreaming about other possibilities, rather than accepting things the way they are. Should we not dream of other possibilities in public relations? Can we not imagine constructing an alternative future for the practice?

What would be the benefit to society if all public relations professionals were ethical, or if ethical public relations professionals were more influential in organizational decision making?

What might be the image of the practice if our professional associations were more insistent on transparency in organizational communications?

What would happen to our image if we aggressively rooted out practitioners and practices that damage the reputation of public relations by doing the wrong thing?

What would it feel like to be a public relations practitioner in a world where the profession was admired and recognized for its relationship- and community-building achievements?

There are endless possibilities if we are willing to dream and then to act. I know that the power of one professional is significant, but the united power of a profession can breathe life into such dreams.

It is time for practitioners to unite as communicators, professionals, advocates, and activists.

It is time to convert our professional words and traditional advocacy efforts into a collective activism that is more engaged in the public world.

It is time for public relations to become a more powerful social force in the name of helping our organizations do the right thing.

I am committed to helping the profession do so.

These are my values, and this is my pledge as a public relations professional.

Appendix: The Dissent Survey

Please choose a number (between 1 = Never and 7 = Always) that indicates how well each of the following items describes the work that you do as a public relations practitioner. Please do not score items highly if others in the department do them, but you do not.

1. I produce brochures, pamphlets, and other publications.
2. I create opportunities for management to hear the views of various internal and external publics.
3. I take responsibility for the success or failure of my organization's communication or public relations programs.
4. I am the person who writes communication materials.
5. I represent the organization at events and meetings.
6. I maintain media contacts for my organization.
7. I make communication policy decisions.
8. I observe that others in the organization hold me accountable for the success or failure of communication or public relations programs.
9. I keep others in the organization informed of what the media report about our organization and important issues.
10. Although I don't make communication policy decisions, I provide decision makers with suggestions, recommendations, and plans.
11. I do photography and graphics for communication or public relations materials.
12. I am responsible for placing news releases.
13. I edit or rewrite for grammar and spelling the materials written by others in the organization.

14. Because of my experience and training, others consider me the organization's expert in solving communication or public relations problems.

15. I am senior counsel to top decision makers when communication or public relations issues are involved.

16. I use my journalistic skills to figure out what the media will consider newsworthy about our organization.

This is a series of statements about how people express their concerns about work. There are no right or wrong answers. Some of the items may sound similar, but they pertain to slightly different issues. Please respond to all items. Considering how you express your concerns at work, indicate your degree of agreement with each statement on a scale of 1 = strongly disagree to 7 = strongly agree.

1. I am hesitant to raise questions or contradictory opinions in my organization.

2. I refuse to discuss work concerns at home.

3. I criticize inefficiency in this organization in front of everyone.

4. I do not question management.

5. I'm hesitant to question workplace policies.

6. I join in when other employees complain about organizational changes.

7. I make it a habit not to complain about work in front of my family.

8. I make certain everyone knows when I'm unhappy with work policies.

9. I don't tell my supervisor when I disagree with workplace decisions.

10. I discuss my concerns about workplace decisions with family and friends outside of work.

11. I bring my criticism about organizational changes that aren't working to my supervisor or someone in management.

12. I let other employees know how I feel about the way things are done around here.

13. I speak with my supervisor or someone in management when I question workplace decisions.

14. I rarely voice my frustrations about workplace issues in front of my spouse/partner or nonwork friends.

15. I make suggestions to management or my supervisor about correcting inefficiency in my organization.

16. I talk about my job concerns to people outside of work.

17. I do not express my disagreement to management.
18. I hardly ever complain to my coworkers about workplace problems.
19. I tell management when I believe employees are being treated unfairly.
20. I talk with family and friends about workplace decisions that I am uncomfortable discussing at work.

Please try to imagine finding that your organization has made a decision you believe is inappropriate. On a scale of 1 = Never to 7 = Always, when would you think it appropriate to take extreme measures—such as leaking information—to undermine a managerial decision under the following circumstances?

1. When the decision is clearly illegal.
2. When the decision is clearly immoral or unethical, such as violating human rights.
3. When the decision is psychopathic or insane and therefore dangerous.
4. When the decision is incredibly stupid.
5. When the decision is insensitive to human needs and feelings.
6. When the decision is inefficient or impractical.
7. When the decision is irritating or annoying.

Now, please try to imagine your response to management decisions in the following situations. On a scale of 1 = Never to 7 = Always, how often would you respond in the described manner to a bad management decision? When management makes a decision that is inefficient or impractical how often would you:

1. Assertively confront management about the inappropriateness of the decision.
2. Work to sabotage implementation of the decision.
3. Agitate others to join you in arguing and working against the decision.
4. Leak information to external stakeholders about the decision.
5. Use facts selectively in making a case against the decision.
6. Stand by and say nothing.

When management makes a decision that is clearly immoral or unethical, such as violating human rights, how often would you:

7. Assertively confront management about the inappropriateness of the decision.
8. Work to sabotage implementation of the decision.
9. Agitate others to join you in arguing and working against the decision.
10. Leak information to external stakeholders about the decision.
11. Use facts selectively in making a case against the decision.
12. Stand by and say nothing.

When management makes a decision that is clearly illegal how often would you:

13. Assertively confront management about the inappropriateness of the decision.
14. Work to sabotage implementation of the decision.
15. Agitate others to join you in arguing and working against the decision.
16. Leak information to external stakeholders about the decision.
17. Use facts selectively in making a case against the decision.
18. Stand by and say nothing.

What do you think it means to "do the right thing" in public relations, when management is making decisions that you believe are inappropriate? [open-ended]

Finally, please answer a few questions about yourself.

Gender   M / F

Age _____

Years in the public relations profession _____

Years working for your current employer _____

Highest level of academic degree BA/BS   MS/MA/MBA   JD/PhD

What is the title of the person to whom you report directly?

> CEO
>
> Chairman
>
> President
>
> Vice President (any level)
>
> Director
>
> Manager
>
> Supervisor
>
> Other (specify)

How often are you directly involved in the organization's decision- and policymaking process?

1 = Never to 7 = Always

What best describes your field of public relations practice?

> Corporate
>
> Agency
>
> Nonprofit
>
> Other (specify)

References

Allen, R. W., Madison, D. L., Porter, L. W., Renwick, P. A., & Mayes, B. T. (1979). Organizational politics: Tactics and characteristics of its actors. *California Management Review, 22*(1), 77–83.

Allison, G. T. (1971). *Essence of decision: Explaining the Cuban missile crisis.* Boston: Little, Brown.

Bachrach, S., & Lawler, E. (1980). *Power and politics in organizations.* San Francisco: Jossey-Bass.

Bahniuk, M. H., Dobos, J., & Hill, S. E. K. (1991). The impact of mentoring, collegial support, and information adequacy on career success: A replication. In J. W. Neuliep (Ed.), *Replication research in the social sciences* (pp. 419–444). Newbury Park, CA: Sage.

Barbalet, J. M. (1985). Power and resistance. *The British Journal of Sociology, 36*(4), 531–548.

Baron, R. A., & Greenberg, J. (1990). *Behavior in organizations.* San Francisco: Jossey-Bass.

Berger, B. K. (1994, November). Revolution at Whirlpool. *Internal Communication Focus—North America, 1*(1), 3–6.

Berger, B. K. (1996a). Revolution at Whirlpool: A case history. In R. L. Dilenschneider (Ed.), *Dartnell's Public Relations Handbook* (4th ed., pp. 197–205). Chicago, IL: The Dartnell Corporation.

Berger, B. K. (1996b, May). Value of a process model for communication. *Communicator—Newsletter of the Council of Communication Management, 13*(5), 1, 3–4.

Berger, B. K. (2005). Power over, power with, and power to relations: Critical reflections on public relations, the dominant coalition, and activism. *Journal of Public Relations Research, 17*(1), 5–27.

Berkowitz, D., & Hristodoulakis, I. (1999). Practitioner roles, public relations education, and professional socialization: An exploratory study. *Journal of Public Relations Research, 11*(1), 91–103.

Bok, S. (1989). *Lying: Moral choice in public and private life.* New York: Vintage Books.

Bolman, L. G., & Deal, T. E. (1991). *Reframing organizations: Artistry, choice, and leadership.* San Francisco: Jossey-Bass.

Bologh, R. W. (1990). *Love or greatness: Max Weber and masculine thinking—A feminist inquiry*. London: Unwin-Hyman.

Brass, D. J., & Burkhardt, M. W. (1993). Potential power and power use: An investigation of structure and behavior. *Academy of Management Journal, 36*(3), 441–470.

Broom, G. M., & Dozier, D. M. (1986). Advancement for public relations role models. *Public Relations Review, 12*(1), 37–56.

Broom, G. M., & Smith, G. D. (1979). Testing the practitioner's impact on clients. *Public Relations Review, 5*(3), 47–59.

Caruth, D., Middlebrook, B., & Rachel, F. (1985, Summer). Overcoming resistance to change. *SAM Advanced Management Journal*, pp. 23–27.

Cheney, G. (1991). *Rhetoric in an organizational society: Managing multiple identities*. Columbia: University of South Carolina Press.

Cheney, G. (1995). Democracy in the workplace: Theory and practice from the perspective of communication. *Journal of Applied Communication Research, 23*, 167–200.

Cheney, G., & Dionisopoulos, G. N. (1989). Public relations? No, relations with publics: A rhetorical–organizational approach to contemporary corporate communications. In C. H. Botan & V. Hazleton, Jr. (Eds.), *Public relations theory* (pp. 135–157). Hillsdale, NJ: Lawrence Erlbaum Associates.

Cheney, G., & Vibbert, S. L. (1987). Corporate discourse: Public relations and issue management. In F. M. Jablin, L. L. Putnam, K. H. Roberts, & L. W. Porter (Eds.), *Handbook of organizational communication: An interdisciplinary perspective* (pp. 165–194). Newbury Park, CA: Sage.

Christians, C. G., Ferre, J. P., & Fackler, P. M. (1993). *Good News: Social ethics & the press*. New York: Oxford University Press.

Cobb, A. T. (1984). An episodic model of power: Toward an integration of theory and research. *Academy of Management Review, 9*, 482–493.

Cohen, A. R., & Bradford, D. L. (1989). Influence without authority: The use of alliances, reciprocity, and exchange to accomplish work. *Organizational Dynamics, 17*(3), 5–17.

Coleman, J. S. (1974). *Power and the structure of society*. New York: Norton.

Coleman, J. S. (1990). *Foundations of social theory*. Cambridge, MA: Harvard University Press.

Colvin, G. (2002, August 12). Wonder women of whistleblowing. *Fortune, 146*(3), 56.

Commission on Public Relations Education. (1999, October). *A port of entry: Public relations education for the 21st century*. New York: Public Relations Society of America.

Corporate profile: The Whirlpool whirlwind. (1994, January). *Inside PR*, pp. 30–34.

Craig, R. (1989). Communication as a practical discipline. In B. Dervin, L. Grossberg, B. O'Keefe, & E. Wartella (Eds.), *Rethinking communication: Vol. 1. Paradigm issues* (pp. 97–122). Newbury Park, CA: Sage.

Cropp, F., & Pincus, J. D. (2001). The mystery of public relations: Unraveling its past, unmasking its future. In R. L. Heath (Ed.), *Handbook of public relations* (pp. 189–203). Thousand Oaks, CA: Sage.

Curtin, P. A., & Boynton, L. A. (2001). Ethics in public relations: Theory and practice. In R. L. Heath (Ed.), *Handbook of public relations* (pp. 411–422). Thousand Oaks, CA: Sage.

Daudi, P. (1983). The discourse of power or the power of discourse. *Alternatives, IX*, 317–325.

Daugherty, E. L. (2001). Public relations and social responsibility. In R. L. Heath (Ed.), *Handbook of public relations* (pp. 389–401). Thousand Oaks, CA: Sage.

Deetz, S. A. (1992). *Democracy in an age of corporate colonization: Developments in communication and the politics of everyday life.* Albany: State University of New York.

Deetz, S. A., & Mumby, D. K. (1990). Power, discourse, and the workplace: Reclaiming the critical tradition. In J. Anderson (Ed.), *Communication yearbook 13* (pp. 18–47). Newbury Park, CA: Sage.

Dozier, D. M. (1992). The organizational roles of communications and public relations practitioners. In J. E. Grunig (Ed.), *Excellence in public relations and communication management* (pp. 327–356). Hillsdale, NJ: Lawrence Erlbaum Associates.

Dozier, D. M., & Broom, G. M. (1995). Evolution of the manager role in public relations practice. *Journal of Public Relations Research, 7*(1), 3–26.

Dozier, D. M., Grunig, L. A., & Grunig, J. E. (1995). *Manager's guide to excellence in public relations and communication management.* Hillsdale, NJ: Lawrence Erlbaum Associates.

Edelman, D. J. (2002, Fall). A challenging time, a bright future. *Public Relations Strategist, 8*(3), 1–3.

Edelman, M. (1964). *The symbolic uses of politics.* Champaign: University of Illinois Press.

Edgett, R. (2002). Toward an ethical framework for advocacy in public relations. *Journal of Public Relations Research, 14*(1), 1–26.

Elsasser, J. (2001, December). A golden age. *Public Relations Tactics, 8*(12), 18.

Falbe, C. M., & Yukl, G. (1992). Consequences for managers of using single influence tactics and combinations of tactics. *Academy of Management Journal, 35*(3), 638–652.

Farmer, S. M., Maslyn, J. M., Fedor, D. B., & Goodman, J. S. (1997). Putting upward influence strategies in context. *Journal of Organizational Behavior, 18,* 17–42.

Ferris, G. R., Fedor, D. B., Chachere, J. G., & Pondy, L. R. (1989). Myths and politics in organizational contexts. *Group & Organization Studies, 14*(1), 83–103.

Fimbel, N. (1994). Communicating realistically: Taking account of politics in internal business communications. *The Journal of Business Communication, 31*(1), 7–26.

Foucault, M. (1988). Social security. In L. D. Kritzman (Ed.), *Michael Foucault: Politics, philosophy, culture* (pp. 159–177). New York: Routledge.

French, J. R. P., & Raven, B. (1960). The bases of social power. In D. Cartwright & A. Zander (Eds.), *Group dynamics* (pp. 607–623). Evanston, IL: Row, Peterson.

Friedman, M. (1970, September 13). The social responsibility of business is to increase its profits. *The New York Times Magazine,* pp. 32–33, 122–126).

Friedman, T. L. (2000). *The Lexus and the olive tree.* New York: Anchor Books.

Gable, T. (2003, Spring). Five major PR issues for the next decade. *Public Relations Strategist, 9*(2), 18–21.

Gandy, O. (1992). Public relations and public policy: The structuration of dominance in the information age. In E. Toth & R. Heath (Eds.), *Rhetorical and critical approaches to public relations* (pp. 131–164). Hillsdale, NJ: Lawrence Erlbaum Associates.

Gaschen, D. J. (2004, July). PR leaders stand up for the profession in Los Angeles. *Public Relations Tactics, 11*(7), 8.

Gass, R. H., & Seiter, J. S. (2003). *Persuasion, social influence, and compliance gaining,* (2nd ed.). Boston: Allyn & Bacon.

German, K. M. (1995). Critical theory in public relations inquiry. In W. N. El-wood (Ed.), *Public relations inquiry as rhetorical criticism* (pp. 279–294). Westport, CT: Praeger.

Goldman, R., & Papson, S. (1998). *NIKE culture*. Thousand Oaks, CA: Sage.

Gong, T. (2000). Whistleblowing: What does it mean in China? *International Journal of Public Administration 23*(11), 1899–1923.

Gower, K. K. (2003). *Legal and ethical restraints on public relations*. Prospect Heights, IL: Waveland Press.

Greiner, L. E., & Schein, V. E. (1988). *Power and organizational development*. Reading, MA: Addison-Wesley.

Grunig, J. E. (1989, Spring). Teaching public relations in the future. *Public Relations Review, 15*(1), 12–24.

Grunig, J. E. (Ed.). (1992). *Excellence in public relations and communication management: Contributions to effective organizations*. Hillsdale, NJ: Lawrence Erlbaum Associates.

Grunig, J. E. (2001). Two-way symmetrical public relations: Past, present and future. In R. L. Heath (Ed.), *Handbook of public relations* (pp. 11–30). Thousand Oaks, CA: Sage.

Grunig, L. A. (1992a). Activism: How it limits the effectiveness of organizations and how excellent public relations departments respond. In J. E. Grunig (Ed.), *Excellence in public relations and communication management* (pp. 503–530). Hillsdale, NJ: Lawrence Erlbaum Associates.

Grunig, L. A. (1992b). Power in the public relations department. In J. E. Grunig (Ed.), *Excellence in public relations and communication management* (pp. 483–502). Hillsdale, NJ: Lawrence Erlbaum Associates.

Grunig, L. A., Grunig, J. E., & Dozier, D. M. (2002). *Excellent public relations and effective organizations*. Mahwah, NJ: Lawrence Erlbaum Associates.

Grunig, L. A., Toth, E. L., & Hon, L. C. (1999, June). *Feminist values in public relations*. Paper presented at the meeting of the Public Relations Division, International Communication Association, San Francisco.

Grunig, L. A., Toth, E. L., & Hon, L. C. (2001). *Women in public relations: How gender influences practice*. New York: Guilford.

Hardy, D., & Clegg, S. R. (1996). Some dare call it power. In S. R. Clegg, C. Hardy, & W. R. Nord (Eds.), *Handbook of organization studies* (pp. 622–641). Thousand Oaks, CA: Sage.

Harrison, D. (1999, July). Assess and remove barriers to change. *HRFocus*, pp. 8, 10.

Hartsock, N. (1981). Political change: Two perspectives on power. In Quest Staff and Book Committee (Eds.), *Building feminist theory* (pp. 3–19). New York: Longman.

Hatch, M. J. (1997). *Organizational theory: Modern, symbolic, and postmodern perspectives*. New York: Oxford University Press.

Hay, P. D., & Hartel, C. E. J. (2000). The influence framework: A theoretical bridge between power and organizational effectiveness. *Australian Journal of Communication, 27*(2), 131–154.

Heath, R. L. (1993). Toward a paradigm for the study and practice of public relations: A rhetorical approach to zones of meaning and organizational prerogatives. *Public Relations Review, 19*(2), 141–155.

Heath, R. L. (1997). *Strategic issues management: Organizations and public policy challenges*. Thousand Oaks, CA: Sage.

Heath, R. L., & Nelson, R. A. (1986). *Issues management: Corporate public policy making in an information society*. Beverly Hills, CA: Sage.

Heyman, W. C. (2004). *A research report: 10 patterns of success in public relations*. (Available from Heyman Associates, 11 Penn Plaza, Suite 1105, New York, NY 10001)

Higginbottom, K. (2002, July 25). Can you afford "an Enron"? *People Management*, pp. 14–15.

Hinkin, T. R., & Schriesheim, C. A. (1990). Relationships between subordinate perceptions of supervisor influence tactics and attributed bases of supervisory power. *Human Relations, 43*(3), 221–237.

Hirschman, A. O. (1970). *Exit, voice, and loyalty.* Cambridge, MA: Harvard University Press.

Holtzhausen, D. R. (2000). Postmodern values in public relations. *Journal of Public Relations Research, 12*, 93–114.

Holtzhausen, D. R., & Voto, R. (2002). Resistance from the margins: The postmodern public relations practitioner as organizational activist. *Journal of Public Relations Research, 14*(1), 57–84.

Hon, L. C. (1997). What have you done for me lately?: Exploring effectiveness in public relations. *Journal of Public Relations Research, 9*, 1–30.

Hullman, K. E. (1995, October). Training 101: Scaling the wall of resistance. *Training and Development*, pp. 15–18.

International Association of Business Communicators Code of Ethics for Professional Communicators. Retrieved May 7, 2005, from http://www.iabc.com/members/joining/code.htm

Jackall, R. (1988). *Moral mazes: The world of corporate managers.* New York: Oxford University Press.

Jackson, P. (1982). Tactics of confrontation. In J. S. Nagelschmidt (Ed.), *The public affairs handbook* (pp. 211–220). New York: American Management Association.

Johnson, M. A. (1997). Public relations and technology: Practitioner perspectives. *Journal of Public Relations Research, 9*(3), 213–236.

Jubb, P. B. (1999). Whistleblowing: A restrictive definition and interpretation. *Journal of Business Ethics, 21*, 77–94.

Judd, L. R. (1989). Credibility, public relations and social responsibility. *Public Relations Review, 15*(2), 34–41.

Kanter, R. M. (1977). *Men and women of the corporation.* New York: Basic Books.

Kassing, J. W. (1997). Articulating, antagonizing, and displacing: A model of employee dissent. *Communication Studies, 48*, 311–332.

Kassing, J. W. (1998). Development and validation of the organizational dissent scale. *Management Communication Quarterly, 12*(2), 183–230.

Kassing, J. W. (2001). From the looks of things: Assessing perceptions of organizational dissenters. *Management Communication Quarterly, 14*(3), 442–470.

Kassing, J. W., & Armstrong, T. A. (2002). Someone's going to hear about this: Examining the association between dissent-triggering events and employees' dissent expression. *Management Communication Quarterly, 16*(1), 39–65.

Kassing, J. W., & Avtgis, T. A. (1999). Examining the relationship between organizational dissent and aggressive communication. *Management Communication Quarterly, 13*(1), 100–115.

Kipnis, D., & Schmidt, S. M. (1982). *Profile of organizational influence strategies.* San Diego: University Associates.

Kipnis, D., & Schmidt, S. M. (1985). The language of persuasion. *Psychology Today, 4*, 40–46.

Kipnis, D., Schmidt, S. M., & Wilkinson, I. (1980). Intraorganizational influence tactics: Explorations in getting one's way. *Journal of Applied Psychology, 65*(4), 440–452.

Knowles, E. S., & Linn, J. A. (Eds.). (2004). *Resistance and persuasion.* Mahwah, NJ: Lawrence Erlbaum Associates.

Koten, J. (Ed.). (2004). *Building trust—Leading CEOs speak out: How they create it, strengthen it, and sustain it.* New York: Arthur W. Page Society.

Kremer, D. (1996). *Accelerating change with business communication.* Littleton, CO: Virginia A. Ostendorf.

Kruckeberg, D. (1998). The future of PR education: Some recommendations. *Public Relations Review, 24*(2), 235–248.

Lauzen, M. M. (1992). Public relations roles, intraorganizational power, and encroachment. *Journal of Public Relations Research, 4*(2), 61–80.

Lauzen, M. M., & Dozier, D. M. (1992). The missing link: The public relations manager role as mediator of organizational environments and power consequences for the function. *Journal of Public Relations Research, 4*(4), 205–220.

Leichty, G. (2003). The cultural tribes of public relations. *Journal of Public Relations Research, 15*(4), 277–304.

Leitch, S., & Neilson, D. (1997). Reframing public relations: New directions for theory and practice. *Australian Journal of Communication, 24*(2), 17–32.

Lesly, P. (1991). Public relations in the turbulent new human climate. *Public Relations Review, 17*(1), 1–8.

Lewis, D. (2002, July). Whistleblowing procedures at work: What are the implications for human resource practitioners? *Business Ethics: A European Review, 11*(3), 202–209.

Lindlof, T. R. (1995). *Qualitative Communication Research Methods.* Thousand Oaks, CA: Sage.

Madison, D. L., Allen, R. W., Porter, L. W., Renwick, P. A., & Mayes, B. T. (1980). Organizational politics: An exploration of managers' perceptions. *Human Relations, 33*, 79–100.

Manheim, J. B. (2001). *The Death of a Thousand Cuts: Corporate Campaigns and the Attack on the Corporation.* Mahwah, NJ: Lawrence Erlbaum Associates.

Marwell, G., & Schmitt, D. R. (1967). Dimensions of compliance-gaining behavior: An empirical analysis. *Sociometry, 30*, 350–364.

Maurer, R. (1998, August). Is it resistance or isn't it? *Manage,* pp. 28–29.

Mayes, B. T., & Allen, R. W. (1977). Toward a definition of organizational politics. *Academy of Management Review, 2*, 672–678.

McLaughlin, J. P. (1972). We are advocates. *Public Relations Quarterly, 17*, 15.

Mechanic, D. (1962). Sources of power of lower participants in complex organizations. *Administrative Science Quarterly, 7*(3), 349–364.

Mickey, T. J. (1997). A postmodern view of public relations: Sign and reality. *Public Relations Review, 23*(3), 271–285

Mickey, T. J. (2003). *Deconstructing public relations: Public relations criticism.* Mahwah, NJ: Lawrence Erlbaum Associates.

Mintzberg, H. (1983). *Power in and around organizations.* Englewood Cliffs, NJ: Prentice-Hall.

Mintzberg, H. (1985). The organization as political arena. *Journal of Management Studies, 22*(2), 133–154.

Molleda, J. C. (2004). Partners in an alliance with a global reach. *Public Relations Strategist, 10*(1), 48–51.

Moore, P. (1994, March). Turning the tide at Whirlpool. *IABC Communication World,* pp. 26–29.

Morrill, C. (1989). The management of managers: Disputing in an executive hierarchy. *Sociological Forum, 4*(3), 387–407.

Motion, J., & Leitch, S. (1996). A discursive perspective from New Zealand: Another world view. *Public Relations Review, 22*(3), 297–309.

Mumby, D. K. (1997, Fall). The problem of hegemony: Reading Gramsci for organizational communication studies. *Western Journal of Communication,* *61*(4), 343–375.

O'Connell-Davidson, J. (1994). The resources and limits of resistance in a privatized utility. In J. M. Jermier, D. Knights, & W. R. Nord (Eds.), *Resistance and power in organizations* (pp. 69–101). London: Routledge.

O'Neil, J. O. (2003). An investigation of the sources of influence of corporate public relations practitioners. *Public Relations Review, 29,* 159–169.

Paine, K. D. (2001). The Old Role of the PR Person Is Over. *Public Relations Strategist, 7*(3), 47.

Pasadeos, Y., Renfro, R. B., & Hanily, M. L. (1999). Influential authors and works of the public relations scholarly literature: A network of recent research. *Journal of Public Relations Research, 11*(1), 29–52.

Pauly, J. J., & Hutchison, L. L. (2001). Case studies and their use in public relations. In R. L. Heath (Ed.), *Handbook of public relations* (pp. 381–388). Thousand Oaks, CA: Sage.

Pfeffer, J. (1981). *Power in organizations.* Marshfield, MA: Pitman.

Pfeffer, J. (1992). *Managing with power: Politics and influence in organizations.* Boston, MA: Harvard Business School Press.

Phair, J. T. (2005, March). Regaining and retaining credibility amid changes and challenges to the profession. *Public Relations Tactics, 12*(3), 22.

Plowman, K. D. (1998). Power in conflict for public relations. *Journal of Public Relations Research, 10*(4), 237–261.

Porter, L. W., Allen, R. W., & Angle, H. L. (1990). The politics of upward influence in organizations. In L. L. Cummings & B. M. Straw (Eds.), *Research in organizational behavior* (pp. 109–149). Greenwich, CT: JAI.

PR blotter: To tell the truth. (2004, February). *Public Relations Tactics, 11*(2), 4.

PR pros find dissatisfaction on the job. (2002, August). *Public Relations Tactics, 9*(8), 9.

Public Relations Society of America. (2000). *PRSA Member Code of Ethics.* New York: Author.

Public Relations Coalition. (2003). *Restoring trust in business: Models for action.* New York: Arthur W. Page Society.

Rakow, L. (1989). From the feminization of public relations to the promise of feminism. In E. L. Toth & C. G. Cline (Eds.), *Beyond the velvet ghetto* (pp. 287–298). San Francisco: IABC Research Foundation.

Rawls, J. (1971). *A theory of justice.* Cambridge, MA: Harvard University Press.

Recardo, R. F. (1995, Spring). Overcoming resistance to change. *National Productivity Review,* pp. 5–12.

Redding, W. C. (1985). Rocking boats, blowing whistles, and teaching speech communication. *Communication Education, 34,* 245–258.

Rothschild, J., & Miethe, T. D. (1994). Whistleblowing as resistance in modern work organizations: The politics of revealing organizational deception and abuse. In J. M. Jermier, D. Knight, & W. R. Nord (Eds.), *Resistance and power in organizations* (pp. 252–273). London: Routledge.

Ruler, B. V., & Lange, R. D. (2003). Barriers to communication management in the executive suite. *Public Relations Review, 29,* 145–158.

Salancik, G. R., & Pfeffer, J. (1977, Winter). Who gets power—and how they hold on to it: A strategic-contingency model of power. *Organizational Dynamics, 5,* 3–21.

Sallot, L. M., Cameron, G. T., & Weaver Lariscy, R. A. (1998). PR educators and practitioners identify professional standards. *Journalism & Mass Communication Educator, 53*(2), 19–30.

Schmidt, S., & Kipnis, D. (1984). Managers' pursuit of individual and organizational goals. *Human Relations, 37,* 781–794.

Schriesheim, C. A., & Hinkin, T. R. (1990). Influence tactics used by subordinates: A theoretical and empirical analysis and refinement of the Kipnis, Schmidt, and Wilkinson subscales. *Journal of Applied Psychology, 75*(3), 246–257.

Seitel, F. P. (2004). *The practice of public relations* (9th ed.). Upper Saddle River, NJ: Pearson Prentice Hall.

Senge, P. M. (1990). *The fifth discipline: The art and practice of the learning organization.* New York: Doubleday/Currency.

Shepherd, G. J. (1992, Winter). Communication as influence: Definitional exclusion. *Communication Studies, 43,* 203–219.

Shoemaker, P. J., Tankard, J. W., Jr., & Lasorsa, D. L. (2004). *How to build social science theories.* Thousand Oaks, CA: Sage.

Sillars, A. L. (1980). The stranger and the spouse as target persons for compliance gaining strategies: A subjective expected utility model. *Human Communication Research, 6,* 265–279.

Smith, M. F. (1997, November). *Public relations from the "bottom up": Toward a more inclusive view of public relations.* Paper presented at the meeting of the National Communication Association, Chicago.

Smith, M. F., & Ferguson, D. P. (2001). Activism. In R. L. Heath (Ed.), *Handbook of public relations* (pp. 291–300). Thousand Oaks, CA: Sage.

Spicer, C. (1997). *Organizational public relations: A political perspective.* Mahwah, NJ: Lawrence Erlbaum Associates.

Sprague, J., & Ruud, G. L. (1988). Boat-rocking in the high-technology culture. *American Behavioral Scientist, 32*(2),169–193.

Tedeschi, J. T., & Melburg, V. (1984). Impression management and influence in the organization. In S. B. Bacharach & E. J. Lawler (Eds.), *Research in the sociology of organizations* (Vol. 3, pp. 31–58). Greenwich, CT: JAI.

Toth, E. L, & Heath, R. L. (1992). *Rhetorical and critical approaches to public relations.* Hillsdale, NJ: Lawrence Erlbaum Associates.

Tucker, J. (1993). Everyday forms of employee resistance. *Sociological Forum, 8*(1), 25–45.

Van Leuven, J. (1999). Four new course competencies for majors. *Public Relations Review, 25*(1), 77–85.

VanSlyke Turk, J. (1989). Management skills need to be taught in public relations. *Public Relations Review, 15*(1), 38–52.

Vigoda, E., & Cohen, A. (2002). Influence tactics and perceptions of organizational politics: A longitudinal study. *Journal of Business Research, 55,* 311–324.

Waldron, V. R. (1999). Communication practices of followers, members, and protégées: The case of upward influence tactics. In M. E. Roloff (Ed.), *Communication yearbook 22* (pp. 251–299). Thousand Oaks, CA: Sage.

Weaver, C. K. (2001). Dressing for battle in the new global economy. *Management Communication Quarterly, 15*(2), 279–288.

Weber, M. (1958). *The Protestant ethic and the spirit of capitalism.* New York: Scribner's.

Werder, K. P. (2003, May). *Responding to activism: An experimental analysis of public relations strategy influence on beliefs, attitudes, and behavioral intentions.* Paper presented at the International Communication Association 2003 Annual Conference, Public Relations Division, San Diego.

Whirlpool Corporation. (1993, November). *Task force report: Communication technology recommendations for Whirlpool Corporation.* Benton Harbor, MI: Author.

Whirlpool Corporation. (1995, April 5). *Communications for Whirlpool leaders: A two-day training program*. Benton Harbor, MI: Author.

Whitwam, D. (1993, January). Whirlpool Management Journal—A new direction. *Whirlpool Management Journal, 1*(1), 2–3.

Williams, S. R., & Wilson, R. L. (1997, Fall). Group support systems, power, and influence in an organization: A field study. *Decision Sciences, 28*(4), 911–937.

Woodward, W. D. (2003). Public relations planning and action as "practical-critical" communication. *Communication Theory, 13*(4), 411–431.

Worldwide standard is in the works for PR ethics. (2003, Spring). *The Public Relations Strategist, 12*(2), 3.

Wrong, D. (1979). *Power: Its forms, bases and uses*. Oxford, England: Blackwell.

Yukl, G., & Falbe, C. M. (1990). Influence tactics in upward, downward, and lateral influence attempts. *Journal of Applied Psychology, 76*, 132–140.

Yukl, G., Guinan, P. J., & Sottolano, D. (1995). Influence tactics used for different objectives with subordinates, peers, and superiors. *Group & Organization Management, 20*(3), 272–296.

Yukl, G., & Tracey, J. B. (1992). Consequences of influence tactics used with subordinates, peers, and the boss. *Journal of Applied Psychology, 77*(4), 525–535.

Author Index

A

Allen, R. W., 4, 8, 56, 62, 152
Allison, G. T., 76, 80
Angle, H. L., 8, 62, 152
Armstrong, T. A., 58
Avtgis, T. A., 57

B

Bachrach, S., 77, 80
Bahniuk, M. H., 111
Barbalet, J. M., 3, 68, 81
Baron, R. A., 12, 61
Berger, B. K., viii, 4, 7, 11, 14, 36, 59, 60,
     61, 66, 73, 80, 126, 133, 152,
     154, 155, 219
Berkowitz, D., 24
Bok, S., 30
Bolman, L. G., 67
Bologh, R. W., 68, 103
Boynton, L. A., 30
Bradford, D. L., 4, 77, 206, 207
Brass, D. J., 4, 80, 232
Broom, G. M., 13, 29, 34, 56, 172, 203
Burkhardt, M. W., 4, 80, 232

C

Cameron, G. T., 24, 37
Caruth, D., 154, 172
Chachere, J. G., 4, 11, 61, 80
Cheney, G., 10, 11

C (continued)

Christians, C. G., 31
Clegg, S. R., 4, 67, 68, 70
Cobb, A. T., 3
Cohen, A., 4, 56
Cohen, A. R., 4, 77, 206, 207
Coleman, J. S., 14, 55
Colvin, G., 153
Craig, R., 10
Cropp, F., 24
Curtin, P. A., 30

D

Daudi, P., 4, 8, 66
Daugherty, E. L., 31
Deal, T. E., 67
Deetz, S. A., 58, 67, 68
Dionisopoulos, G. N., 10
Dobos, J., 111
Dozier, D. M., 2, 3, 10, 13, 14, 16, 29, 34,
     56, 97, 172, 173, 200, 201, 203,
     219, 227

E

Edelman, D. J., 4, 218
Edelman, M. 80
Edgett, R., 55
Elsasser, J., 218

F

Fackler, P. M., 31

267

Falbe, C. M., 108, 109, 113
Farmer, S. M., 108, 110, 113
Fedor, D. B., 4, 12, 61, 80, 108, 110, 113
Ferguson, D. P., 59, 60
Ferre, J. P., 31
Ferris, G. R., 4, 12, 61, 80
Fimbel, N., 4, 61
Foucault, M., vii, 66, 201, 203
French, J. R. P., 4, 76
Friedman, M., 31
Friedman, T. L., 221

G

Gable, T., 219
Gandy, O., 68, 221
Gaschen, D. J., 240
Gass, R. H., 112, 246
German, K. M., 10, 11, 80
Goldman, R., 221
Gong, T., 153
Goodman, J. S., 108, 110, 113
Gower, K. K., 33
Greenberg, J., 12, 61
Greiner, L. E., 3, 4, 12
Grunig, J. E., 2, 3, 10, 29, 34, 56, 60, 67,
    68, 97, 172, 173, 200, 201, 219,
    227
Grunig, L. A., 2, 4, 7, 10, 29, 34, 56, 59,
    60, 66, 68, 71, 77, 97, 172, 173,
    200, 201, 219, 227
Guinan, P. J., 4, 200

H

Hanily, M. L., 29
Hardy, D., 4, 67, 68, 70
Hartel, C. E. J., 3, 4, 12, 59, 61, 152
Hartsock, N., 68
Hatch, M. J., 77
Hay, P. D., 3, 4, 12, 59, 61, 152
Heath, R. L., 10
Heyman, W. C., 25, 77, 88, 107, 227
Higginbottom, K., 153
Hill, S. E. K., 111
Hinkin, T. R., 4, 170
Hirschman, A. O., 47
Holtzhausen, D. R, 4, 7, 8, 10, 14, 60, 66,
    71, 77, 78, 203, 205, 206, 207,
    239
Hon, L. C., 68, 200
Hristodoulakis, I., 24

Hullman, K. E., 154, 172
Hutchison, L. L., 237

J

Jackall, R., 12, 63, 64, 201
Jackson, P., 60
Johnson, M. A., 81
Jubb, P. B., 153
Judd, L. R., 28

K

Kanter, R. M., 4, 7, 8, 68, 77
Kassing, J. W., 57, 58, 153, 171, 172, 174
Kipnis, D., 4, 108, 109, 111, 113, 121,
    170
Knowles, E. S., 53
Koten, J., 238
Kremer, D., 122, 134
Kruckeberg, D., 200

L

Lange, R. D., 15, 36
Lasorsa, D. L., 73, 74
Lauzen, M. M., 3, 14, 36, 37, 78, 149,
    200, 205
Lawler, E., 77, 80
Leichty, G., 9, 10
Leitch, S., 4, 10, 68
Lesly, P., 53
Lewis, D., 153
Lindlof, T. R., 38
Linn, J. A., 53

M

Madison, D. L., 4, 62
Manheim, J. B., 154
Marwell, G., 112
Maslyn, J. M., 108, 110, 113
Maurer, R., 172
Mayes, B. T., 4, 56, 62
McLaughlin, J. P., 1, 2, 201
Mechanic, D., 4, 205
Melburg, V., 4
Mickey, T. J., 10, 60
Middlebrook, B., 154, 172
Miethe, T. D., 153

Subject Index